Doing Business in Russia and the Other Former Soviet Republics

Accounting and Joint Venture Issues

by

Adolf J.H. Enthoven, Ph.D.
Jaroslav V. Sokolov, Ph.D.
Alexander M. Petrachkov, Ph.D.

A study carried out on behalf of the
Institute of Management Accountants
Montvale, New Jersey

Published by

Institute of Management Accountants
10 Paragon Drive
Montvale, NJ 07645-1760

Claire Barth, Editor

Foreword

On May 19, 1992, *The New York Times* carried a front-page story with the headline "Chevron to Spend $10 Billion to Seek Oil in Kazakhstan." The article indicated that the undertaking was "one of the largest joint ventures between a Western company and a former Soviet republic." This agreement with Kazakhstan, said *The Times*, "would pave the way for more Western investment in the former Soviet republics by showing that a large corporation can, despite the region's instability, conclude a major deal."

It was this potential for economic partnership, when so little was known about Soviet accounting systems, that motivated the Committee on Research (COR) of the Institute of Management Accountants (IMA) to consider research in this subject area in 1990. The COR desired to provide guidance to its IMA member practitioners on the management accounting aspects of joint ventures. Fortunately, at that time Adolf Enthoven, director of the Center for International Accounting Development at The University of Texas at Dallas, and his colleagues from the former Soviet Union also thought this gap needed to be filled.

What has been developed through this research is a handbook that is required reading for all who are interested in or desire to be partners in the Commonwealth of Independent States (CIS). This book, organized in three sections, covers the Soviet accounting system and the accounting for joint ventures and appraises the future of accounting and auditing in the CIS. To help readers understand the development of the Soviet accounting system and the political and socioeconomic aspects of change in the Soviet Union, detailed appendices are provided. So, too, are a glossary of Soviet accounting terms and a bibliography.

In this study you will learn of *perestroika*, which refers to the opening of the Soviet economy to foreign investment and the restructuring of its economy. You will discover that:

- The departure from a centralized economic mechanism to a market economy has been legalized;
- The Soviet accounting system and its standard chart of accounts was designed to provide information necessary for the centralized planning and control of the Soviet economy;
- New regulations have reduced difficulties for business enterprises operating under free market conditions.

iii

Still needed, however, as this study indicates, are a sound theoretical base and conceptual framework for the accounting standard setting process.

Guidance in the preparation of this research was kindly provided by the Project Committee:

David W. Vogel, *Chairman*
E.I. duPont de Nemours & Company
Wilmington, Delaware

John Karabec   Ray Vander Weele, CMA
IBM Corporation   Christian Reformed Church
Tarrytown, New York   Pension Fund
                                          Grand Rapids, Michigan

This report reflects the views of the researchers and not necessarily those of the Institute, the Committee on Research, or the Project Committee.

Patrick L. Romano
Director of Research
Institute of Management Accountants

Preface

The principal aim of this study is to depict the structure and process of accounting and auditing in what was formerly known as the Soviet Union (the Union of Soviet Socialist Republics—USSR), with particular attention directed to the areas of cost (or management) accounting, financial accounting, and joint venture accounting elements and issues. We hope to give American and other Western business managers, accountants, economists, government administrators, and potential foreign joint venture partners interested in operating in Russia and the other former Soviet republics an insight into the "Soviet" accounting system and its procedures.

More specifically, our study is geared to attaining a clearer understanding of the Soviet accounting and auditing structure and process and their underlying economic, political, and historical accounting aspects. Another objective is to give Soviet business people, accountants, government officials, and others an insight into their own system. It is hoped that this study will lead to the effective merger of Soviet accounting with international accounting and auditing standards and practices. We have tried to show where adaptations are needed in the Soviet accounting system, practices, training, education, and research. Such adaptations will make accountancy for enterprises in Russia and the other republics more effective as an information measurement system to facilitate economic analysis, policy, and decision making at both the micro and macro economic levels. We felt such an appraisal also would benefit foreign businessmen, accountants, and economists planning to operate in, or interested in, the republics of the former Soviet Union.

While originally we intended to focus our study on the "managerial accounting" aspects, during the course of our evaluations it became apparent that financial and cost accounting have been interwoven so tightly in the Soviet Union that our approach needed to be broader, on the one hand, and narrower, on the other, than management accounting. Also, management accounting, as it is conceived of in the West, does not exist as yet in similar form in the Soviet Union.

At the end of December 1991, 11 of the 12 remaining republics of the former Soviet Union (the original 15 included the three Baltic states—Estonia, Latvia, and Lithuania) formed the Commonwealth of Independent States (CIS). The largest republic in the CIS is the Russian Federal Republic (Russia), which has more than 50% of the former Soviet Union population and more than 60% of its national product. However, other republics in the CIS, such as Ukraine,

Kazakhstan, and Byelorussia (Belarus), also play a vital economic and political role.

At the time we finalized our study (early 1992), many political, military, and economic issues still were to be resolved within the CIS, including, among others, accounting and auditing regulations and procedures. These accounting and auditing issues are expected to be resolved in a satisfactory and harmonious way, however.

Most of the accounting formats, charts of accounts, and related statements and procedures, which Russia already has adopted, in all likelihood also will be adopted by the other members of the CIS. Each republic may well make its own minor modifications without hampering the overall scope and content of the formats, charts, procedures, and regulations. The common historical heritage and joint socioeconomic interests of the republics will assure synchronized development of accounting standards. The Soviet accounting methodology and organization as of December 1991 (the date of formal disintegration of the USSR) is the common ground for future accounting developments in the new independent states. This study *reflects* the accounting practice in all the former Soviet republics.

Although our study might appear to apply mainly to Russia, because that republic has adopted the accounting rules and charts of the former Soviet Union, it applies equally to all the other republics of the CIS as well. As of early 1992, however, many of these republics had not yet officially adopted (or adapted) these formerly centralized Soviet procedures and charts.

Throughout the text we have used the term "Soviet Union," but the reader should recognize that we are referring to what will be known as the republics of the Commonwealth of Independent States. We also have maintained both the term "Soviet accounting," for the accounting system and practices of the republics up to the present, and "Soviet accountants" for those trained and practicing in the system. The transition of many procedures and guidelines from the former centralized Soviet Union to the more decentralized CIS will be a gradual one. Whether the CIS in its current form will last is doubtful. It may well be superseded by a different eco-political structure.

We believe this transformation from the Soviet Union to the CIS has minimal impact on the nature of our study for three principal reasons: (1) The republics all have—and intend to maintain—a common accounting system; (2) Economic interaction and transactions will remain strong, requiring better accounting methods, especially due to greater privatization and economic restructuring; and (3) The trend in all these republics is toward greater internationalization of their accounting systems for market conditions and for needed foreign investments. However, it also is possible that the CIS may resort back to a more structured political and economic model.

The need for this study became apparent to us at a conference in Moscow in June 1989 that dealt with "Accountancy for Joint Venture Operations." The conference was sponsored jointly by the United Nations Centre for Transnational

Corporations (UNCTC) and the Soviet Chamber of Commerce and Industry, with active participation from the Soviet Ministry of Finance and principal accounting academics from the USSR. At that time, and during follow-up appraisals in the USSR, we clearly felt that little was known about Soviet accounting internationally, while Soviet accountants were not fully cognizant of Western (international) accounting developments. We thought this gap needed to be filled, particularly in view of the further integration of the Soviet economy with the economies of the outside (largely Western) world. We had no specific plan, however, nor the necessary means to implement our ideas.

Fortunately, the Committee on Research of the Institute of Management Accountants, IMA (formerly known as the National Association of Accountants, NAA) also clearly recognized the need for a comprehensive research study on this subject.

Joint ventures undoubtedly will play a major role in the economic restructuring and development of Russia and the other CIS republics. One of the problems faced by joint ventures between foreign and Soviet firms has been the incompatibility of Soviet accounting with the reporting requirements of foreign investors. A difficulty exists in operating a profit-oriented enterprise in a business environment that still preserves many features of a formerly centralized economy with many rigid features.

Those who attempt to establish joint ventures with foreign firms in the CIS encounter major difficulties. Among the problems, a significant obstacle is the lack of mutual understanding between businessmen and accountants of different countries. From a psychological perspective, it is understandable that investors, when introduced to the Soviet accounting system, note only the differences and as a rule assume that what is unfamiliar is bad. The reasons for these differences often are neglected, though sometimes the differences are well justified. To understand each other's problems and to help each other in learning accounting procedures used in different countries will require good will on the part of both Soviet and foreign accountants. If our study fosters better understanding of Soviet accounting practice among accountants internationally, it will have accomplished one of our major purposes.

Also, understanding the changing business climate, the long-term trends, and the emerging realities is a must for any potential investor or interested party. Future accounting developments in the CIS will very much depend on these socioeconomic conditions and changes. We therefore have provided our readers with a broad overview of political, economic, and legal developments in the Soviet Union.

We recognize that we have not covered all necessary accounting aspects in specific detail, while some changes may not have occurred at the time the study was finished (May 1992). We have tried to make it as current and relevant as possible, however, including outlining certain future trends.

During the preparation of this study we interacted extensively with each other during visits to the Soviet Union or to the United States and by extensive correspondence between visits. In our opinion, this active dialogue has greatly benefitted the contents of the study.

   We look forward to receiving your comments.

Professor Jaroslav V. Sokolov
Chair of the Accounting Department
St. Petersburg Institute of International
   Commerce and Economics
Member of the Board,
   Association of Accountants of the
   Russian Federation
Russia (CIS)

Professor Adolf J.H. Enthoven
Professor of Accounting
Director, Center for International
   Accounting Development
The University of Texas at Dallas
USA

Professor Alexander M. Petrachkov
Director, Department of International Economic Relations
Kiev State University
Permanent Expert to the Ukrainian Parliament
Ukraine (CIS)

Acknowledgments

During the preparation of this study, we received very valuable advice and assistance from the members of the Committee on Research of the Institute of Management Accountants. They are David W. Vogel, chairman, John Karabec, Patrick Romano, and Ray Vander Weele. We are extremely grateful for the assistance and continuous support received from the Committee on Research.

We would like to thank our families and colleagues for the many hours away from home or office that we devoted jointly or individually to preparing and evaluating the underlying material. We also wish to express our appreciation to those who actively assisted in putting this material together, both in the Soviet Union and the United States. We are especially appreciative to Professor Valery V. Kovalyov, deputy rector at the Institute of Commerce and Economics (St. Petersburg), who assisted in various parts of the study. His extensive knowledge helped us enormously in our writings. Others who played a significant role in putting this study in its current form are Helen Tkachy, Vladimir Rusinov, Svetlana Aseeva and Ruslan Korzh, all from the Soviet Union; Angela Hildenbrand, secretary of the Center for International Accounting Development; and Janice Jantz, Johnnye Heaton, Julie Bell, and Anita Stover, of The University of Texas at Dallas. We are especially appreciative to Claire S. Barth, senior editor at the Institute of Management Accountants, for the extensive editing she carried out for this study. It has been a pleasure working with her.

About the Authors

Adolf J.H. Enthoven

Adolf J.H. Enthoven, Ph.D., is professor and chairman of the Accounting Department and director of the Center for International Accounting Development at The University of Texas at Dallas. He is vice president of The International Consortium on Governmental Financial Management and an officer in the American Accounting Association. Formerly he was director-Europe for Coopers & Lybrand (international certified public accountants) and a senior investment officer with the World Bank. He has been a consultant to the U.S. Agency for International Development, the U.S. General Accounting Office, the World Bank, the United Nations, and the Ford Foundation on international accounting educational and structural developments.

Dr. Enthoven previously taught at the University of Illinois, the University of North Carolina, and Harvard University. He has written eight books and numerous articles in the area of accounting and economic policy.

Jaroslav V. Sokolov

Jaroslav V. Sokolov, Ph.D., is professor and chair of the Department of Accounting at the Leningrad Engels Soviet Trade Institute. He is a member of the board of the Soviet Association of Accountants, member of the Accounting Methodology Council of the Ministry of Finance of the USSR, and president of the Accountant's Club of Leningrad (St. Petersburg).

Dr. Sokolov served as consultant to the Ministries of Trade of the USSR and Russia and to various organizations and companies. He is also a member of the international section of the American Accounting Association and the International Academy of Accounting Historians. He is the author of more than 150 publications, including 14 books and monographs on accounting methodology and history, and serves as a member of the editing boards of Finance and Statistics Publishing House and the magazines *Accounting* and *Soviet Trade* (Moscow).

Alexander M. Petrachkov

Alexander M. Petrachkov, Ph.D., is associate professor of international economics at the Ukrainian Institute for International Relations, Kiev State University, Kiev, Ukraine. He was a visiting scholar at The University of Texas at Dallas and a visiting professor at the Graduate School of Management, University of Dallas at Irving.

Dr. Petrachkov is permanent expert of the Commission on Foreign Affairs, Supreme Soviet (Parliament) of Ukraine and former member of the Accounting Methodology Council of the Soviet Ministry of Finance. He is a coorganizer of conferences on doing business in the Soviet Union and is the author of more than 40 publications, including monographs and book chapters. Dr. Petrachkov currently is employed at the Treasury and Investments Branch of the International Labour Office, Geneva, Switzerland.

Table of Contents

Doing Business in Russia and the Other Former Soviet Republics

Organization of the Study and Overview of the Soviet Accounting System

The book has been divided into three related parts and three appendices. The overall aims of Part I (Chapters 1, 2, and 3) are:

- To describe the documents that form the legal basis of Soviet accounting, as well as peculiarities of the organization of control and "revision" (audit) in the Soviet system.
- To explain the differences between Soviet and Western organization of accounting and principles of accounting methodology.
- To describe the principles of Soviet cost calculation and its various aspects in different branches of the national economy.

Specifically, Part I explores the underlying principles of the Soviet accounting system and its vital chart of accounts (Chapter 1), followed by a description of the aspects and requirements of accounting, reporting, and auditing in Russia and other CIS republics (Chapter 2). Chapter 3 reviews cost accounting procedures and norms, emphasizing the important point that Soviet cost/management accounting as yet is not considered a separate system or even branch of accounting.

Part II explores the extensive area of Soviet accounting that applies to joint ventures (Chapters 4 and 5). It also describes the legal environment for joint venture operations in the former Soviet Union and points out typical features of taxation related to joint ventures.

Part III presents an overall appraisal of Soviet accounting and auditing and some thoughts on the future of accounting in the republics (Chapter 6). This part covers the education, skills, and experience that accountants of various grades have. It also evaluates future accounting development requirements in Russia and the other CIS countries, including a training program for accountants for joint ventures in the CIS.

One purpose of this study has been to provide an extensive insight into the prevailing system of cost and financial accounting and auditing. Another has been to set forth a framework for further analyses and decision making regarding desirable directions in Soviet accounting, especially in the context of attracting more extensive foreign investment. We expect the overall system, including systems in the respective republics, to move toward a synthesis of the former

Soviet system with the Western (international) system, with slight variations among the respective republics.

Appendix A gives an overview of the political and socioeconomic aspects of change in the former Soviet Union. It analyzes the changing business environment and trends in political, economic, and social development under *perestroika* and describes their probable influence on the organization of accounting and auditing in the CIS.

In Appendix B we give a sketch of the historical development of accounting and auditing in Russia. This section traces the development of peculiarities of Russian and Soviet accounting through many centuries and outlines the evolution of the principles of cost accounting and cost calculation. It tries to show that traditional ways of thinking of Russian accountants conform to classic Western European accounting. Appendix C addresses issues of accounting education in the CIS. A glossary and a bibliography also are included.

We felt it would be a good idea to give a brief overview of the Soviet accounting system in this introductory chapter. Describing the features of the system and comparing it with the Western accounting system provides a background for the more technical chapters that follow.

An Overview of Accounting in the USSR

The Economic Climate

Since 1987, the Soviet Union has been opening its economy to foreign investment as part of the needed restructuring of its economy called *perestroika*. This restructuring also involved decentralization of individual enterprises and a move toward a market economy. The Soviets have been eager to cooperate with Western companies to revamp and restructure the Soviet economy. They recognize that international (largely Western) technology, know-how, and capital investment are much needed. The Soviets have greatly liberalized the laws and regulations for attracting foreign investment, essentially in the form of joint venture investments. As a result, business enterprises, and particularly joint ventures, already have achieved some freedom and are expected to gain even greater freedom from central control. New systems in areas such as taxation, credit and interest rates, banking, and pricing and marketing are likely to bring joint venture enterprises more in line with market forces.

In June 1990, the Supreme Soviet of the USSR passed a resolution calling for the introduction of market-oriented mechanisms. Accounting is the basic infrastructure of business in any market-oriented economy, so the transition from a centrally planned to a market-oriented economy requires a modernization of the accounting system. Without a proper accounting system, firms, as well as investors and the public, are not able to evaluate business performance and prepare sound costs.

The Western reader should take into account, however, that the Soviet Union was a state with a socialist structure. The accounting objectives and functions have been different from those of the West because of distinct socioeconomic conditions and objectives. These differences may remain for the time being while the transformation process takes place. In setting principles or norms, for example, Western countries have been motivated by profit making, while in the Soviet Union the focus has been more on physical production to serve public requirements. It is important for the Western reader and investor to understand the structure and process of the Soviet system and its objectives in its socioeconomic context.

The Soviet Accounting System

The Soviet accounting system in general was designed to provide economic/ statistical information necessary for central planning and for controlling the economy. This prime function has been of a dual nature: (1) to control operations to achieve plan targets through the economic use of resources and (2) to protect socialist property. The accounting system, therefore, has been used as an instrument of national economic management.

The Soviets have been applying a single accounting system with three subsystems:

- Statistical record keeping for aggregate economic data, including volume of production, cost of production, productivity, productive capacity, and resources;
- Operational-technical record keeping, which physically monitors the movement of materials and products within a plant; and
- Financial record keeping dealing with assets, liabilities, revenues, and expenses in financial terms.

The main feature or requirement of Soviet financial accounting is that it should be realistic, that is, accurate and objective and based on actual accounting documents. The accounting system also should be uniform so that all enterprises provide comparable information to central planners. Accounting information should be timely to adjust the production process to meet planned targets. Finally, the accounting system should be efficient—that is, the cost of information should not be excessive.

Comparability is achieved by using the standard chart of accounts, by which various pieces of accounting information are accumulated and systematized. The present chart of accounts for business activities was approved originally in March 1985 by the USSR Ministry of Finance (Minfin), which accounting reports to, and by the USSR Goscomstat, the State Committee for Statistics (the statistical office). The chart contains both summary accounts (that is, aggregated, combined, or first-level) and subaccounts (second-level) that are used in bookkeeping, depending on the requirements of control and reporting. This chart was revised in October 1990 and again in October 1991. It was adopted in Russia in December 1991.

Balance sheets and income statements are drawn up, based on the chart of accounts. The objective of these financial reports is to provide information about the financial position and performance for a given period. The financial reports must fully reflect the results of all economic operations, as well as the availability of cash, fixed assets, and inventory.

The organizational structure of an enterprise can be seen as a functional departmentalization (the process of allocating work to departments within the company). Management gets some instructions and regulations necessary to manage the company. The chief accountant is instructed to make the balance sheet and the income statement, which have to be forwarded to the Ministry of Finance of the USSR (and now of Russia), the local authorities, top management, and the State Committee for Statistics (SCS). Though in theory they all need different information, in practice they all get the same balance sheet and income statement. Financial accounting information normally is not used for management accounting. Cost accounting in the Soviet Union has been part of financial accounting. As explained in Chapters 1 and 2, costing is used only to calculate the production cost, not for managerial planning and control needs.

Managers have their own system of so-called operational accounting (see Chapter 3). The director of the plant has a special team of supervisors whose main task is to control the fulfillment of the plans. The supervisors know how many goods and machines are needed on a daily basis and give their information every day to the director, so the daily volume of production is known. The items are calculated in quantity, not in money. The director cares mainly about production volume and is not significantly concerned with how financial resources are spent. This system of operational accounting is for state enterprises. Joint ventures, however, are more concerned about the costs of production. Because their goal is to make profit, they can influence price setting.

Accounting for Joint Ventures

The Ministry of Finance and the SCS enumerated specific features of the regulations for joint ventures in May 1988, August 1989, June 1990, and October 1991. The regulations determine the procedure and forms of financial reports, including valuation of investments, fixed assets, inventory, cash, and settlements, and detect divergences between book value and physical inventory. They also cover revenue recognition; creation of reserves; financial investments; writing off assets, deficits and losses, debts, and uncollectible accounts receivable; exchange rate translations; dates and addresses for submission of reports; consideration and approval of reports; ways of introducing alterations; and amendments to reports.

In addition to the mandatory financial reports, the SCS requires joint ventures to submit a special report to local statistical authorities and to the ministry (department) that authorized the formation of the joint venture.

Internationalization of Soviet Accounting

A joint venture enterprise in the Soviet republics should be able to function as an independent economic entity with the same characteristics as those of business enterprises operating under free market conditions. The accounting rules and regulations applicable to Soviet state-owned enterprises were not suitable for joint ventures. Many existing and potential Western partners of Soviet joint ventures found it difficult to accommodate themselves to accounting practices based on the concepts and principles developed for state-owned enterprises. Those difficulties have been reduced as accounting principles or standards were modified to suit business enterprises operating under free market conditions.

The Soviet system may have worked adequately for the requirements of a tight, centrally planned economy, but the advent of *perestroika* and the simultaneous need for attracting Western joint venture partners require a reorientation of the prevailing Soviet accounting-statistical systems. This process started in 1990 when accounting regulations for joint stock companies and securities and the quarterly reporting formats for all Soviet enterprises were adopted. Furthermore, the various republics intend to have their own specific guidelines, although presumably following the general established framework. The Soviet republics clearly recognize that joint venture operations require bringing the accounting system in line with international norms and, accordingly, that accountants need to understand Western accounting methodology and practices.

To achieve such harmonization, the existing Soviet accounting system, including its chart of accounts, had to be and still needs to be further adapted. Soviet authorities have been quite willing to modernize their system using international standards or the common language of the international business community.

What is needed most of all is the development of a sound theoretical base for Soviet accounting, a conceptual framework that should contain fundamental concepts and assumptions capable of guiding the setting of standards for financial reporting and managerial decision making. The incorporation of international standards into such a framework would be warranted; however, domestic standards have to be seen in the context of the socioeconomic structure and environment—a careful process of induction and deduction. Such an evaluative process demands theorists and practitioners well versed in accounting concepts and methods.

Therefore, the standard-setting process in the Soviet republics may take some time yet. The Soviets intend to appraise carefully both which Western norms are suitable to their socioeconomic structure and the extent to which Western standards can be incorporated into their system. Most officials and educators in the Soviet Union are aware that the existing rules must be modified and also that academicians and practitioners need to be updated and upgraded into Western accounting.

Divergence from Western Accounting

Until 1930, the main objective of the accounting system in the USSR was to calculate profit and income. After 1930, this objective changed to fulfilling plans and safeguarding valuables (material and monetary assets) to prevent theft. Enterprises belonged to one of the ministries, a situation implying that all profits were paid to those ministries and, hence, that the enterprises could not manage their own financing. Authorities said that their system of pricing, not the good operations of the enterprises, earned profit. A universal chart of accounts was created and had to be used in all kinds of enterprises. The principle of valuation was acquisition (historical) cost. The government fixed prices, and inflation did not formally exist.

Differences between Soviet and Western accounting have been the result of both historical traditions and the distinct Soviet economic system. In the USSR, to serve national planning aspects the accounting system has been subject to strict centralized control and a uniform chart of accounts. The accounting methodology also is different. For example, assets have a historical value base; such concepts as LIFO and FIFO or accounting for changing prices, e.g., current value, are not well known. Land was excluded from the balance sheet because it belonged to the state. Know-how and goodwill also were not recognized.

In Western accounting, income determination based on accrual accounting is the underlying element, and so the matching concept plays a crucial role. Revenues are recognized as earned, and expenses are recognized when incurred. Soviet accounting until recently did not follow this matching concept and also differed from Western practices in the way it handled such basic accounting concepts as assets and liabilities, in addition to revenues and expenses. Both systems, however, use the double entry system.

Many issues, such as matching revenues with expenses, the calculation of production costs, the calculation of profits, and the recognition and valuation of assets and liabilities, still need to be resolved. In regard to production costs, clarification is needed about what constitutes a product cost and a period cost, a direct cost and an indirect cost, and a fixed cost and a variable cost. Soviet accounting ignored the differences between period costs and product costs. All expenses are accumulated in inventories, which are overvalued by international standards, often resulting in material differences in profits and losses. Because of Soviet accounting practice for unfinished products and general expenses, Soviet profits are overvalued by 12% to 20%, by Western standards.

Determination of profit and its distribution are important issues yet to be clarified for Western joint ventures. Underlying income determination and its distribution is the measurement of costs. In Soviet accounting, the cost of production includes almost every cost of the enterprise, not just raw materials, direct labor, and factory overhead, as in the West.

Soviet cost accounting also differs greatly from Western accounting; Soviet accounting is hardly aware of such notions as "different costs for different purposes," in other words, variable (direct) costing. The prevailing notion is that all costs (expenses), whether fixed or variable costs, product or period costs, are to be reflected in the cost method. Cost accounting as a tool for managerial decision making and control is not used effectively, although it is well known in certain quarters.

Nonproduction expenses, which in the West would be expensed as a general overhead, are apportioned to the cost of production. Accordingly, total cost includes both direct and indirect costs. Under international practice, general overhead costs are treated as period costs, not as product costs. In Soviet accounting, the general overhead costs are included in product costs and are carried forward in the value of finished products, as well as of unfinished products. This practice results in overestimation of profits. On the other hand, according to Soviet accounting principles rent for production facilities is not included in the production cost but is taken up directly in the income statement. As a rule, this approach results in a decrease in the cost of production and an understatement of inventories. Other issues yet to be worked out are the choice of inventory valuation methods, the valuation of contributed assets, and the valuation of local inputs.

Soviet accounting regulations require the creation of a number of "special funds" at Soviet enterprises. (Fund accounting is a major feature of the Soviet system.) In joint ventures, such fund accounting effectively would reduce the Western partner's profit share. This requirement is not mandatory for joint ventures, however, and is left to the partners' discretion. The only mandatory requirement is that part of before-tax profits be transferred to a reserve fund that must be built up to a maximum of 25% of the joint venture's statutory fund (capital stock).

Part I
The Soviet Accounting System

Chapter 1

Principles of the
Soviet Accounting System

Until now, all Soviet accounting has been considered financial accounting. Accordingly, accounting has not been divided into financial and managerial (cost) disciplines. Cost accounting is considered a constituent and a consequence of financial accounting.

This chapter gives an overview of the basic regulations pertaining to accounting, while Chapter 2 examines the financial accounting statements and procedures in more detail. In Chapter 3, cost accounting and cost analysis are discussed.

Methodology of Financial Accounting

Since the economic reform of A. Kosygin went into effect in 1964, the previously dominant goal of controlling plan fulfillment has been steadily losing significance, to the point that it has almost disappeared. That goal has been replaced by two new principal goals: (1) control for safeguarding materials and monetary values and (2) control of business transactions.

The first goal arises from the legal functions and the second from the economic functions of accounting. Although the same accounting elements—documentation, inventory taking, chart of accounts, double entry, balance sheet, calculation, valuation, and reporting—are used whether measuring the legal or the economic functions, they are interpreted in different ways.

The Accounting Elements

Documents form the legal foundation for recording transactions according to the Soviet-Russian rules of bookkeeping. No entry should be made unless a bookkeeper has a primary document.

Inventory taking is the sole means of controlling the physical safety of assets and their valuation. It is the main method of supervising the persons who are financially responsible for assets. Under the labor contract, assets always are entrusted to a financially responsible person who has no bond—that is, a person

11

under contract for financial responsibility cannot be bonded under (Soviet) law. Thus, inventory taking is the only means of control.

The *chart of accounts* provides the nomenclature of accounts and correspondence among them.

Double entry is a traditional accounting concept accepted in all developed countries.

The *balance sheet* is the basic reporting form that predetermines the chart of accounts and has as its basis the accounts of the general ledger. Accounts comprise summary (main)[1] and analytic (supporting) accounts. During the entire Soviet period, the balance sheet has been defined as the instrument that shows the assets of an enterprise, along with the funding sources for those assets, at a definite moment in time. That is, the balance sheet is a statistical conception of groups of assets correlated in balance with their respective liabilities.

Calculation is the computation of cost per unit of finished products or services rendered. Pricing in Soviet accounting has been determined not by supply and demand but by adding a charge (margin) on cost (grossing up on cost). Calculation receives much attention because price and profit are directly proportional to planned cost, while net revenue and therefore bonuses are inversely proportional to the difference between planned and actual cost.

Valuation at cost has been typical in Soviet accounting since the period of the new economic policy (NEP), beginning in 1921.

Reporting includes balance sheets and report forms approved by the Ministry of Finance and State Committee for Statistics (SCS). The purpose of the Soviet financial reporting system is to furnish government control agencies with concise information. The system uses accounting indicators such as direct labor to reflect business activities of enterprises and organizations during a particular period. Reporting indicators are shown similarly on a number of reporting forms, and the same item can be traced through two or more forms. One of the tasks of an accountant is to verify that such indicators are the same on all forms.

Accounting reporting is based on the following principles:

- *Intersectoral unity.* The basic reporting forms are in common use throughout the national economy, with certain exceptions for joint ventures.
- *Documentary basis.* Data taken from primary documents are the basis of all reporting data.
- *Logical consistency.* The same indicator should not be different on different forms.

The Chart of Accounts

Accounting experts are unanimous in assigning pivotal importance to account categorization and the double entry system. A uniform chart of accounts was

---

[1]The Russians refer to this account as "synthetic."

adopted on March 28, 1965, by Decree No. 40 of the Ministry of Finance, coordinating with the SCS. This "chart of accounts for accounting of business activities of enterprises, associations, and organizations, and instructions for its implementation" provides for standard nomenclature so that accounts correspond. The latest chart of accounts for all enterprises was adopted in October 1991 and also was adopted officially by the Ministry of Finance of Russia in December 1991. The chart of accounts is the key point of Soviet and Russian accounting methodology, with the balance sheet and all other report forms flowing from the accounts. Each account has its own two-digit code, and a number of accounts have subaccounts.

The complete chart of accounts is given at the end of this chapter. The accounts are divided into nine sections, according to the principle of circulation of assets:

- Section 1—Long-Term (Fixed) Assets and Investments,
- Section 2—Raw Materials,
- Section 3—Production Costs and Expenses (Work-in-Process),
- Section 4—Finished Products, Goods, and Sales,
- Section 5—Monetary Assets,
- Section 6—Settlements (Accounts Receivable, Accounts Payable),
- Section 7—Financial Results and Profit Utilization (Profit and/or Loss),
- Section 8—Funds and Reserves (Ownership),
- Section 9—Bank Credits and Financing (Liabilities).

Accounts included in these first nine sections are called balance sheet accounts, that is, all transactions are reflected by the double entry system. Off-balance sheet accounts constitute a tenth section. They disclose either values not owned by an enterprise (leased property, goods on consignment, goods delivered to an enterprise by mistake) or symbolic values (for example, unsold theater tickets). Transactions registered in off-balance sheet accounts are shown by single entries. The chart of accounts provides:

- An interrelated classification, grouping, and generalization of information on business activities of enterprises;
- A unified methodological basis for the organization of accounting in the whole national economy;
- An effective system of control of indicators for business activities;
- Common understanding when accountants transfer from one industry to another.

Organizational Structure and Regulation of Accounting

The centralization of accounting methodology derives to some extent from the Soviet constitution. Article 131 reads, "Within the framework of its authority the

Council of Ministers of the USSR . . . elaborates and carries out measures on . . . the organization . . . of a single accounting and statistical system." The Council of Ministers is obligated "to carry out measures" intended to organize accounting and statistics in the country. To that end, three regulations on accounting, "Regulation on Main Accounting," "Regulation on Chief Accountants," and "Regulation on Accounting Statements and Balance Sheets," have been approved by decrees.

Regulation on Main Accounting

By means of the "Regulation on Main Accounting" the State Committee on Statistics directs the way accounting is done, authorized by the Council of Ministers. The Ministry of Finance is responsible for determining accounting policy and procedure. Because the Ministry controls the state budget, it must define the calculation method of the most important quantitative indices, particularly those relating to the income of an enterprise. The Ministry of Finance also issues interdepartmental regulations and instructions. On the basis of these general regulations and instructions, other ministries and lower-level departments issue instructions, amended for their specific operations, that all the subordinate enterprises, institutions, and organizations are required to follow.

Regulation on Chief Accountants

The "Regulation on Chief Accountants" was approved by decree of the Council of Ministers of the USSR on January 24, 1980. It consists of chapters on: (1) general provisions, (2) chief accountants' duties, (3) rights of chief accountants, and (4) responsibilities of chief accountants. These rules remain in existence in the Russian Federation and presumably throughout the CIS.

The chapter on general provisions points out that the regulation encompasses chief accountants of associations, factories, organizations, and institutions. Besides doing bookkeeping, these people prepare complete financial statements, including data from subordinate factories; bookkeeping statements; and chief accounts of centralized accounting. On methodological issues, the chief accountant of such an entity is subordinate to the chief accountant of the superior (higher-level) organization, and on administrative issues, only to the director. Soviet accounting segregates duties to safeguard assets. The chief accountant is responsible for supervising personnel and recording transactions. He or she does not have physical custody of materials, cash, or inventory and may not authorize any distribution of assets or payment of invoices. Although a chief accountant usually has a specialized higher education, in some cases three years of work in accounting can serve as a substitute for the educational requirement.

The second chapter of the Regulation enumerates in detail the duties of the chief accountant. In summary, he or she is responsible for the timely, true, and fair representation of whatever is the subject of the accounting. The chief accountant must maintain strict control over the use of manpower, material, and monetary resources. For that purpose, documents supporting the receipt or issuance of cash, inventories, invoices, notes, and checks must be signed both by the directors and by the chief accountants of associations, factories, organizations, and institutions (or by persons authorized by them). Delegation of signature authority must be registered, by order.

A special procedure is provided for settling conflicts that may arise between a director and a chief accountant. If a chief accountant is ordered by a director to conduct a transaction that is contrary to statute or policy, he or she is required to notify the director in writing of the questionable character of the proposed transaction. On receiving from the director a second written instruction to authorize the transaction, the chief accountant carries it out, but at this point full responsibility lies with the director. The chief accountant immediately must report the possible infraction in writing to the director of the superior body, and the superior director then makes a determination about the disputed matter and notifies the subordinate director of the decision.

According to the third chapter, on the rights of chief accountants, the chief accountant determines the duties of his or her subordinates. The list of those employees who are responsible for preparing source documents and who have the authority to sign them must be submitted to and approved by a chief accountant. A chief accountant has substantial power with respect to the appointment, resignation, and promotion of employees.

The fourth chapter of the Regulation stipulates the responsibilities of chief accountants. To some extent, the regulation concerning chief accountants serves as a code of ethics for the profession. The chief accountant is personally responsible for neglect of accounting services, distorted presentations of accounting reports, acceptance of documents for transactions that deviate from established procedure on distribution of assets, errors in the reconciliation of bank accounts, and erroneous statements of receivables and payables. The chief accountant is also responsible for violation of procedures for writing off losses and receivables, ill-timed audits and physical inventory of factory departments, preparation of unfair documentation by the accounting department, and other violations of rules and instructions regulating the accounting service. The chief accountant and the director are jointly accountable for determination of financial and production activity, for any violation of rules and instructions, for ill-timed collection of cash from the employees (required by the People's Control Committee resolutions), and for failure to timely submit their accounting statements.

Regulation on Accounting Statements and Balance Sheets

The "Regulation on Accounting Statements and Balance Sheets," approved by the decree of the Council of Ministers on June 29, 1979, consists of five chapters on: (1) general provisions, (2) rules for the preparation of accounting statements and balance sheets, (3) inventory of balance sheet items, (4) the procedure for writing off damaged and spoiled items (as well as debts and losses), and (5) the procedure for presentation and approval of accounting statements and balance sheets.

Chapter 1 stresses that the Regulation applies fully to factories operating on the self-financing principle. Business entities covered by the regulation on socialist state-owned factories can apportion their structural departments on separate balance sheets. Thus, the use of a separate balance sheet for each production department of a factory is permitted but not required.

Chapter 2 states the recording requirements for business transactions. They can be summarized as full disclosure and reconciliation of data in summary and analytic accounts.

Chapter 3 classifies 18 groups of assets that require physical inventories. The frequency of inventory taking, as well as the inventory deadline, is stipulated for each group. For example, the inventory of fixed assets must be taken not earlier than November 1, and the inventory of investments, not earlier than December 1. Thus, the figures on the annual balance sheets are checked by physical audit of the values. When the personnel with responsibility for physical assets change, different inventory procedures are specified. Ministries and departments can change the number of required inventories with the approval of the Ministry of Finance of the respective republics.

Chapter 4 sets out write-off procedures. It specifies which kinds of factories and organizations can initiate write-offs and which accounts can be written off the balance sheet. The chapter also outlines the procedure for calculating the amount of the values written off and the periods during which the write-off is to be carried out. Special attention is devoted to the reconciliation of the data derived from the physical inventory with the data from accounting registers.

Chapter 5 explains the order for submitting accounting reports, along with the submission dates. The reports are to be submitted, first, to the superior organization (or owners of the joint venture); second, to local financial agencies; third, to the local body of the State Committee on Statistics; and fourth, to the bank (if a factory has a current account with that bank). Quarterly reports are submitted not later than the 12th day of the month following the last month of the reported quarter, and annual reports are submitted not later than January 20 of the following year.

Associations that have an intricate organizational structure with a large number of subordinate entities located in various regions of the country are allowed five extra days to submit their reports. The date of the postmark on the envelope is considered to be the date of submission in the case of a factory that sends its reports by mail.

Representatives of the financial institutions have the right to take part in the meetings at which reports are examined. All the interested parties must be notified about the examination date at least three days before the meeting. Financial institutions have the right to demand an explanation of the reported data if they notify both the factory and its superior bodies of their concern within

15 days of receiving the reports. If the local financial agencies, the local office of the State Committee on Statistics, and the bank do not receive a reply message expressing disagreement with their respective reports within 10 days after a factory's superior organization has received them, they are considered to be accepted.

In case of a disagreement, a factory will submit reports and a balance sheet to its administrative authority within 10 days of receiving the disputed report. Before the resolution of the dispute, only the decisions approved by the financial bodies are to be implemented. If reports that already have been submitted and approved need to be corrected, these corrections will be included in the first quarterly report following the annual report. If the annual report has not been approved by the time the need for corrections is apparent, the corrections are posted to December of the last accounting year.

Regulation on Documents and Document Circulation in Accounting

A fourth regulation, the "Regulation on Documents and Document Circulation in Accounting," was approved by the Ministry of Finance of the USSR on July 29, 1983. The Regulation consists of six chapters on: (1) general provisions, (2) trial (source) documents, (3) registers, (4) correction of errors in trial documents and registers, (5) organization of circulation of documents, and (6) storing of trial documents and registers.

The first chapter gives a brief survey of the contents of the Regulation.

Chapter 2 describes trial documents, each of which, as a minimum, must contain the name, date, transaction explanation, measures, and the position and printed names of the persons who have signed the documents. Document entries can be made only in ink, indelible pencil, or ballpoint pen or by a typewriter or computer.

The factory director, after consultation with the chief accountant, issues the list of persons who have the authority to sign trial documents. The number must be limited, especially if materials in great demand or of high value are involved. Passwords or codes are acceptable substitutes for signatures on computer-generated documents. All the documents supporting cash receipts, payments, or payroll transactions must be canceled with the notation "collected" or "paid" made with a stamp or in writing, and this date must be referenced.

The third chapter explains the order of data transfer from the checked and processed trial documents to the registers, a process that can be accomplished either manually or by a computer. The procedure of data transfer from the registers to the accounting forms also is discussed.

Chapter 4 stresses that erasures and unexplained corrections are inadmissible. Corrections in cash payment and cash receipt vouchers are not tolerated in any form, and corrections in bank documents are executed only in conformity with a special instruction.

Chapter 5 recommends that general accountants design document circulation schedules in the form of charts or tables.

Chapter 6 determines the order of storing of documents before they are deposited in archives or in special cabinets or safes in the accounting department. The chief accountant appoints employees to be responsible for each phase of storage. Documents that are stored and issued under strict supervision must be kept in safes or secured premises. Documents are divided and stored according to the date of issuance. The transfer of the documents to the archives is the duty of an accountant general.

Documents can be withdrawn from an enterprise only under investigation by the Office of the Public Prosecutor or by court order. Withdrawal of documents is registered with the record of evidence, a copy of which is kept at the enterprise. With the approval of the bodies withdrawing documents, the workers of the enterprise can have copies, which must state the grounds for, and the date of, the withdrawal. If documents are lost or damaged, the director issues an order appointing a commission to investigate the incident. The commission must submit a report of the investigation for examination and approval by the director, and a copy is sent to the superior organization.

The regulations described above are the most important normative documents. Various branch agencies have issued many instructions regulating accounting procedures on the basis of such documents.

The Soviet and Russian National Chart of Accounts

The following chart of accounts was adopted October 30, 1991, and also applies to joint ventures. Accounts 03 to 09, 16, 47, 48, 52, 58, 75, 82, 86, 87, 97, and 007 were added, and all sections were restructured. The Russian Ministry of Finance and Economics adopted it in December [letter No. 18-05, December 19, 1991].

Account Number and Name	Subaccount Number and Name
Section 1: Long-Term (Fixed) Assets and Investments	
01 Tangible fixed assets	Different kinds of assets accounted for separately
02 Depreciation of tangible fixed assets	1. Depreciation of owned assets 2. Depreciation of leased assets
03 Leased assets	
04 Intangible assets	Different kinds of assets accounted for separately
05 Amortization of intangible assets	

06	Long-term financial investments	1. Shares and stock 2. Bonds 3. Long-term loans

07	Equipment to be installed	1. Domestic 2. Imported

08	Capital investments	1. Construction and acquisition of tangible fixed assets—planned cost 2. Expenditures not included in the planned cost of tangible fixed assets 3. Young livestock transferred to main herd 4. Acquisition of livestock 5. Dispatch of livestock

09   Leasing claims receivable

Section 2: Raw Materials

10	Materials	1. Raw materials 2. Purchased semifinished goods and parts 3. Fuel 4. Tare materials 5. Spare parts 6. Other materials 7. Materials delivered for processing elsewhere 8. Construction materials and parts

11   Feedstock

12	Low-value and short-life items	1. In warehouse 2. In circulation 3. Temporary (untitled) assemblies

13   Depreciation of low-value and short-life items

14   Revaluation of material assets

15   Procurement and acquisition of material assets

16   Variances in cost of materials

17   ....

18   ....

19   ....

Section 3: Production Costs and Expenses

20   Basic production

21	Self-produced semifinished goods	
22	....	
23	Auxiliary production	
24	....	
25	General production costs	
26	General and administrative overheads	
27	....	
28	Defective products (rejects)	
29	Service sector	
30	Noncapital work	1. Temporary (titled) construction 2. Temporary (untitled) construction 3. Other noncapital work
31	Prepaid expenses	
32	....	
33	....	
34	....	
35	....	
36	....	
37	Production (works, services) output	
38	....	
39	....	

Section 4: Finished Products, Goods, and Sales

40	Finished products	
41	Goods (merchandise inventory)	1. Goods in warehouse 2. Goods in retail trade 3. Tare materials 4. Purchased goods 5. Goods for hiring out
42	Trade surcharge	1. Trade surcharge (discount, markup) 2. Suppliers' discount for reimbursement of transportation costs.
43	Sales expenses	
44	Distribution costs	
45	Goods dispatched (delivered)	

46 Sales

47 Sales and disposal of fixed assets

48 Sales of other assets

49 ....

Section 5: Monetary Assets

50 Cash in hand

51 Cash in bank (business account)

52 Foreign currency account   1. At home
                                          2. Abroad

53 ....

54 ....

55 Other bank accounts   1. Letters of credit
                                          2. Checking accounts

56 Money documents

57 Cash in process of transfer

58 Short-term financial investments   1. Bonds and other marketable securities
                                          2. Deposits
                                          3. Credits receivable

59 ....

Section 6: Settlements (Accounts Receivable, Accounts Payable)

60 Settlements with suppliers
    and contractors (accounts
    payable)

61 Settlements with suppliers for
    advances paid them

62 Settlements with buyers and   1. Cash settlements
    customers (accounts receivable)   2. Planned settlements
                                          3. Notes receivable

63 Settlement of complaints

64 Settlement with buyers for
    advances received from them

65 Settlements for property
    and personal insurance

66 ....

67	Settlement of payments other than to the state budget	By types of payments
68	State budget settlements	
69	Social insurance and social security settlements	1. Social insurance settlements 2. Pension settlements 3. Medical insurance settlements
70	Wage settlements (payroll)	
71	Settlements with accountable persons	
72	....	
73	Other settlements with employees	1. Goods sold on credit 2. Loans 3. Material damage
74	....	
75	Settlements with owners	1. Settlements of inputs to the statutory fund 2. Settlements of income
76	Settlements with debtors and creditors	
77	....	
78	Settlements with subsidiaries	
79	Intraorganizational (intrafirm) settlements	

Section 7: Financial Results and Profit Utilization (Profit and/or Loss)

80	Profits and losses	
81	Utilization of profit	1. Contributions to the state budget from profits 2. Other utilization
82	Reserves (provisions) for doubtful debts	
83	Profits of future periods (deferred revenues)	1. Deferred revenues 2. Future payments of debts for cash deficits of previous periods 3. Difference between cost and amounts received from those responsible for missing material assets
84	Deficits and losses from damage to material assets	

Section 8: Funds and Reserves (Ownership)

85	Statutory fund	
86	Reserve fund	
87	Retained earnings	1. Reporting year 2. Previous years
88	Special-purpose funds	By types of funds
89	Provisions (reserves) for future expenditures and payments	By types of reserves

Section 9: Bank Credits and Financing (Liabilities)

90	Short-term bank loans	By types of loans
91	....	
92	Long-term bank loans	By types of loans
93	Bank loans for employees	By types of loans
94	Short-term credits	
95	Long-term credits	
96	Special-purpose financing and allocations	
97	Leasing liabilities	
98	....	
99	....	

Off-Balance Sheet Accounts

001 Rented or hired assets

002 Custody of material assets

003 Materials registered for processing

004 Goods on consignment

005 Equipment registered for assembling and installation

006 Strictly accountable blank forms

007 Bad debts written off as losses

008 Securities and guarantees received

009 Securities and guarantees issued

Head of Department of Accounting Methodology   Nikolai V. Panteleev

Chapter 2

Accounting, Reporting, and Auditing

In this chapter, accounting and auditing elements are analyzed in more detail, and characteristics of Soviet accounting are compared with those of the West.

Principles Underlying Financial Reporting

Reporting is necessary only for external purposes, for the administrative agencies that make management decisions for the enterprises. Reports are submitted to superior organizations, financial and banking institutions, and agencies of the State Committee for Statistics (SCS), each of which focuses on different aspects of the reports. Superior organizations, for example, owners, analyze the reports to obtain information for planning, to evaluate performance, to aid in management decision making, and to assure the continued protection of assets. Financial institutions determine the sums due for payment according to the budget, calculate whether financial subsidies are required, and find out what financial reserves are available for the use of enterprises. Banks verify the security of loans and the proper use of the wage fund. SCS agencies summarize the reports to provide general information about the national economy, either in its sectoral or in its regional aspects.

Financial reports are the source of most statistical information in Russia and other republics. The state regulates the composition and the structure of these reports. The Ministry of Finance (Minfin), in coordination with the SCS, carries out methodological supervision of reporting; determines its volume, structure, and forms; and also prepares instructions for filing. The procedure for report preparation and submission is set out in the "Regulation on Accounting Statements and Balance Sheets" (described in Chapter 1). SCS agencies have the right to cancel departmental reporting that is not in accordance with acting statutory regulations.

Reporting Requirements

Financial reports should meet the following requirements:

- *Conformity to regulations.* Reporting is carried out according to statutory regulations and presented within strictly determined periods of time.

- *Consistency with plan.* Performance according to plan is monitored via common indicators. In other words, the time frame and mathematical formulae used to calculate the actual reported statistics are the same as those used in doing the planning.
- *Effectiveness.* Statistics shown in reports can be used to influence business transactions, and irrelevant information is disregarded.
- *Efficiency.* The expenses incurred in obtaining information about each operating statistic should not exceed the benefit to managerial decision making.
- *Timeliness.* Information should be made available to managers while it is still relevant to decision making.
- *Accuracy.* All figures and dates reported should be accurate.
- *Clarity.* Reporting should use simple, conventional terminology, and the forms and statistics reflected in the reports should be presented logically.
- *Accessibility.* Reports should be accessible to any individual or organization because there is no principle of commercial secrecy.
- *Reliability.* The data used in reporting should have a foundation in fact.

There are five levels for reporting information: (1) general ledger, (2) summary (main) account registers, (3) analytic (supporting) account registers, (4) primary documents, and (5) inventory data.

When accountants prepare reports, data from the general ledger should equal the results from registers of summary accounts. Data from summary and analytic accounts should correspond, and all primary data from both analytic and summary accounts should be supported by primary documents.

Given these requirements, it follows that an accounting cycle is necessary for correlating the reports with the conditions that gave rise to them. Factors such as documentation and inventory must coincide with reporting. Administrative agencies determine the length of the accounting cycle, which can last for a month, a quarter, or a year. The cycle can match the cycle for the preparation of balance sheets, or it can be shorter. The former was the case until 1985; then the Ministry of Finance retained the monthly accounting period but abolished monthly balances.

Monthly cycles are necessary for: (1) paying monthly bonuses, (2) presenting monthly statistical reports, (3) assessing intermediate results of business activities, and (4) matching balances of analytic accounts and summary accounts.

The Ministry of Finance Regulation 26B of June 17, 1991, established the following new annual reporting formats for Soviet enterprises (the Ministry of Finance of Russia adopted these formats in December 1991):

- The Balance Sheet (Format No. 1),
- Statement of Financial Results and Their Uses (Format No. 2),

- Statement of Property (Format No. 5),
- Statement of Availability and Flow of Enterprise's Funds (Format No. 10).
  (These reporting formats can be found at the end of this chapter.)

The regulation also requires the inclusion of an explanatory note of 15 to 20 pages.

The annual report is to be submitted not later than March 1 following the reporting year, to three parties: the owner(s), the top authority, and the bank (if provided by credit arrangement). Joint ventures are subject to less reporting, and Minfin approves their reports separately.

The Balance Sheet

The balance sheet is the central and most important reporting form because it contains a full and detailed description of both assets of the enterprise and sources of their creation. The form has two columns, one for the beginning and the other for the end of the period, so readers can draw conclusions about changes in assets for the accounting period.

All other reporting forms only clarify the balance sheet or provide more details and analysis.

The overall balance sheet structure is shown in Table 2-1, and the required detailed format is presented at the end of this chapter. An examination of the structure of a balance sheet and the interrelations among its horizontal sections reveals the sections described below.

Table 2-1
GENERAL STRUCTURE OF THE BALANCE SHEET

ASSETS	LIABILITIES
No. of Balance Sheet Section	No. of Balance Sheet Section
I Fixed assets	I Sources of assets (own resources)
II Inventories and expenses	II Bank credits for inventories and expenses
III Monetary assets, settlements, and other assets	III Various bank loan payments and other liabilities

Section I. Assets include fixed assets, intangible assets, and noncirculating assets. They also include allocations of profit to the budget and to reserves of interministerial payments (current assets taken from the enterprise). Noncirculating assets do not yet exist within an enterprise or organization but are counted for control purposes. They frequently are referred to as "withdrawn" assets. Essentially they comprise investments and settlements of various kinds.

Sources of assets shown on the liabilities side are the statutory fund, profit, and depreciation of fixed assets.

Section II. Inventory that cannot yet be sold—production stock, work-in-process, overhead costs on ending inventories of goods, finished products, and other stock and expenses—is shown on the assets side.

On the liabilities side are loans secured by assets and items regulating the valuation of goods disclosed on the assets side of the same section. Bank credits secured by stock, expenses, and foreign currency are the most important liability. Also on this side are reserves for future expenses and payments and also depreciation of low-value items.

"Trade discount on unsold goods" is important for trade companies. Because this item is merely potential profit, it cannot be shown as earned profit. It will be earned only after the sale of goods.

Section III. Monetary assets, securities, and settlements connected with the transformation of assets into money are shown on the assets side. Included here are monetary assets in rubles and foreign currency, disposal of long-term bank credits in rubles and foreign currency, goods delivered, services rendered, settlements with debtors and creditors, expenses exceeding the value of special funds and special-purpose financing, and financial investments in other enterprises and other assets.

On the liabilities side are accounts payable (which comprise short-term loans and long-term bank credits, settlements with creditors for goods and services, promissory notes on commercial credits, credit advance payments, liabilities on wages and insurance, and funds owed to the budget and other creditors) and the complex of items shown under Section I of Liabilities. Also on the liabilities side are sources of assets of purpose-oriented financing and purpose-oriented receiving because, although they belong to the enterprise, their use is strictly limited and intended for a specific purpose. Therefore, they are "withdrawn" from the general funds and are shown in Section III of Liabilities but not in Section I (assets used for loans to workers, special-purpose funds and special-purpose financing, deferred revenues, and other liabilities).

Logical Interrelationships on the Balance Sheet

Several logical interrelationships are established among sections of the balance sheet (see Table 2-1). In theory, the balance expresses equalities of internal links between assets of an enterprise and sources of these assets. Violation of any equality indicates deviation from the legal order of assets.

The first equation is the basic condition of business activities: (1) Assets (A) (I + II + III) = Liabilities (L) (I + II + III). The sum of the first three sections of assets equals the sum of the first three sections of liabilities, thus expressing the balance of the main activities of an enterprise or a company. The equality shows that the sources of assets are equal to the assets available.

The second equation is possible if the equality is broken: (2) A (I + II + III) > L (I + II + III). In this case, part of the funds are used to finance the regular operations (activities).

In the third equation, (3) A (I + II + III) < L (I + II + III), current assets have been withdrawn to support capital investment. The occurrence of this inequality testifies to the temporary withdrawal of current assets from circulation.

The fourth equation shows the existence of an excess of earned and allocated funds over fixed and noncirculated (nonliquid) assets: (4) A I < L I.

All fixed assets are owned by (that is, they are under the operating control of) an enterprise. Leased assets are counted in the lessee's balance sheet.

When business activities are being analyzed, owned assets often are treated in the same manner as assets of legal and actual persons that are at the enterprise's disposal. Included are indebtedness to customers and clients for advance payments received and to unions for payments, wages, and deductions for social insurance reserves for future expenses and payments, and funds remaining free for economic stimulation.

In sum, the balance sheet as the basic reporting form is characterized, from the accounting point of view, by the existence of two balances—one at the beginning of the year or quarter and the other at the end of the year or quarter. Hence, it is always possible to compare changes in accounting indicators (operating statistics).

Preparation of the Balance Sheet

It is necessary when setting up a balance sheet to understand its connection with the chart of accounts and the inventory. The chart of accounts is the source of all data used in the balance sheet.

The preparation of the balance sheet has four stages. *First,* all intercompany payments are checked. For example, a plant pays for materials delivered to its subsidiaries and posts to its own account revenues from the sale of goods produced by these subsidiaries. Such payments during a month are accounted for in the plant's accounting department, and the sum of the turnover and the amount of the balance of separate subsidiaries and of the plant in general should be equal. In case of inequality, errors are identified and corrected. Payments between the plant and its superior agency are verified in the same way. *Second,* payments to financial institutions are checked. Regulation of loan accounts is the *third* stage, and in the *fourth* stage, the financial result (profit or loss) is determined.

After the fourth stage, the general ledger accounts are closed. As a rule, the general ledger is kept on special sheets of paper. Sometimes each page opens with a subaccount, but very often a page of the general ledger opens instead with a summary (main) account, the order recommended in the methodological literature. In the latter case, however, the direct link between the general ledger and the balance sheet is lost. The accountant has to go back to the data from day-to-day operations to record several items on the balance sheet separately for each summary account that combines several subaccounts.

All balance sheet items should be confirmed by sums of balances of general ledger accounts. The "Regulation on Accounting Statements and Balance Sheets" and also the established accounting period require that data be provided by the first of each month to reconcile the supporting accounts as well as the activity and the remainder of the summary accounts. For this purpose, the accountant should prepare activity reports on each summary account. The purpose of these reports is to verify that summary and supporting accounts correspond and to show that all balances are confirmed by the entries in the accounts and primary documents.

In addition to the balance sheet, the "Statement of Financial Results and Their Uses" (see page 41) shows the financial results during the period, the utilization of profit, and the payments to the state budget. Section 1, "Financial Results," reflects the profits and losses. Section 2 shows the "Utilization of Profit." Section 3, "Payments to the State Budget," shows the various tax payments made. Section 4, "Costs Taken Into Consideration for Tax Exemption Purposes," reflects the series of costs to be eliminated for tax calculation purposes.

Analyzing Financial Statements

Analyzing financial statements consists of four steps:

1. Profitability is estimated by two ratios: ratio of profit to owner's resources and ratio of profit to balance sheet total;
2. Solvency is estimated by the following ratio: Accounts Payable less Accounts Receivable divided by Material Current Assets Balance plus Cash;
3. Liquidity is estimated by expert opinion: Estimated Realization Value of Assets less Accounts Payable;
4. Turnover velocity is determined by general ledger data; the number of days in which each account balance is completely changed can be calculated.

Control and "Revision" (Auditing)

Auditing has a different meaning in the Soviet Union than in the West. There are no auditors, in the Western meaning of that term. Auditors in the West work as independent associations of experts who guarantee the reliability of accounting information to shareholders and creditors. Because there are no shareholders in the Soviet Union (as yet) and nearly every creditor is a state enterprise, only designated state agencies are entitled to audit accounting statements. There is, however, a system of complex "parallel control" over the economic activity of enterprises. The state subsidizes the organizations exercising this control.

- *Branch agency control.* Each superior branch agency is required to audit the enterprises subordinate to it. Superior bodies use audits to maintain discipline among subordinates rather than for real investigation. Therefore, Soviet audits do not provide the assurance of adherence to accounting standards that Western audits do. In joint ventures, only partners have the right to audit.
- *The people's control.* The people's control is an autonomous control system that can check all kinds of enterprise activity. As a rule, however, joint ventures are not checked by this system.
- *Financial control.* Financial control is exercised by the branches of the Ministry of Finance and is oriented toward ensuring that taxes dictated by the budget are paid.
- *Credit control.* Banks carry out credit control to maintain the solvency of enterprises and, thus, security for credit.

The branches of the Ministry of Interior Affairs verify the legality of business transactions in order to uncover violations of the criminal code related to property plundering or corruption. The only organization entitled to perform audits of the financial activities of a joint venture is Inaudit (controlled by Minfin), and it does so at the joint venture's expense.

The idea of shifting the inspection function away from a central institution is emerging, along with the establishment of departmental auditing boards and the penetration of the term "audit" into financial and bank controls. However, for the reasons described at the beginning of this section, genuine auditing activity with competition among independent firms has not become widespread at the present time.

Comparison of Soviet and Western Accounting

The differences between the Soviet and Western accounting systems are explained both by historical traditions and by peculiarities of the economic systems. Historical traditions continue to influence the formation of the professional views of Soviet accountants, whereas economic reality determines their behavior in everyday life.

Strict centralized control over all the accounting methodology, exercised by the Ministry of Finance and branch ministries, is the most important characteristic and influences all other circumstances. Such control enables the state to focus all the financial, material, and labor resources of the country on solving the problems deemed most critical. Any other approach would permit some officials to use state property for their local, and sometimes personal, interests.

Methodological differences in Soviet and Western accounting can be divided into three groups: (1) organization, (2) general methodology, and (3) cost accounting.

Organization

The organization of Soviet accounting was strictly centralized, resembling the command over a huge army. Enterprises submitted reports and balance sheets on a quarterly basis to: (1) financial bodies levying taxes, (2) banks lending money to the enterprise, (3) branches of the SCS responsible for accumulation of data from the entire country, and (4) superior organizations. Each of the four reporting groups has its own consolidation structure that culminates in national reporting. Each republic now has its own rules, although these formats are expected to be retained in the republics constituting the CIS.

Thus, we can say that, first, the data at the microlevel (the enterprise) are equal to the macrolevel data, and, second, statistical data for the Soviet republics as a whole are based on the information registered in the bookkeeping system. Although the alternative versions of data contained in numerous reporting forms are not allowed, this fact does not mean that there are no differences in the accounting systems of the myriad Soviet enterprises. Such differences obviously exist, but they are of little consequence. They are attributable to differences in the economic activities of those enterprises, as well as to the habits and preferences of the accountants employed there.

The complete absence of auditing until a few years ago is another peculiarity of Soviet accounting practice. The concept of auditing was contrary to the traditional ideas about control. According to Lenin's views, accounting and control were not private affairs but matters of national concern. Likewise, until recently, no joint stock companies existed. The only nationwide bank automatically loaned money to nearly all enterprises. Bankruptcy did not occur, and no enterprise was ever closed as unprofitable. Hence, there was no need to defend the rights of shareholders and creditors.

General Methodology

The general methodology of Soviet accounting is based on the double entry principle, but the system has some significant peculiarities. Valuation is based largely on historical cost. This approach, which dates back to the 17th century, is a national feature of Soviet accounting. Assets have a legal and an economic valuation base. Values are recorded at the documented purchase price (including delivery and installation) or at the amount invested in the asset (in-house fabrication). Though the economic basis may be disputed because incurred losses still are included in the assets, the valuation at historical cost is recognized as a basic accounting concept. Where values are in constant flux, as is the case, for example, with fresh produce, those values are written off at the average price of acquisition. The principles of last in, first out (LIFO) and first in, first out (FIFO) are unknown to Soviet accounting practice. The principle of conservatism is not used in Soviet accounting practice either. Any deviation from valuation at cost leads to misrepresentation and falsification of the economic nature of the balance sheet.

Another important difference lies in the interpretation of income. In the Soviet accounting system, income is considered a monetary amount; that is, income is cash. In many Western accounting systems, however, income is not cash but the right to receive cash. For this reason, Soviet accountants have a completely different understanding of the moment of sale for finished goods and provided services (recognition of revenue). From the Soviet accountant's point of view, the moment of sale is the moment when a seller receives cash from a buyer, whereas from the Western accountant's point of view, the moment of sale is the moment that goods are shipped or legally transferred. The act of shipping transfers ownership and creates for the seller the right to receive income. Soviet civil law recognizes the latter, but the accounting recognition of revenue occurs only from the moment of cash receipt—no money, no income. Under the conditions of the administrative and command system, this practice had a control function because it prevented overestimation of accounts receivable or falsification of income.

Many Western businessmen are inclined to overstate the significance of the differences in the moment of sale in Soviet accounting and in the West, perhaps because they believe that the Western method shows higher profit than does the Soviet method. However, it is debatable which is the more reliable predictor of profit—the payment that already has been made or the payment that has been promised. A difference of opinion between a Western partner and a Soviet (CIS) partner to a joint venture can be resolved by a provision in the joint venture contract whereby the Soviet practice regarding the moment of sale is followed, but the Western partner's share of the profit is slightly increased. Acceptance of the Western practice would lead to the growth of fictitious accounts, which in turn could create artificial amounts of receivables and cause overestimated profit.

Accounting for assets also differed in the past. Western colleagues frequently were surprised by the Soviet methodology for depreciation of fixed assets. In Soviet accounting the depreciation fund account is opened by debiting an expense account and crediting the fixed assets depreciation account. Simultaneously, the statutory fund (capital) account was debited and the amortization fund account was credited. The first entry, whereby an expense account is debited and the depreciation fund is credited, reflects real expenses on depreciation. The second entry had a purely statistical character, making it possible to estimate the carrying value of fixed assets. Recent changes have eliminated the second entry for both joint ventures and domestic enterprises.

The availability of a production development fund is another peculiarity of Soviet practice. This fund is formed by depreciation amounts and partial allocations of pretax profit. Because this account contains both resources for the renewal of fixed assets and some extra resources, it creates the possibility of financing various undertakings from part of a joint venture's pretax profits.

The economic incentive fund is designed to provide bonuses for the most active employees. Unlike in Western enterprises, where bonuses are included in costs, in Soviet accounting this fund is an allocation from profit. Bonus payments, if included in costs, would increase the cost and, correspondingly, the price of products. (Prices in Russia and the other republics are not yet determined by supply and demand but on the basis of cost and planned charges (margins). However, this practice does not apply to joint ventures, which have the right to establish their own prices.)

The availability of a reserve fund in Soviet accounting does not contradict the practice of some European countries, although many countries do not have any such fund. Soviet accounting practice includes the so-called balance sheet adjustment, which implies the allocation of the entire profit from the accounting year. There are no retained earnings as in Western enterprises, but there is still no significant methodological difference because in Soviet accounting retained earnings actually are disclosed under the reserve fund.

The same adjustment implies writing off annual losses. They must be covered by the enterprise's own resources, for example, from the reserve fund (which is designed especially for such purposes), the economic incentives fund, or from the statutory fund. In some cases, owners may need to make additional investments. In the West, losses of the accounting year can be carried forward to the next year. The Soviet reserve fund makes this practice unnecessary.

Other peculiarities of Soviet accounting practices are:

- No sales discount is provided for prompt payment, such as 2% if a bill is paid within 10 days (2/10).
- Taking inventories is a purely financial accounting procedure.
- Extra cash on hand is payable to the state budget.
- Bank statements are forwarded to enterprises daily.
- Controllers are required to sign all financial documents and, therefore, are liable for all results of transactions.
- Industrial groups (including agencies and amalgamations) sum up their subsidiaries' data without the necessary eliminations, instead of consolidating them.
- Ledger accounts are subdivided into balance sheet accounts and off-balance sheet accounts. Off-balance sheet accounts also are used to account for assets (values) that are not the property of enterprises but that they use (such as leases). For example, owned cars will appear on account 01, leased cars on account 001; purchased merchandise is debited to account 41, merchandise on consignment to account 004.

Another important peculiarity of Soviet accounting is in its education principles, more precisely, textbooks. They are differentiated by level (university or college) or by sector of the economy (manufacturing, construction, retail trade, and so on).

Cost Accounting

Even greater peculiarities arise in the area of cost accounting (for details on Soviet costing, see Chapter 3). Various ministries and branch agencies issue their own departmental instructions. The main goal is to ensure what the officials regard as the correct method of cost calculation of the finished products, because prices in the CIS are fixed by charges (margins) on cost, which determine profits on the planned costs of produced goods. This practice gives management the incentive to overestimate the planned cost. Then the accounting department calculates the actual cost, which, as a rule, is lower. (It is easy to obtain the planned cost by overestimating work-in-process recorded in the basic production account.) This result leads to distribution of bonuses to management for "good" budgeting and to employees for high-level output.

Thus, "norm" accounting usually does not reveal deviations until after the transaction has been carried out, making it a very poor tool for effective decision making. This fact explains why, despite all the promotional efforts by accounting theorists, Soviet norm accounting has not become a management tool. (Norm costing is the best previous average cost.)

In relating cost accounting to calculation of costs and then to price formation, Soviet accountants do not take into account the centers of responsibility and their costs. They do not use the direct costing method, and they lack the concept and practice of managerial accounting (as it is known in the West). All internal accounting used for managerial purposes is called "operational" accounting. It is not conducted by accountants and is by no means connected with accounting offices.

Since the 1930s, the authors of Soviet instructions on cost accounting have been influenced greatly by Marx's theory on "labor costs necessary for society." Discussions still analyze whether this or that kind of expense is relevant to society's needs. If the answer is yes, those expenses are included in the costs; otherwise they are not. In different periods of accounting history and in different industries, the same type of expense has been attributed to the basic production account, to the sales account, and even (rather frequently) to the profit and loss account.

Based on the above discussions, we can understand why, for example, interest, start-up costs, or research and development expenses are charged directly to the profit and loss account, whereas in the West those expenses are considered an integral part of production costs.

Another peculiarity of Soviet accounting concerns the absence of provisions for doubtful debts (accounts). Although such provisions are indisputable in theory and undoubtedly necessary in practice, their use may lead to two undesirable consequences: (1) deliberate understating of profit and (2) artificial overstating of accounts receivable for the purpose of decreasing profit.

Finally, it is necessary to say a few words about classification of expenses. Costs are classified as direct and indirect. The former are attributed directly to certain products, whereas the latter are accumulated first in certain temporary "operative" accounts and then distributed among products, as a rule in proportion to basic wages and salaries. Fixed and variable costs are known in the former Soviet Union in theory but are never used in practice.

The Detailed Balance Sheet Format

Annual Report Format Only for Soviet Enterprises (Except Joint Ventures)*

As per annex
to the letter of the Ministry of Finance
of the USSR
of 17 June, 1991, N26B

Balance sheet
on _____ , 199__

		CODES
	Format No. 1	
Enterprise	per OKUD**	0710001
Supervising body	Date (YY, MM, DD)	
Sector of industry	per OKPO**	
Unit of measurement: thousands of rubles	per OKONH**	
	Control total	

Address _____

Date of dispatch	
Date of receipt	
Term of submission	

---

*Note: This *annual* format is for Soviet (Russian) enterprises only but is similar to the *quarterly* report format that now must be prepared for all enterprises including joint ventures (with and without foreign investment). The reporting for joint ventures and all domestic enterprises gradually is being standardized.
**Russian abbreviations used for statistical purposes.

ASSETS (*AKTIV*)	Code of the Line	At Beginning of Year	At Year End
1	2	3	4
I Fixed assets and investments			
Fixed tangible assets (01)*	010		
Intangible assets (04)	020		
Investments and advance payments (08, 61)	030		
Equipment to be installed (07)	035		
Long-term financial investments (06)	040		
Utilization of profit (81)	050		
. . . .	060		
Settlements with owners (75)	065		
Property settlements (76)	070		
Losses (80)	080		
Total of Section I	090		
II Inventory and expenses			
Production stocks (10, 12)	100		
Work-in-process (20, 21, 23, 29, 30)	110		
Selling overheads on ending merchandise inventory (44)	120		
Prepaid expenses (31)	130		
Finished products (40)	140		
Merchandise inventory (41)	150		
Other inventories and costs	160		
Total of Section II	170		
Including goods in process of transfer	171		
III Cash, settlements, and other assets			
Cash in hand, including petty cash (50)	200		
Cash in bank (business account) (51)	210		
Foreign currencies in bank (52)	220		
Other bank accounts (55)	230		
Money documents and other cash (56)	240		
Securities and other short-term financial investments (58)	250		
Utilization of credits (82)	270		
Settlements with debtors (short-term and long-term):			
For goods and services (76)	300		

*Figures in parentheses refer to the account numbers of the chart of accounts presented in Chapter 1.

ASSETS (*AKTIV*), Cont'd	Code of the Line	At Beginning of Year	At Year End
1	2	3	4
Notes receivable (59)	310		
Advance payments (61)	320		
With the state budget	325		
Other debtors	330		
Receivables from employees for bank loans (73)	340		
Expenses not secured by special funds and purpose financing (87, 88, 96)	350		
Other assets	360		
Total of Section III	370		
. . . .	380		
Total balance	390		

LIABILITIES (*PASSIV*)	Code of the Line	At Beginning of Year	At Year End
1	2	3	4
I Sources of owned assets			
Statutory fund (85)	400		
Depreciation of fixed tangible assets (02)	410		
Depreciation of short-life and low-value items (13)	420		
Financing of investments (93, 94)	430		
Property settlements (76)	440		
Special funds and purpose financing (87, 88, 96)	450		
Reserve for future expenses and payments (89)	460		
Amortization and maintenance fund (86)	470		
Deferred income (83)	480		
Markup on unsold merchandise	490		
. . . .	500		
Profit (80)	510		
Total of Section I	520		

LIABILITIES (*PASSIV*), Cont'd	Code of the Line	At Beginning of Year	At Year End
1	2	3	4
II Credits and loans			
Short-term credits (90)	600		
Medium-term credits (91)	610		
Long-term credits (92)	620		
Credits not repaid in time	630		
Short-term loans (95)	640		
Long-term loans (95)	650		
Total of Section II	660		
III Settlements and other liabilities			
Accounts payable:			
For goods and services (60)	700		
Notes payable (66)	710		
For advances received (61)	720		
To the state budget (68)	730		
To the extrabudgetary stabilization funds (65)	735		
For social insurance (69)	740		
To employees (salaries)(70)	750		
To other creditors	760		
Liabilities to provide loans for employees	765		
Other liabilities	720		
Total of Section III	780		
. . . .	790		
Total balance	800		

_____

DIRECTOR (signature)

_____

CHIEF ACCOUNTANT (signature)

Statement of Financial Results and Their Uses

**The Quarterly Format (Includes Joint Ventures)
and the Annual Format (Does Not Include Joint Ventures)**

Format No. 2

CODES
0710002

From January 1 to _____ , 199___   Per OKUD

Enterprise . . . .   Date (YY, MM, DD)

Sector of industry . . . . . .   UKPO

Supervising body . . . .   OKONH

Unit of measurement: thousands of rubles   Control total

Address_____

I FINANCIAL RESULTS

Name of Item	Code of the Line	Profits (incomes)	Losses (expenses)
1	2	3	4
Revenue (gross income) from sales	010		X
Sales tax	015	X	
Turnover tax	020	X	
....	030		
Production (distribution) costs	040	X	
Profit (loss) from sales	050		
Profit (loss) from other sales	060		
Nonoperational revenues and expenses	070		
including: income from securities and participations	071		X
Total of profits and losses	080		X
Profit (loss) of the reporting year	090		

II UTILIZATION OF PROFIT		
Name of Item	Code of the Line	At End of Period
1	2	3
Payments to the state budget	200	
Allocations to the reserve (insurance) fund	210	
Utilized for:		
Production development	220	
Social development	230	
Incentives	240	
Charity and sponsorship	250	
Other purposes		
(e.g., cost of fines and sanctions)	260	

III PAYMENTS TO THE STATE BUDGET			
Name of Item	Code of the Line	Accrued	Actually Paid
1	2	3	4
Rental payments	300		
Income tax	310		
Including:			
Profit within established rate of return			
(profitability)	320		
Allocations for labor resources	330		
Allocations for utilization of natural resources			
and damage to environment	340		
Turnover tax	350		
Sales tax	355		
Export tax	360		
Import tax	365		
Tax on revenues	370		
Individual income tax and tax on			
single persons	380		
Transportation tax	385		
Other tax	386		
Economic sanctions (fines for			
overdue liabilities)	390		

IV COSTS TAKEN INTO CONSIDERATION FOR TAX EXEMPTION PURPOSES		
Name of Item	Code of the Line	Actual Costs of Period
1	2	3
Production development, research, and start-up technology costs, development of experimental activities	500	
Payment of governmental credit as part of centralized state investment programs, including expenditures for reinvestment	510	
Environmental protection costs	520	
Maintenance of health and old-age institutions, kindergartens, health resorts, sports utilities, etc.	530	
Allocations to help construct agricultural installations and purchase agricultural equipment	540	
. . . .	550	
. . . .	560	

DIRECTOR (signature)

CHIEF ACCOUNTANT (signature)

Statement of Property

Format Established by Ministry of Finance, USSR,
For the Annual Financial Statement for Russian Enterprises

As of January 1, 199___

Registered name of enterprise . . . . .

Sector of industry . . . .

Units of measurement:
per thousands of rubles . . . .

	CODES
Format No. 5	
per OKYD	0710005
Date (YY, MM, DD)	
per OKNO	
per OKONH	
per OKNO	
Control total	

Name of Item	Code of the line	Balance at beg. of year	Accumulated inflow	Outflow	Balance at end of year
1	2	3	4	5	6
I Tangible fixed assets					
Buildings	010				
Construction and creations	020				
Driving gear	030				
Machinery and equipment	040				
Tools, appliances, and other items	050				
Working animals	060				
Productive livestock	070				
Long-term plantation	080				
Other types of fixed assets	090				
Total of Section I	100				
II Unfinished building (construction)	110				

INFORMATION (Notes)

Name of Item	Code of the line	Amount
1	2	3
From line 100, col. 6:		
Fixed assets provided for lease	210	
Value of leased tangible fixed assets	220	
From line 110, col. 4:		
From own sources of assets	230	
From long-term loans	240	
From other credits	250	
From line 040 and 250, col. 4 of Balance Sheet—financial		
investments to the statutory fund of other enterprises	260	
for temporary use of other enterprises	270	
Average number of employees	280	
Funds for consumption including:	290	
Wages and other forms of compensation	291	
Premiums, bonuses, and other financial incentives	292	
Income from stocks of other enterprises and		
return on investments in other enterprises	293	

DIRECTOR (signature)   CHIEF ACCOUNTANT (signature)

Statement of Availability and Flow of Enterprise's Funds

Format Approved by the USSR Ministry of Finance
for the Annual Statement

	Format No. 10		CODES
	per OKYD		0710010
As of January 1, 199__	Date (YY, MM, DD)		
Registered name of enterprise	per OKNO		
Sector of industry	per OKONH		
Units of measurement: thousands of rubles	per OKNO		
	Control total		

Item	Code of the line	Balance (+) [over-expenditure (-)] at the beginning	Entered— accrued increase during the year	Expended (transferred) decrease during the year	Balance (+) [over-expenditure (-)] at end of year
1	2	3	4	5	6
Statutory fund	010				
Amortization fund	020				
Reserves fund	030				
Development and improvement fund	040				
Social expenditure fund	050				
Premium and bonuses fund	060				
. . . .	070				
Repair fund	080				
Provisions (reserves) for future expend-itures and payments	090				

Item	Code of the line	Balance (+) [over-expenditure (-)] at the beginning	Increase during the year	Decrease during the year	Balance (+) [over-expenditure (-)] at end of year
1	2	3	4	5	6
Special finance from budget	100				
Special-purpose finance from the nonbudget funds of economic stabilization	110				
. . . .	120				
Total	130				

Item	Code of the line	From budget	From nonbudget funds for economic stabilization
1	2	3	4
Received:*			
To finance centralized investments	150		
To finance scientific research and development	160		
To cover losses	170		
For production and social development	180		
For other purposes	190		

*The flow of the assets received from budget and nonbudget funds for economic stabilization is recorded on lines 150-190.

Item	Code of the line	Recorded calculated amount	Used by enterprise	Transferred to funds
1	2	3	4	5
Allocated for social needs:				
To social insurance fund	200			
To pension fund	210			
To employment fund**	220			

**The compulsory allocations to the state employment fund on wages are recorded on line 220.

_____

DIRECTOR (signature)

_____

CHIEF ACCOUNTANT (signature)

Chapter 3

Cost Accounting and
Statistical Reporting

General Overview of Soviet Cost Accounting

Western authorities' concept of Soviet accounting as primarily managerial is erroneous because Soviet accounting methodology is uniquely financial accounting methodology. Internal operational management systems are a conglomerate of very different methods independent of each other. Therefore, it is difficult to speak yet about "management accounting," although cost accounting and cost analysis are practiced extensively, mostly by administrators.

Many authorities in the West tend to overestimate the role of central planning and management in the Soviet economy. The simplistic view of Soviet enterprise is that it is no more than a unit within the economy as a whole. That was Lenin's conception of the Soviet economy before 1921, but after that, the idea was no longer valid. In reality, any Soviet enterprise was a legal person and taxpayer, but, until recently, financial and economic freedom of enterprises was restricted severely, and accounting methodology always remained highly centralized.

Perestroika had an impact on accounting by giving birth to management accounting (as an extension of operational accounting). There are, however, important reasons to believe that future Soviet management accounting will be very different from Western practice. Probably accounting (actually, financial accounting) will deal mostly with official, legal data; unofficial, not legally binding data will be the subject of management accounting.

Although the various states in the CIS have the right to develop their own financial and cost accounting methodology, indications are that great uniformity will continue. Development in common will occur in view of the shared historical evolution of accounting, the close interaction between the various republics' economies, and the necessity to adhere to internationally accepted standards and practices, especially in view of the closer integration of the CIS economy with Western economies.

As conveyed above, what is called management accounting in the West does not exist in the Soviet Union (now CIS) as either a comprehensive concept or a clear discipline and practice. However, aspects such as accounting for flows of funds within an entity, cost formation and calculation, intrafirm payments, and unit efficiency analysis do exist. Such functions are performed by the administrative staff, not by accountants, who are engaged solely in financial accounting. The training of specialists in the above-mentioned administrative aspects of accounting falls into three subject-matter areas (described below):

- Operational accounting,
- Cost accounting and cost calculation,
- Analysis of economic (business) activities.

Operational Accounting

For purposes of our study, we shall use the term "operational accounting" and follow its terminology, although it might better be referred to as "financial statistics on operations." Operational accounting has no conceptual accounting basis, but certain features can be identified.

1. Data are provided rapidly. This feature has given its name to this type of information processing because in Russian the word meaning "operational" derives from the same root as the word meaning "fast." The speed with which data are provided is considered the principal merit of operational accounting. This feature also distinguishes operational accounting from financial accounting and its strict recording procedures. In practice, however, speed often is not easy to achieve. The time lag between events and their recording is sometimes significant. This drawback, typical of financial accounting, is often present in operational accounting as well.

2. The objectivity of information is not maintained as strictly in operational accounting as it is in financial accounting. Usually, operational accounting requires no documented evidence, and data may be transmitted verbally. Utility prevails over legal validity in data flows.

3. Approximations can be used for operational accounting data. Rapid estimates often are more important than accurately calculated numbers; that is, speed prevails over accuracy.

4. Operational accounting very characteristically uses ratios, whereas financial accounting deals only with numbers in rubles. Different ratios help in organizing and consolidating substantial data flows for managerial purposes.

5. Operational accounting information often deals with events and numbers that are possible rather than certain.

6. The acceptable degree of informality of data depends on the probability that an event will occur. The more unexpected the event, the more informative the data can be. For example, reporting on the theft of five rubles may be more important than reporting an ordinary purchase of merchandise for 5 million rubles. Therefore, the information about five stolen rubles has priority and may be reported faster to the management.

7. In operational accounting, data are recorded and reported selectively, based on their relevance to managerial decision making. Financial accounting, however, records all data about operations of a company.

Operational accounting is very specialized, according to its application. It exists in various forms—such as technical operational accounting, manufacturing operational accounting, and selling operational accounting—according to the industry or activity and therefore often merges with the planning and control of operations of a technical and administrative nature.

Operational accounting achieves management control through: (1) execution of contracts, (2) meeting plan goals, (3) "dispatcherization," (4) internal reporting, (5) special-purpose reporting, and (6) projections.

Execution of Contracts

Most Soviet enterprises have commercial (sales and purchases) departments, where clerks keep tremendous numbers of files. Computers are used widely now, so every contract is entered into a separate file that holds all basic information about products, terms of delivery, prices, and so forth. Commercial clerks record receipts and deliveries of goods and the execution of contracts. These data are summarized every 90 days to show the amount of merchandise supplied, both by vendors and by the enterprise itself. Relevant data then are transferred to the management for decision making.

Under the centralized economic mechanism, contracts between Soviet enterprises were concluded in accordance with government plans. Even more important than plans were the so-called funds—centrally distributed supplies of materials. The State Committee on Planning, or Gosplan, was the highest authority in assigning funds to enterprises. Thus, contracts were made in accordance with fund assignment, and there was no freedom of choice for the contracting parties. The system of funding coexisted with the contractual nature of business links, but those links operated as quasi-contracts.

Today, funds have been replaced by the so-called state purchase orders. The role of these orders is expected to decrease in the state-controlled sector of the economy, and enterprises will have more freedom in using their products.

Meeting Plan Goals

Independent of whether plans are imposed on enterprises by the government or internally, the management keeps a close watch over their realization. Every manager receives daily reports with compiled information about how plans are carried out. Relevant data—often rough estimates—usually are collected by phone and are discussed during so-called operational meetings for decision-making purposes. In practice, this procedure is the Russian version of managerial or, rather, operational accounting.

The computerization of Soviet enterprises makes managerial data flows and managerial decisions more effective. Computers also facilitate instant quantification of ratios and projects, often allowing the general managers to know more about the performance of departments and sectors than their direct supervisors, who are not able to make projections. Computers also give general managers more power over subordinates, because managers can choose which data may be disclosed to subordinate supervisors. Operational accounting data flows within enterprises have a serious drawback—to the extent that numbers are not supported by objective evidence, they well may be overestimated or underestimated during transfers. The only way to combat data falsification is to compare the data with the exact numerical information provided by the organization's accounting offices at the end of accounting periods. If such comparisons reveal falsifications, those responsible are subject to administrative punishment.

Every enterprise has full discretion in choosing ratios and indicators, such as solvency, liquidity, and return on investment. This freedom of choice brings operational accounting closer to financial and operational analysis.

Dispatcherization

"Dispatcherization" (rapid communication of data) provides control over the flow of assets (materials, semifinished goods, and so on) within enterprises. Data used are an integral part of operational accounting information and have nothing to do with financial accounting or decision-making (managerial) accounting.

Internal Reporting

When the management wants to establish tighter control over the flows of assets, the assets also are measured in monetary terms (by multiplying the quantity by price per unit). In this case, persons responsible for handling inventories, for example, are considered materially responsible for them, that is, liable for them. The concept of material responsibility of individuals within state enterprises is one of the basic aspects of Soviet financial accounting. According to Soviet labor laws, employees' responsibilities can be full or partial. Full responsibility can be borne by the individual or by groups. Managers usually are held partially responsible for conduct that causes damage to their enterprises, but the liability cannot exceed the manager's average monthly salary.

By special agreement with the administration, certain employees are bound by law to bear full responsibility for covering all possible damage or loss. If damage or loss does occur, the person in charge of specific assets has to provide written explanations. If the explanations are sufficient and comprehensive, the person may be freed from financial liability, and the damage or loss is posted to the income and loss account. If the explanations are not considered sufficient, however, the person is liable to cover full damage or loss. In case of serious material responsibility, the amount is distributed evenly among the members of the group. In cases of both individual and group responsibility, the position of the manager of the unit where loss has occurred is a delicate one. He or she has to cover the damage when the culprit has not been identified, even though the manager might suspect someone. In the case of group responsibility, the manager pays equally with others, even though only one person may have stolen assets.

Both individual and group material responsibility motivate employees within a structural task unit to set up a system of internal reporting. The manager of the unit controls all assets assigned to the unit (for example, merchandise inventory, materials, and tools) and distributes them among the members of the unit against receipts. At the end of the work day, the remaining materials and tools are returned and the receipt is signed.

In retail trade, this procedure of internal control is widespread. At the end of each trading day, salespeople return the balance of merchandise, together with copies of receipts for the goods sold, to their manager. The sales people usually must cover any deficit on the spot. However, internal reporting data are not legally binding and are not considered by courts as proof of theft or other crimes.

Use of personal computers allows an expansion of the responsibilities of each individual employee. However, legal responsibility lies with the entire group of employees and the manager.

Special-Purpose Reporting

The centralized system obligated Soviet enterprises to provide administrative agencies of different levels and competence with miscellaneous information about different aspects of their activities. Very often the data required by these agencies are not even recorded at the enterprise, so special research is conducted and data are collected. The Soviet government often prohibited such administrative inquiries about enterprises, but until very recently such special-purpose reporting was very common.

Projections

One of the most important functions of operational accounting is to provide management with data about developments. In this function, it is similar to the planning and analyzing of business operations. The role of projections has increased with the use of computers.

In operational accounting, projections are made in three principal forms:

1. *Expert estimates.* On a periodic basis, the management asks the most competent employees for their opinions about expected developments, future sales, opening markets, and other matters. The peculiarity and attraction of such projections is that they are based more on intuition and expertise than on analysis of past events. The inquiries are made according to random and/or pattern schemes, then documented and processed on computers.

2. *Extrapolation.* Future events are predicted as a continuation of past trends. Extrapolation gives positive results only in cases where market relations are

stable. The drawback of extrapolation is that it depends much on past events, and future developments might not necessarily be the same. Modern methods of extrapolation consider only the most recent events.

3. *Matrix forecasts.* All possible interrelations between two indicators (for example, between revenues and expenses) are listed in a matrix. Some of the elements of the matrix are filled in with real data, others with established numerical values computed with ratios. Because computed values have different degrees of probability, allowances must be determined in each case.

We have considered the most important goals of Soviet operational accounting but have restricted the listing to those goals that demonstrate that operational accounting constitutes the basis for management of Soviet enterprises. We shall turn now to what is more properly known as cost or management accounting, although the latter concept still is somewhat farfetched in the CIS.

Cost Accounting and Cost Calculation

Cost accounting and cost calculation form the second component of Soviet managerial accounting. Accounting for expenditures (costs) is considered an integral part of Soviet financial accounting, thus making it different from Western practice. This entire aspect of accounting is considered no more than the extension of Account 20, Basic Production (see page 19). The accounting procedure is not much different from that of Account 10, Materials, or other accounts. However, as the following review shows, Soviet accounting devotes great attention to accounting for expenditures and to calculation of the cost of finished products.

Basics of Cost Accounting

Costs are expenditures of material, labor, and financial resources for the production of goods or services. This formula was transformed, however, by Marx's theory that both costs and prices in the end are determined by labor expenditures. Marxist views have influenced Soviet accounting theory a great deal. According to his theory, all finished products are expenditures of past labor (materials and depreciation) and current labor (wages and profit). Such an approach to cost has dramatic practical implications; that is, accounting for expenditures is considered a tool for calculating costs of every specific item (whether a product, a semifinished product, a process, or a service).

Moreover, cost calculation was believed to be the necessary precondition for correct price formation. This concept of price formation can be expressed by a formula: $P/T = 1$, where P = price and T = social labor expenditures. When P and T are in balance ($P = T$) everything is considered all right. An imbalance causes inflation and shortages of goods.

Thus, prices are determined as costs increased by ratios set specifically for every sector of the economy or class of goods. In practice, this method leads enterprises to increase costs because the higher their costs, the larger their profit. Managerial logic is as follows: Establish the planned costs as high as possible, then decrease actual costs against planned costs and at the same time derive higher profits from high planned costs. As a result, actual profits will be increased even more by the difference between planned and actual costs.

Actual amounts of wages, bonuses, economic stimulation funds, and taxes depend on the amount of profit. The accountants' task is to compute the profit so that it is as high as possible while the actual costs remain at the minimum level. The higher the planned costs, the easier it is to achieve this goal. This practice is the primary reason that waste and inefficient use of resources were so prevalent in the Soviet economy.

All the negative effects of this system have been discussed widely in recent years and described as the "waste mechanism." However, at the same time government policies were aimed, not at reviewing the theory but at expanding the authority of the enterprises' management over most of their profits and all depreciation amounts. Widespread use of so-called contractual prices between enterprises (determined by supply and demand, not by plan) also increases the amount of profits available to these enterprises. The transition to a market economy that has begun in the Soviet Union will lead to further liberalization of prices. Under these circumstances, the role of cost accounting will be more important than ever.

It is also worthwhile to note that the approach described is still largely typical of Soviet accounting: Accounting for expenditures is considered the initial stage of cost calculation. During the last decade, however, a trend has been growing toward separate approaches, whereby accountants are responsible for expenditure accounting and planners and technocrats are in charge of cost calculation.

Methods of Calculating Cost of Finished Products and Services

The six methods of calculating cost in the Soviet Union are classified according to three criteria:

- By the scope of costs per unit: direct variable (partial cost) and full cost (including almost all costs);
- By the evaluation method of costs per unit: actual costs, norm (standard or prefixed) costs, and aggregated costs (actual expenditures calculated in proportion to norms);
- By objects of calculation per unit of finished goods: the *pozakazny* method (calculation of costs per order) and the *poperedelny* method (calculation of costs at every stage of production of certain goods).

The first classification is purely theoretical because the full cost principle has been adopted officially in the USSR. The list of costs is subject to frequent change

Table 3-1
METHODS OF CALCULATION OF COST OF FINISHED PRODUCTS AND SERVICES

Evaluation Methods	Objects of Calculation	
	Pozakazny (by orders)	*Poperedelny* (by stages)
Actual costs	Method 1: Actual cost of finished goods	Method 2: Actual cost of finished goods at every stage of manufacturing
Norm costs	Method 3: Norm cost of finished goods	Method 4: Norm cost of finished goods at every stage of manufacturing
Aggregated costs	Method 5: Variance of actual costs from norm costs for the full production line	Method 6: Variance of actual costs from norm costs at every manufacturing stage

by the government, however, so that certain costs at times are included in the list and at other times are posted to profit and loss. The relationship between the other two classifications is shown in Table 3-1.

All six methods require debiting Account 20, Basic (Main) Production, at the end of every accounting period by all amounts accumulated on accounts such as Account 23, Auxiliary Production, Account 25, General Production Costs (Overhead), and Account 26, General and Administrative Overheads.

Accounting offices often maintain files for every product for cost-calculation purposes. Direct costs are recorded in the files, and indirect costs are allocated from Accounts 23, 25, and 26 in proportion to one of the bases, usually direct labor. This approach has been justified primarily by ideology because, according to Marxist theory, labor determines costs and prices. As a result, costs are higher for labor-intensive products (which, as we have noted already, are more profitable to Soviet enterprises) and lower for high-technology and capital-intensive goods.

Let us consider all six methods of calculating cost in more detail.

1. *Actual cost by orders.* This method is used most commonly in manufacturing. At the end of each month accountants debit the total unfinished goods to Account 20, Basic (Main) Production. They compute the total from the results of inventories of unfinished products in the shops. These products are valued at cost (acquisition cost plus transportation cost). The amount of unfinished production computed in such a way becomes the ending balance of Account 20. Then they add the beginning balance to all monthly expenses. Finally, they

subtract the ending balance from this sum to obtain actual costs of production of finished goods during the accounting period. This procedure is a part of financial accounting because the amount of actual costs is used further to compute the financial result—profit or loss.

All individual costs determined from files and relevant to Account 20 then are summed and divided by the number of produced goods. The result shows the cost of a unit of production.

The procedure described above is the usual one for scale production. In every case, the object of cost calculation is a specific order of goods (the manufacturing department issues such orders to the shops for a certain amount of goods).

2. *Actual cost by stages.* This method provides cost calculation not of finished goods but of unfinished goods at every manufacturing stage. Discussions about whether to calculate the cost of semifinished goods have been prominent in accounting periodicals. Only the cost of finished products is calculated, and the cost of materials and parts consumed in the shops is subject to operational accounting, as described in the previous section. Theoreticians tended to tout the virtues of "semifinished goods accounting," but practitioners preferred "no semifinished goods accounting" because it is less time consuming.

3. *Norm cost by orders.* Soviet norm accounting, based on previous average actual costs, is considered the most efficient method of cost accounting. In contrast to the previous methods, norm accounting organizes special branches for "technical and economic norming" (standardization) within enterprises. These branches are responsible for establishing norms (standards) for all expected expenditures.

Actual costs are written off according to these norms, but primary documents reflect full amounts of actual costs, including variances. This practice is supposed to ensure better control. The deviations of actual costs from norms are posted to subaccounts.

Norm cost accounting is supposed to be the most efficient management tool because eventual variances automatically signal disruptions in the planned production process. The practical difficulty in applying norm cost accounting lies in the great variety of factors causing deviation of actual costs from norm costs. Accounting for variances is the main practical problem.

Norms, which determine the variance rates, are calculated from averages of previous actual costs. It is typical of management at all levels to make these norms higher in order to have access to more resources. However, the growing instability of the economic environment and disturbances in the production process cause almost constant revision of norms. Under these circumstances, cost accounting is almost useless. For this reason, norm accounting is very much praised in theory but is seldom used in practice.

4. *Norm cost by stages.* This method combines the two previous ones. Theoretically, it is an excellent management tool. In practice, however, it is infeasible for the reasons described above.

5. *Aggregated cost by orders.* This broadly used and very convenient method

has emerged as a way of avoiding the practical difficulties of norm cost accounting. According to this method, planned cost is calculated for each aggregated product group, after which costs are computed for the whole output of finished products. Then the total actual costs are compared to planned costs. Eventual deviations are spread over all product lines. For example, if an enterprise produces A, B, and C, and actual costs turned out to exceed planned costs by 5%, the individual cost of every product line will be increased by 5%. Sometimes, costs are distributed in this way not only at total cost level but for every planned cost item.

From the point of view of Soviet managers, this method is convenient because it does not require maintaining complex analytical accounts and cost calculation files. At the same time, it makes reporting on cost much easier.

6. *Aggregated cost by stages.* A development of the previous method, this one is based on a preliminary computation of the planned cost of semifinished goods. It is seldom used in practice because it adds nothing to achieving one of the main goals of an enterprise—fast and easy reporting of costs—which the previous method provides.

Each of the six methods described above may have to deal with the problem of determining and allocating so-called complex costs. Complex costs are those that create several product lines at the same time. Such calculations are aimed at computing costs even in those cases where they cannot be determined in practice.

Cost Accounting Within Economic Entities

To increase economic initiative at lower levels of management, some structural task units within certain enterprises can use so-called internal cost accounting procedures. These structural task units (such as a manufactured item or a department) are granted certain amounts of current and long-term assets by the general management of the enterprise. Usually, leasing contracts formalize such arrangements. From the moment of formalizing, structural task units account for their operations separately or, in Russian terminology, have their own balance. The company itself, together with all its task units, continues to be one legal entity. From the legal point of view, the separate unit's balance sheet and other financial statements are not valid. Nor do structural task units have any authority to engage in transactions with other companies on their own, unless their company's management grants the units such authority.

Because these internal units engage primarily in intrafirm transactions, all such flows of goods and services are valued at transfer prices or at cost determined according to internal cost accounting. The transfer prices consist of raw product costs determined at the supply shop, the value added at the machine shop, and the planned "profit" of the manufacturing shop, which actually is a sort of markup to planned, or norm, costs of the shop (norm costs serve as a basis when the norm cost by orders or the norm cost by stages method is used).

Flows of goods and services are recorded in special intrafirm accounts. The recipient of goods can make a claim against the supplier on the quality and/or quantity of the transferred products. Intrafirm arbitrators make the final decision on the claim. If the recipient wins the dispute, the ruble amount of the claim is transferred from the supplier's account to the recipient's account.

At the end of the accounting period, the accounting office of the enterprise computes the so-called internal cost accounting profit for each structural unit. The amount of profit determines the salaries of the employees.

The practical problem with internal cost accounting is that intrafirm transactions become somewhat independent from the operations of the overall companies. It is fairly common for structural units to increase the markup on costs of their products, on various grounds. As a result, the share of "internal profit" of shops increases transfer prices, although the company's overall real profit is determined only as a result of transactions with third parties. Quite frequently, the total of internal profits of structural units exceeds the amount of the company's profit.

It may even happen that the company as a whole shows a loss, although its units have earned internal profits. This complication is serious because, as discussed above, employees' salaries within units are linked to internal profits.

Accounting for Cost of Finished Products and Services

According to Soviet accounting principles, only those expenditures that are not taxed are considered costs. This fact explains why tax laws, primarily the Soviet Union law of June 14, 1990, determine the composition of costs. Because provisions of this law apply to all enterprises, independent of their ownership, cost accounting (or, rather, cost calculation) is uniform for all companies. However, decrees and acts of governmental agencies contain different provisions relating to financial and cost accounting for different types of companies. For example, costs of issuance, distribution, and purchase of securities and losses from writing off "underdepreciated" assets are not tax deductible and are not debited to Income Summary accounts. On the contrary, for joint ventures these expenses are charged against profit and debited to Account 80, Profit and Loss. Such provisions are set forth in the guidelines relating to the composition of costs to be included in the cost of production (services) issued November 30, 1990.

The guidelines, like the tax law, classify all expenditures in three categories: (1) those included in the cost of production and services, (2) nonrealization losses, and (3) expenses charged to the post-tax retained earnings. The first are costs as such and are debited to Account 20, Basic (Main) Production, and later posted to Account 46, Sales. The second are debited to Account 80, Profit and Loss. The third are debited to Accounts 81, Utilization of Profit; 96, Special-Purpose Financing; and 87 and 88, Special Funds. Production costs are further classified as material costs, labor costs, state social security expenses, health security expenses, depreciation of fixed assets, and other costs. The State Committee for Statistics publishes manufacturing costs annually on a per item basis.

Material costs include materials, supplies, parts used for production, packaging and sales, maintenance and repairs, start-up operations, and items for personal security. Fuel, lubricants, energy, parts, and depreciation of low-value and short-lived items also are included in the material costs, as are services rendered by third parties and supplementary production costs. Material cost items are valued at the acquisition (historical) cost, including the invoice price, bank interest, transportation and fees, installation costs, and commissions.

Until the mid-1980s, Soviet accounting for inventories was based on stable wholesale prices determined by the government and published in official price lists. Because of their stability and uniformity, these prices served as a convenient basis for analysis of inventory flows. The state-fixed price of each lot was debited to different inventory accounts: Account 05, Supplies; 06, Fuel; 08, Parts; and so forth. Differences between official list prices and costs of lots were accumulated in special variance accounts by different product lines. Inventories were charged to production and sales at accounting (list) prices. At the end of every month before closing entries, all the variances were debited to the same account in which particular inventory items were charged initially. Therefore, material costs were finally valued according to the average cost of every lot.

At present, the loosening of governmental control, with inflation, makes material cost accounting more complicated. Prices vary significantly not only in the private sector but also among state-owned enterprises. Because the Minfin, which used to issue mandatory decrees for all occasions and all matters, did not foresee sharp price increases this time, Soviet accountants were left without guidelines to cope with new accounting complications and tax inspections.

According to the Statement on Financial Reports and Balance Sheets issued by the Soviet Council of Ministers in 1979, inventories must be valued at actual cost. Cost is not determined by average prices, however. Total acquisition cost of an inventory lies in the range between values determined by FIFO (at the bottom) and LIFO (at the top) methods. Soviet accounting regulations permit the choice of any value within this range as inventory cost. Tradition and lack of relevant knowledge keep Soviet accountants from using inventory valuation methods other than average cost. Also, auditing and tax inspections act against enterprises' freedom to choose valuation methods.

Depreciation of low-value and short-lived items also has certain peculiarities. The enterprises themselves establish the depreciation rules. Most often they depreciate such items on a 50% basis, though the methods may vary. For example, the cost of special clothes is charged evenly to expenses every month during their normal life, but special tools are depreciated according to rates linked to production unit output. Some items are written off in the first year, but their value can be charged to costs of special funds when the funds are the sources of financing of such items. The entry will be the following:

Dr Accounts of Costs (20, etc.)
    Cr Account 12, Depreciation of Low-Value and Short-Lived Assets

The typical Soviet accounting practice of depreciating 50% of low-value and short-lived items exaggerates the allowances and partially immobilizes the profits of an enterprise.

Labor Costs

Besides direct and indirect labor of full-time employees, labor costs include all monetary and nonmonetary disbursements to persons operating under contracts with the enterprise. These costs include all bonuses, premiums, and allowances such as provision of free accommodation, meals and special uniforms, special rewards, and all kinds of payments to part-time employees.

Wages in the public (state) sector are determined according to grades fixed by ministries and agencies. In the private sector, companies determine wages and salaries independently. Salaries are determined by overall performance and also can depend on length of service, hours worked, or productivity. "Accord" payments are one form of the latter. Structural task units within state-owned enterprises, such as brigades, often use so-called labor-participation ratios (LPR). These individual ratios increase or decrease the basic salary grades for each worker according to actual wages, depending on the worker's performance. The overall total of individual wages must equal the total payment to the whole brigade for the work it has performed. An example is shown in Table 3-2.

Most Soviet industrial workers in the public sector are employed according to payroll schemes based on productivity. Premium payments are often integral parts of such schemes.

According to labor law, compensation payments are not included in labor costs but are charged to so-called other costs, most of which are determined by special norms and rates. For example, compensation for business trips is limited to transportation, living costs, and per diem costs. Both housing expenses and per diem costs are limited by special regulations of the Council of Ministers, depending on where the employee was sent on business. Compensation for use of special tools, cars, and other items belonging to employees also is determined by the regulations, based on depreciation rules.

Compensation amounts not provided by current legislation are not included in costs and are charged to net profit; thus they are not tax deductible. For example, if an enterprise compensates employees for extra charges (in comparison to government norms) incurred during business trips, they are debited to Account 81, Utilization of Profit, or 88, Special-Purpose Funds. Moreover, such compensation is treated by the tax law as additional payments to employees, is added to their salaries, and is subject to individual income taxes.

Taxes

All enterprises are subject to social security and other taxes. Revenues realized through such taxes are directed to various social welfare and benefit funds. The social security tax of 26%, established by presidential decree at the end of 1990, is a ratio of total wages and salaries of the enterprise, and the resulting amount is charged to the enterprise's costs. Part of these allocations goes to the Federal Pension Fund, and the remainder is designated for different allowances specified by labor laws. The latter allowances cover temporary disabilities, including illness, pregnancy, and childbirth; child care; funeral allowances; and others. Low-income families receive special allowances for children.

Trade union committees at the enterprises use norms established by branch unions to devise the rules for the use of such funds. Funds not consumed by the enterprises are returned to the branch unions. The branch union normally compensates enterprises for overdrafts.

Table 3-2
CALCULATION OF MEMBERS' WAGES USING LPRs

Name	Basic Salary Grade (Rubles)	LPR	Wages Based on LPR	Total Earnings	Calculation of Individual Wages	Wages Payable
Kuznetsov	200	1.5	300	---	$\frac{2000}{1520} \times 300$	394.74
Popov	300	1.0	300	---	$\frac{2000}{1520} \times 300$	394.74
Ivanov	400	0.8	320	---	$\frac{2000}{1520} \times 320$	421.05
Sidorenko	500	1.2	600	---	$\frac{2000}{1520} \times 600$	789.47
	1400	X	1520	2000	X	

The transition to a market economy (growth of the private sector) and dramatic growth in the number of contracts between companies and individuals have led to disputes between enterprises and tax authorities. Fiscal agencies tend to classify these contracts as so-called employment contracts, but enterprises consider them "civil contracts," or contracts between legal entities (the Soviet Union was a civil law country). Neither the companies nor the tax authorities are perfectly correct in applying the civil code. Thus, enterprises often cite various "civil" agreements (transportation, construction, consultancy, and joint operations) in addition to labor or employment agreements. On the other hand, tax authorities tend to consider everybody's earnings as salaries and insist on accruing allowances for social security on such earnings. Though tax authorities are interested in increasing budgetary income, by insisting on more social security allowances they increase companies' costs and, therefore, decrease the taxable income.

Besides social security taxes, all enterprises are subject to payment of allowances designated for the so-called economic stabilization fund established by former President Mikhail Gorbachev. The rate of such allocations is 11% of overall wages of the enterprise. Legislation also mentions compulsory allowances for health security. However, no official regulation covers such deductions, and they seldom are taken.

All the above-mentioned allocations are mandatory for joint ventures and other legal persons with foreign participation.

Depreciation of Fixed Assets

Depreciation rules for joint ventures are different from those for regular local enterprises. Regulations for regular enterprises permit only the straight-line method of depreciation on a monthly basis, plus uniform depreciation rates. Machinery, plants, and equipment are depreciated until their asset values have been written down completely and the reserve balance equals acquired cost. Thereafter no depreciation will be allowed. Some items, such as historical sites and buildings, can be depreciated for an indefinite time. No depreciation is allowed for unfinished construction, creating inconveniences for companies engaged in long-term construction, nor is it allowed for cattle or library books.

The tax law of 1990 (Article 3) permits charging to expenses only the depreciation of the so-called main productive assets. Depreciation of auxiliary fixed assets (such as items designed for recreation) is considered to be profit utilization expense and is debited to Account 81.

Accelerated depreciation is permitted only for assets used in the production of computers, new materials, and equipment or that lead to increases in exports. However, accelerated depreciation seldom is used because the vagueness of the provisions authorizing it often leads to disputes with tax agents.

The situation is quite different for joint ventures. Depreciation "rules" established for joint ventures give them a degree of freedom hardly possible in many other countries. In fact, if a joint venture's statute states that the venture itself chooses depreciation rules, the venture is not legally bound to follow any Soviet-Russian rules and may choose to apply any rate and any depreciation method. According to Soviet-Russian joint venture legislation, depreciation is no longer a matter of public policy but of private preference. Under these circumstances, some joint ventures have chosen to depreciate their fixed assets at extremely low rates, thus increasing profits and dividends to partners. At the same time, the underdepreciated residual values of fixed assets at their disposal are charged to losses and therefore are not taxed.

Joint ventures, like corporations and companies given limited liability by Soviet law, can amortize intangible assets, including goodwill. The terms of amortization are determined by the useful lives of such items. When the useful life is unknown, the item must be amortized for 10 years. Because Soviet-Russian rules do not allow capitalization of launching (start-up) costs, such costs are not amortized but are charged directly to expenses.

Other Costs

Soviet-Russian enterprises and joint ventures differ significantly in how they treat the accounting for other costs. For instance, insurance expense of state-owned enterprises is included only partially in costs. It is a mandatory payment determined by the government at a rate based on fixed and current assets. Voluntary insurance expense cannot be charged to costs and is debited to profit utilization as it is incurred (Account 81).

In contrast, joint ventures include all kinds of insurance expenses in costs (see also Chapter 4), and some are mandatory, a significant incentive for joint ventures as compared to regular Soviet enterprises. Actual, but not accrued, insurance payments can be included in costs, however, both by joint ventures and by Soviet-Russian companies.

Russian tax law allows charging interest to cost only on short-term loans that are not overdue. Interest on long-term and overdue loans is deducted from post-tax profits. Another peculiarity of Soviet-Russian legislation is that it regulates only bank loans and ignores credit from companies and individuals. Thus, most financial operations of Soviet enterprises are not regulated by law. Some other divergences are related to interest. For example, interest on commercial credit, according to Minfin Letter 133 of November 30, 1990, is included in costs, but there is no special regulation for joint ventures. According to the specialized foreign trade companies (in the Russian abbreviation, V/Os) of the Ministry of Foreign Economic Relations, interest due on commercial credit is to be accounted for as deferred expense, and after payment it is to be charged to sales overhead.

Soviet accounting rules provide no adequate treatment for discounts on securities and notes. Fundamental Soviet regulations require accounting for all items at acquisition cost, that is, including all expenses related to acquisition. All commissions paid to banks and other parties are included in costs.

However, tax agents sometimes refuse to recognize certain payments to banks as expenses because they do not consider such payments as disbursements to third parties. For this reason, Minfin pointed out in its Regulation 142 of December 29, 1990, that all kinds of commissions to banks are expenses.

Rental payments are included in costs according to the amounts fixed in rental agreements. Long-term lease payments usually are determined on the basis of depreciation of fixed assets and are accounted for by the lessee.

Other costs of Soviet enterprises include various disbursements to third parties, such as advertising, consulting, legal, and auditing fees, as well as administrative expenses. The latter include so-called representation costs (expenses for luncheons, parties, open houses, souvenirs, and the like). These costs are "normed" (standardized), meaning that expenses exceeding such norms are charged against net profit and are not tax exempt. The Minfin has freed joint ventures from limits on representation costs.

Other costs also include maintenance and repair of fixed assets. Maintenance costs can be financed from reserves that were established by enterprises at rates based on the book value of fixed assets. In this case, "other costs" include monthly allowances for maintenance, rather than actual maintenance costs. Joint ventures have a greater variety of "other costs," including deficiencies in inventories and other assets when no party can be identified as being responsible for such deficiencies. Regular enterprises reflect such deficiencies of goods as losses.

Different categories of expenses permitted to be included in costs are classified according to the regulations of different sectoral ministries. For example, in manufacturing, costs are classified as follows:

- Materials and supplies,
- Recyclable materials,
- Purchased inventories,
- Fuel and energy for technological purposes,
- Direct labor of workers,

- Indirect labor of workers,
- Social security deductions,
- Start-up and launching costs,
- Maintenance of equipment,
- General manufacturing overhead,
- General overhead,
- Losses due to poor quality (substandard production),
- Other production overhead, and
- Nonproduction overhead.

The first five items constitute direct costs. All other costs are indirect costs. So-called nonproduction overhead is accounted for separately. It arises from the sale of finished products and includes packing, transportation, and other costs that, according to the terms of the contract, are borne by the shipper.

Extraordinary expenses are accounted for separately on the debit side of Account 80, Profit and Loss. They include ecological disasters, sanctions and fines, losses from the sale of fixed assets, losses from previous periods, and negative foreign currency translation differences. Joint ventures can add two more items—allowances for bad debts and losses from sales of intangible assets.

Finally, disbursements that do not affect the amount of balance sheet profit, such as dividends and taxes, are debited to Account 81, Utilization of Profit. Table 3-3 shows the classification of manufacturing costs debited to Account 20, Basic (Main) Production.

Analysis of Business Activities

Analysis of business activities is the third component of Soviet managerial accounting after operational accounting and cost accounting and calculation. It is more an extension of operational accounting, as referred to previously, than it is financial analysis. Until very recently, the main goal of analysis was (and for many Soviet enterprises still is) control over fulfillment of state-fixed plans. Currently, analysis of profitability is more important, and a future field of analysis is solvency and liquidity of enterprises. However, cases of bankruptcy already exist. In the old command economy, bankruptcy was conceptually impossible. State-owned enterprises were obligated to fulfill plans in nonmonetary terms by any means, though financially the enterprises could be in constant loss. The state budget covered these losses.

In Soviet accounting for enterprises, the variance analysis is the main aspect of control over profitability. Two measures of profitability are used—return on sales (used by enterprises) and return on assets (used by academic analysts).

Costs are analyzed in order to reduce them. When they rise, as is usually the case, management's goal is to prove to planning agencies that the increases were justified because of growth of input costs and better quality of finished goods.

Analysis of financial and position performance is only now emerging in this transition period of the Soviet economy. Both simple and sophisticated methods of analysis are practiced. Enterprises use three simple basic methods: the balance method, the index (growth rate) method, and the ratio method. Researchers use more sophisticated and less practically applicable correlational and regression methods. The first three methods are discussed briefly below.

1. The balance method is linked to control over plan fulfillment. It usually compares planned items with actual ones. (See Table 3-4 on page 68.)
2. The index method is basically a factorial analysis based on factors variance analysis. (See Table 3-4.)
3. The ratio method is used increasingly today. The debt-equity ratio, rate of return on sales, and sales-inventory ratio are much the same as in market

Table 3-3
MANUFACTURING COSTS DEBITED TO ACCOUNT 20

CLASSIFIED ELEMENTS OF COSTS/ COST ITEMS	MATERIAL COSTS	LABOR COSTS	SOCIAL SECURITY	DEPRECIATION OF FIXED ASSETS	OTHER COSTS
Materials & supplies, semiproducts, purchased items, fuel, energy	Material expenses for technological purposes	---	---	---	---
Direct (principal) wages	---	Wages of workers for actual labor hours	---	---	---
Indirect (additional) wages	---	Wages of workers for nonoperational hours, leaves, business trips, etc.	---	---	---
Social security deductions	---	---	Allowances at a fixed rate to principal & additional wages	---	---
Start-up costs	Material start-up costs	Labor costs	Social security allowances from relevant wages	Depreciation of plant & equipment engaged in start-up	Consulting costs, etc.
Maintenance & repair costs	Material maintenance costs	Wages of workers engaged in maintenance	Relevant allowances	Depreciation of equipment	Fees for consulting expertise, rentals & leases, & insurance
General manufacturing overhead	Material cost of maintenance of plant & equipment	Wages of shop masters, engineers, & service personnel	Relevant allowances	Depreciation of plant & equipment	Reporting of buildings, fees, rentals & leases
General overhead	Material costs of maintenance & of general & administrative services (offices, warehouses, etc.	Wages of management, general & administrative services	Relevant allowances	Depreciation of general & administrative services facilities (offices, etc.)	Insurance, rentals & leases, fees, general & administrative expense (most classified earlier), amortization of intangible assets, etc.
Technological and "poor quality" losses	Costs of spoiled items or substandard products	Wages attributable to spoiled items & repair costs	Relevant allowances	Depreciation pertinent to spoiled products	Other costs related to production of spoiled or substandard items
Nonproduction costs	Packing costs of finished products	Wages pertinent to loading, transportation, & storage of finished goods	Relevant allowances	Depreciation of plant & equipment related to storage, packing	Transportation, storage & other freight-in fees & transportation

economies. Soviet enterprises manage the velocity (sales inventory) ratio, considered to be of primary importance, in two principal ways, one based on management of inventories in natural weights and measures and the other on accounting for storage costs.

Another ratio often used in Soviet accounting is the following:

$$\frac{\text{Equity - Fixed Assets}}{\text{Fixed + Current Assets}}$$

The result shows the share of the so-called owned current assets. This ratio often is planned (ministries used to impose it on enterprises). The bank often would check this ratio before opening a credit line for an enterprise. Measuring solvency and liquidity is becoming more important for enterprises today. For example, the current ratio is calculated in the following way:

Table 3-4
PERFORMANCE—BALANCE AND INDEX METHODS

Balance method—analysis of merchandise flows. Merchandise flow is represented by the following equation:

$B_b + A = S + B_e$ where B_b = merchandise inventory beginning; A = purchased inventory; S = goods sold; and B_e = merchandise inventory ending. Therefore the balance method relationships are expressed as follows:

(1) Planned inventory $B_b + A = S + B_e$
(2) Actual inventory $B_{bl} + A_l = S_l + B_{el}$
(3) Difference—balance $B_b - B_{bl} + A - A_l = S - S_l + B_e - B_{el}$

Since planned sales are the determinant, this formula also can be expressed algebraically as:

(4) $S - S_l = B_b - B_{bl} + A - A_l - B_e - B_{el}$

Index method—computed outputs. Output is represented by the following equation: $V = Q \times P$ where V = output, Q = number of workers, and P = average productivity. Therefore the index method relationships are expressed as follows:

(5) Historical output $V_h = Q_h \times P_h$
(6) Actual output $V_a = Q_a \times P_a$

To indicate the change in output due to changes in the number of workers, this additional formula is used:

(7) Change in output $V_t = Q_a \times P_h$

Both theory and practice of the index method are based on index relationships.

$$\frac{C + I + Cr + D}{P + S + B + AP + PL + CE}$$

where C = cash; I = inventories; Cr = credit received in bank and authorized for payments; D = accounts receivable, net; P = accrued wages; S = accrued social security allowance; B = accrued payments to the state budgets; AP = accounts payable (for inventories); PL = payment of loans; and CE = current expenditures (disbursements).

Entries Related to Cost Accounting

The following entries to T-accounts illustrate typical transactions in Soviet cost accounting. The numbers of the accounts correspond to the national chart of accounts (see page 18).

(1) Supplies were purchased at acquisition cost.

10 Materials		60 Accounts Payable	
(1) 2000			(1) 2000

(2) Supplies were delivered to the manufacturing shops.

10 Materials		20 Basic Production	
(1) 2000	(2) 1200	(2) 1200	

(3) Finished goods, at planned cost, were delivered to the warehouse.

20 Basic Production		40 Finished Goods	
(2) 1200	(3) 900	(3) 900	

(4) Finished goods were shipped to customers.

40 Finished Goods		45 Goods Delivered	
(3) 900	(4) 500	(4) 500	

(5) Payments were received from customers for goods.

51 Cash in Bank		46 Sales	
Beg. Bal. 3000			
(5) 550			(5) 550

(6)   The cost of finished goods is charged to sales.

45 Goods Delivered	
(4) 500	(6) 500

46 Sales	
(6) 500	(5) 550

(7)   Suppliers' accounts were paid (for the goods shipped).

51 Cash in Bank	
Beg. Bal. 3000	(7) 2000
(5) 550	

60 Accounts Payable	
(7) 2000	(1) 2000

(8)   Wages to manufacturing workers (principal) are accrued.

20 Basic Production	
(2) 1200	(3) 900
(8) 400	

70 Payroll Settlements	
	(8) 400

(9)   26% social security allowance is accrued to wages accrued.

20 Basic Production		69 Social Security & Pension Settlements	
(2) 1200	(3) 900		(9) 104
(8) 400			
(9) 104			

(10) An allocation of 11% of accrued wages is made to the Stabilization Fund. The Stabilization Fund is established by the federal government as a centralized resource. Allocations to this fund are, in fact, an indirect tax on enterprises.

20 Basic Production		68 Settlements with State Budgets	
(2) 1200	(3) 900		(10) 44
(8) 400			
(9) 104			
(10) 44			

(11) Depreciation of machinery is accrued.

25 General Production Costs		02 Depreciation of Fixed Assets	
(11) 200			(11) 200

(12) Depreciation of the buildings of manufacturing shops is accrued.

25 General Production Costs		02 Depreciation of Fixed Assets	
(12) 100		(11) 200	
		(12) 100	

(13) Depreciation of offices and warehouses is accrued.

26 General Overhead		02 Depreciation of Fixed Assets	
(13) 50		(11) 200	
		(12) 100	
		(13) 50	

(14) Wages to manufacturing workers are accrued.

25 General Production Costs		70 Payroll Settlements	
(12) 100		(8) 400	
(14) 100		(14) 100	

(15) Social security allowances are accrued—26% of wages is accrued.

25 General Production Costs		68 Settlements with State Budgets	
(12) 100		(9) 104	
(14) 100		(15) 26	
(15) 26			

(16) Allocation to the Stabilization Fund is accrued—11% of wages of manufacturing workers is accrued.

25 General Production Costs		68 Settlements with State Budgets	
(12) 100		(10) 44	
(14) 100		(16) 11	
(15) 26			
(16) 11			

(17) Salaries of management office employees are accrued.

26 General Overhead		70 Payroll Settlements	
(13) 50			(8) 400
(17) 50			(14) 100
			(17) 50

(18) Social security allowance is accrued—26% of accrued wages of management office employees.

26 General Overhead		69 Social Security & Pension Settlements	
(13) 50			(9) 104
(17) 50			(15) 26
(18) 13			(18) 13

(19) Allocation to the Stabilization Fund is accrued—11% of wages of office management employees is accrued.

26 General Overhead		68 Settlements with State Budgets	
(13) 50			(9) 104
(17) 50			(15) 26
(18) 13			(18) 13
(19) 5.50			(19) 5.50

(20) Individual income tax on employees is accrued.

70 Payroll Settlements		68 Settlements with State Budgets	
(20) 70	(8) 400		(9) 104
	(14) 100		(15) 26
	(17) 50		(18) 13
			(19) 5.50
			(20) 70

(21) Cash was withdrawn from account in bank for payment.

51 Cash in Bank		50 Cash in Hand	
Beg. Bal. 3000	(7) 2000	(21) 480	
(5) 550	(21) 480		

(22) Wages were paid in cash to employees.

70 Payroll Settlements		50 Cash in Hand	
(20) 70	(8) 400	(21) 480	(22) 480
(22) 480	(14) 100		
	(17) 50		

(23) Cash was transferred to social security agencies.

51 Cash in Bank		69 Social Security & Pension Settlements	
Beg. Bal. 3000	(70) 2000	(23) 143	(9) 104
(5) 550	(21) 480		(15) 26
	(23) 143		(18) 13

(24) Cash was transferred to government budgetary agencies.

51 Cash in Bank		68 Settlements with State Budgets	
Beg. Bal. 3000	(7) 2000	(24) 218.50	(9) 104
(5) 550	(21) 480		(15) 26
	(23) 143		(18) 13
	(24) 218.50		(19) 5.50
			(20) 70

(25) At the end of the month, maintenance expense is charged to the Main Production account.

20 Basic Production		25 General Production Costs	
(2) 1200	(3) 900	(11) 200	(25) 200
(8) 400			
(9) 104			
(10) 44			
(25) 200			

(26) At the end of the month, manufacturing shop expenses are charged to Main Production.

20 Basic Production		25 General Production Costs	
(2) 1200	(3) 900	(12) 100	(26) 237
(8) 400		(14) 100	
(9) 104		(15) 26	
(10) 44		(16) 11	
(25) 200			
(26) 237			

(27) At the end of the month, general and administrative expense is charged to Basic Production.

20 Basic Production			26 General Overhead		
(2)	1200	(3) 900	(13)	50	(27)118.50
(8)	400		(17)	50	
(9)	104		(18)	13	
(10)	44		(19) 5.50		
(25)	200				
(26)	237				
(27)	118.50				
Turnover	2303.50				
Ending Bal.	1413.50				

At the end of the period, an inventory is taken, and the amount of work-in-process is established and documented. This amount is debited to Account 20 as Ending Balance, 1413.50.

(28)Actual production costs (890 rubles) are debited to Account 40, Finished Goods.

40 Finished Goods			20 Basic Production		
(3) 900		(4) 500	(2)	1200	(3) 900
(28)[10]*			(8)	400	(28) [10]*
			(9)	104	
			(10)	44	
			(25)	200	
			(26)	237	
			(27)	118.50	
			Turnover	2303.50	
			Ending Bal.	1413.50	

*Note: The entry of 10 rubles is made in red ink and indicates actual economy in costs as against planned cost. The economy is supposedly due to economy of materials or increase in productivity. Earlier, in transaction (3), finished goods were entered at planned cost. It is only at the end of the month that actual costs can be recorded. The computations are shown below.

900.00	Planned cost of finished goods
890.00	Actual cost of finished goods
10.00	Economy in costs
2303.50	Total actual costs of the month
1413.50	Work-in-process
890.00	Actual cost of finished goods

(29) The economy in costs is debited to Account 45 (in red ink).

40 Finished Goods		45 Goods Delivered, Services Rendered	
(3) 900	(4) 500	(4) 500	(6) 500
(28) [10]	(29)[5.50]	(29) [5.50]	

Some of the finished products, with the actual cost of 494.50, were sold. The amount of economy is computed proportionately between the inventory and sales. Total economy is 10 rubles as shown above.

(30) Actual cost of sales is debited to Account 46.

45 Goods Delivered, Services Rendered		46 Sales	
(4) 500	(6) 500	(6) 500	(5) 550
(29)[5.50]	(30)[5.50]	(30)[5.50]	

Note: This operation reveals the final actual net profit from sales—55.50 rubles.

Soviet accounting methodology leads to permanent overestimation of earned profits primarily for two reasons: very low depreciation rates and partial allocation of costs to inventories (transaction 28). The profit is overestimated on the average by 12% to 20%.

Part II
Accounting for Joint Ventures
in the Soviet Union

Chapter 4

Establishing Joint Venture Operations in the Soviet Union

The Nature of Joint Venture Operations

Although specific regulations concerning joint venture investments in the Soviet Union (CIS) may be drawn up by individual republics in the future, it is expected that the general framework as described in this chapter will remain intact and be adopted by the republics.

A recent study by various international organizations,[1] in a chapter called "Foreign Direct Investment in the U.S.S.R.," states:

> Few, if any, countries offer as potentially attractive opportunities for large-scale foreign direct investment as the U.S.S.R.: a vast international market; a critical need for an efficient and expanded consumer goods industry; enormous natural resources whose efficient exploitation would yield large benefits both to the U.S.S.R. and to foreign investors; new, untapped business opportunities resulting from the conversion of the defense industries; a woefully underdeveloped services sector—including the basic distribution system and business-related services—where foreign know-how would be extremely valuable; and a general need to import foreign technology, managerial skills, and experience in operating in a market environment.

> This potential notwithstanding, foreign direct investment in the U.S.S.R. has been minimal to date in terms of foreign capital actually invested, and is unlikely to expand significantly in the absence of a dramatic improvement in the country's political, economic and regulatory environment. One, but not the principal, reason for this disappointing performance is the inadequacy of the regulatory framework for foreign investment. More fundamental from a foreign investor's viewpoint are overall political and legal uncertainty, economic risk, and the lack of functioning input markets and basic infrastructure in such areas as finance and telecommunications.

> Against this background, it is clear that there are great potential benefits to the U.S.S.R. from increased participation of foreign investors in the development of the

---

[1] *A Study of the Soviet Economy*, International Monetary Fund, World Bank, Organization for Economic Cooperation and Development, European Bank for Reconstruction and Development; OECD, Paris, 1991, Volume 2, pp. 75-80.

U.S.S.R. and its integration into the world economy. Indeed, by providing favorable feedbacks to the process of economic reform, success in attracting substantial flows of foreign investment could be crucial in the transition to a market economy. It is also evident that the difficulties to be overcome in achieving this are considerable.

Commenting on the activities of joint ventures established in the USSR, the authors continue:

The equity joint venture has been to date the principal form of foreign direct investment in the U.S.S.R. This form is characterized by an equity ownership in a separate legal entity by the foreign partner(s) of up to 99 percent, reflecting a commensurate investment of capital. As a general rule, joint ventures are subject to the same laws and practices as other Soviet business entities, but there are a variety of important exceptions in areas such as supply and distribution, taxation, wages and management rights.

The enabling legislation for joint ventures was passed in January 1987 and by mid-1990 there were 1,754 registered joint ventures with a total registered initial capital of around rub 4 billion. This figure is, however, a poor indicator of the volume of convertible currency funds that has actually been invested in joint ventures. Although convertible data are not available in this respect, it can be reasonably estimated that the stock of foreign investors' convertible currency contribution is unlikely to exceed the equivalent of rub 500 million and may indeed be substantially less.

(Note: A new form of investment that can be expected to play an increasing role is the purchase of shares by foreigners in existing or new Soviet enterprises or cooperatives. Contract joint ventures, consisting in essence of a joint project between foreign and Soviet partners without ownership interests and obligations in a new entity, also may become more common; and wholly owned foreign enterprises are permitted by the presidential decree of October 26, 1990.)

The initial stage of joint venture development was marked by steady growth, as would be expected as the first wave of negotiations bore fruit. The initial enthusiasm has become tempered, however, by the realization of the problems posed by economic disorganization and bureaucratic resistance. Growth has slowed noticeably since late 1989 in terms of the number of new ventures and, to an even greater extent, initial capital investment. Furthermore, of the 1,754 joint ventures registered at the end of June 1990, only 541 actually are operating and producing goods or services. An additional 162 (mainly in the service sectors) reportedly are paying their workers but have not yet entered the production phase. All in all, the number of ventures that can be said to be operational is 703, or about 40% of the total registered at that time.

The average joint venture tends to be small by both international and Soviet standards. More than half the operating ventures employ 50 or fewer persons, and fewer than 10 ventures have more than 1,000 employees. These ventures, however, accounted for approximately 15% of the overall volume of production recorded in the first half of 1990, while the 470 joint ventures with a work force of up to 200 employees contributed just over half of the total production. The limited size of joint venture operations is even more evident when measured in terms of capitalization. Indeed, from the outset, Soviet officials have noted with disappointment that, from their perspective, joint ventures have tended to be seriously undercapitalized. The statistics bear out this impression.

In some cases, joint ventures appear to have been set up primarily, if not exclusively, because they provide a relatively inexpensive and quick way to establish a physical presence in the USSR. This factor seems to be the most important one for smaller foreign companies, which often find it easier to identify a Soviet partner willing to establish foreign ties than to traverse the many bureaucratic obstacles to setting up a legal representation in the USSR. The positive economic impact of this "illusory" form of direct investment is likely to be marginal.

Legislation concerning direct foreign investments also has been passed. In the following sections, specific attention will be paid to the critical functional aspects to be addressed in entering into joint venture agreements in the CIS.

Historical Background

Decree No. 49, issued by the Council of Ministers in January 1987, marked the beginning of joint venture operations in the USSR. This decree was one of the first major steps in the country's process of economic reform, and it was introduced well before any other significant changes in the Soviet economy were launched. At that time, even the key word—*perestroika*—had a different meaning than it has today. In early 1987, Soviet leaders were not speaking of a transition to a market economy. Market instruments at that time were considered supplementary to the basic centrally planned model of the economy, and the political climate then was very different. Keeping this fact in mind will help observers understand the nature of the difficulties that joint ventures in the Soviet Union still encounter.

The process of joint venture creation in the Soviet Union passed through at least three major stages. The *first stage*, from January 1987 to approximately August 1988, was characterized by the introduction of different regulations based upon Decree No. 49. During that time, the Ministry of Finance registered no more than 60 to 70 joint ventures.

The *second stage* began in the fall of 1988. The period from September 1988 through January 1990 saw a dramatic growth in the number of joint ventures registered—approximately 1,000—an average of about 60 new entities per month, or two every day. Decree No. 1405, issued in December 1988, introduced major liberalization measures relevant to joint venture creation, organization, and operation. It had a significant impact on this process.

The *third stage* may have begun in the first months of 1990. As of April 1, 1991,

3,400 joint ventures were registered in the USSR, but only 948 (28%) were operating. The operating joint ventures, broken down by sectors, are as follows:

- Manufacturing—42%,
- Services—27%,
- Retail trade—9%,
- Restaurants—9%,
- Research & development—8%,
- Construction—5%.

Joint ventures have generated much less foreign technology and currency earning than expected, and their imports have exceeded their exports. (More than one-fourth of the exports are fish products and seafood.) Many of the joint ventures actually entered into shady deals, either price abuses or currency speculations. Since 1989, the federal government has imposed more restrictions than liberalizations on joint ventures.

A review of current joint venture activities discloses the principal reasons for their establishment and operation:

- To obtain tax advantages,
- To give Soviets easy access to the West (including travel privileges and dollar earnings),
- To gain publicity,
- To establish a market presence and watch Soviet developments so as to secure a future position in the Soviet market,
- To earn high profits (well above Western margins) due to currency exchange/ price differences,
- To gain access to Western consumer goods or Soviet raw materials and commodities.

Many such ventures were started as a result of personal contacts (or sympathies) between Soviet and foreign individuals rather than because of market research or the like.

The *fourth stage*, that began in the spring-summer of 1991 is characterized by increased legislative activity in the republics concerning different aspects of international business, especially foreign investments. The regulations are becoming much more liberal (e.g., 100% foreign ownership is now allowed).

Basic Regulations for Joint Venture Operations

Decree No. 49

As mentioned above, Decree No. 49 of January 1987, followed by a dozen different orders and instructions of different Soviet agencies and ministries, laid the initial legal foundation for joint ventures. These regulations were formally valid until September 1, 1991—the date the law on foreign investments in the Russian federation became effective. However, despite the collapse of the old USSR after the failed coup in August 1991, many former Soviet regulations related to foreign business are valid—either formally (because they are recognized by new Russian legislation) or informally (until they are replaced by new ones). This fact greatly increases the complexity of the legal environment for foreign Russian operations during the "post-Soviet" transition period. Soviet-Russian legislation on joint venture operations from 1987 to 1991 may be summarized as follows:

Participants in the joint venture may be one or several Soviet and foreign legal persons. Joint ventures are legal persons under Soviet law. The law on property passed in February 1990 allowed foreign natural (actual) persons to establish joint ventures in the USSR.

The founding documents (the agreement between the partners and the statute), together with a feasibility study upon request, must be submitted to a regulatory body that registers joint ventures. Registration with local authorities or a branch ministry is now allowed. Previously, only the Council of Ministers of the USSR could grant such permission. The agreement and feasibility study then also must be registered with the Ministry of Finance (formerly Soviet, now Russian).

Shares in the statutory funds are negotiated and valued by agreement between the partners. Initially, the foreign partner's share was limited to 49%, but this restriction was lifted in December 1988. Since 1991, 100% foreign subsidiaries are allowed. To protect the interests of the minority partners, crucial decisions concerning joint venture operations require the unanimous vote of the board of directors.

Property that foreign partners brought as part of their share in the statutory fund is not subject to customs duties. Imports of joint ventures for their own needs or for further development of operations, as well as personal belongings of employees, are duty free and exempt from input taxes. On the other hand, Decree No. 203 of March 7, 1989, prohibits importation of goods destined for sale to third parties in the USSR.

Foreigners may now hold top executive offices in the joint venture. The board of directors can make decisions on any issues covering the operations of the joint venture, including personnel, wages, investments, and allocation of profit to funds. Most crucial decisions, which are to be specified in the treaty or the statute, should be unanimous.

Earnings in foreign currencies may be repatriated after taxation. The tax holiday has been extended to two years after the declaration of profits (previously this period covered the two years after the creation of a joint venture, during which time the venture often had losses).

Joint ventures are allowed to engage in any kind of foreign business transaction.

Other Orders and Instructions

A number of orders and instructions followed Decree No. 49 and are relevant to different fields of activity of joint ventures. They are listed below:

- *Registration:* Instruction of the Ministry of Finance of November 24, 1987.
- *Assessment and valuation of property:* Order by State Committee on Prices of February 4, 1988.
- *Accounting and reporting:* Letters of the Ministry of Finance and State Committee on Statistics of February 22, 1987; May 3, 1988; and August 9, 1989.
- *Taxation:* Instruction of the Ministry of Finance of May 4, 1987, and November 30, 1987.
- *Procurement:* Order of the Gossnab (State Committee for Supplies) of June 4, 1987.
- *Insurance:* Instruction of the Ministry of Finance of June 5, 1987.
- *Banking operations:* Orders of Gosbank (State Bank of the USSR) and Vneshekonombank (Bank for Foreign Economic Relations) of September 22, 1987, and August 31, 1988.

A major difference from the former Soviet practice applied to joint ventures is that the whole board of directors and the management are to resolve all issues concerning hiring and firing, payroll, and premiums. Social guarantees cannot be less than those provided by Russian legislation.

Law on Foreign Investments

The Russian law on foreign investments passed on July 4, 1991, became valid on September 1. It introduced the notion of "enterprises with foreign participation," synonymous with "joint ventures." It allows 100% foreign-owned enterprises, as well as branches of foreign companies. In addition to the points listed above, the law establishes the following provisions:

1. Foreign investors obtain treatment no less favorable than that nationals receive.
2. Foreign investments are guaranteed against nationalization and expropriation (in exceptional cases such decisions must be taken by the Supreme Soviet).
3. Losses and damages to foreign investors are compensated fully, quickly, and effectively.
4. Proceeds in rubles from foreign investments may be reinvested in Russia or converted into dollars at market rates.
5. Foreign investments exceeding 100 million rubles must be approved by the Council of Ministers within two months.

6. The Ministry of Finance is obligated either to register an enterprise with foreign investment or to notify it of the reasons for refusal within 21 days. Refusals may be based only on violation of law and may support a course of action in court.

7. Wholly owned subsidiaries and joint ventures with foreign shares exceeding 30% are not subject to licensing of exports of their own products and imports for their own needs.

8. Revenues from exports of an enterprise's own products in foreign currencies are not subject to foreign currency taxation.

9. Foreign investors are allowed to purchase shares, stock, and securities of Russian enterprises both with foreign currencies and with rubles earned from operations in Russia. In case of conversion of foreign currencies into rubles for the purpose of such acquisition, the exchange rate must not be lower than the rate used by Gosbank for foreign economic transactions.

Some of the special regulations and procedures concerning joint ventures, covering accounting, reporting, and taxation, are discussed in more detail below.

Principal Obstacles Facing Joint Ventures

Despite continuing liberalization, major barriers to further development of joint ventures in the Soviet Union still remain. For example, the nonconvertibility of the ruble is a major problem. These obstacles can be grouped as follows:

Establishment and Launching Problems

Red tape. Despite liberalization of the registration process, bureaucrats both at the local level and at the Ministry of Finance sometimes are unwilling to relinquish control of the situation and create artificial obstacles in the process of registration. These complications are much eased now because of restrictions imposed on terms of registration by the laws on enterprises and foreign investments.

Underdeveloped infrastructure. Office space and housing for employees are difficult to find, communication facilities are inadequate, the level of services is low, and consumer goods are in short supply.

Problem of assessment of property as part of partners' investment in the statutory fund of a joint venture. The use of improper methods of evaluation, lack of information about international market prices, and lack of professional assessors usually lead to overestimation of values of property, land, and equipment. Growing inflation complicates the situation even more.

Lack of mutual understanding between partners. A major problem is that partners speak different languages; have different backgrounds, especially in the fields of management and marketing; and often either are not very confident about each other or, on the other hand, tend to have a euphoric view of the joint venture project.

Operational Problems

Management. Management problems are closely related to the preceding problems. Even once the joint venture is established, it still may encounter major managerial problems. Western businessmen are not very familiar with peculiar Soviet "tricks" in business, and Soviet managers, though successful in Soviet enterprises, often are not knowledgeable about running a profit-oriented business. This issue leads to a broader one, discussed next.

Lack of specialists. There is a lack of relevant specialists in international business transactions, marketing, and so on. In addition, many people in the Soviet Union consider joint ventures to be an area in which to make a lot of money, not to work hard.

Deficiencies in the banking services for joint venture operations. The very rigid and conservative Soviet banking system in general is inflexible in terms of loans, accounting, provision of guarantees as to credit worthiness of Soviet partners, and leasing services.

Difficulties in procuring supplies. This problem was not particularly anticipated before the introduction of joint venture legislation in the USSR. It was widely considered that Soviet enterprises mostly needed know-how and technology, while raw materials were in abundance. Now joint ventures are facing two serious problems: one of a more general nature resulting from the deterioration of the situation in the Soviet markets for capital and consumer goods, and the second, the peculiar problem that Soviet raw materials or semifinished goods do not meet Western standards. A well-known example is that McDonald's had to create its own farming and processing facilities before it could open its restaurant in Moscow.

Accounting and reporting differences. Accounting and reporting differences still remain a big obstacle and are discussed in detail in the next paragraphs.

End-of-Period Problems

Distribution of profits. The Soviet system of distributing profits is very different from international practice. Retained earnings are practically unknown. All profits always used to be allocated to funds, and Soviet enterprises encounter major difficulties in using cash from different banking accounts. A state-owned enterprise must justify every expenditure to meet the goals of a fund to which cash has been allocated. Also, an inspector of the Ministry of Finance can cause problems.

Private enterprises have more freedom, but even so, anti-inflation measures restrict access to cash. Joint ventures are required to allocate profits to funds, including a special reserve fund, as do "normal" Soviet enterprises. A reserve fund is mandatory, but the allocation of profits to the production development fund (or other fund) is at the discretion of the board of directors. At the same time, until 1992 no retained earnings were allowed, so the partners had to divide all profits as dividends if they wanted to avoid interference in the joint venture's affairs by Gosbank and the Ministry of Finance.

Repatriation of profits. Foreign investment legislation guarantees repatriation of profits to foreign partners, provided they pay the usual 20% tax on the amount transferred abroad. Until recently the most infamous problem for joint ventures was, and partially is, the nonconvertible ruble. Joint ventures are required to be self-supporting in currency. The best way to earn hard currency is to export joint venture products or at least find a demand that can be met by payment in hard currency in the Soviet Union. A growing number of joint ventures, such as hotels, restaurants, and retail stores, earn hard currency providing services for foreign visitors (and legally for Russians since the fall of 1990). Many foreign partners used to solve this problem by purchasing raw materials or other goods in the Soviet market for rubles they earned as their share of profits, but the Ministry of Foreign Economic Relations and other central administrative agencies now restrict most exports very severely.

A growing number of joint ventures use the opportunities that have arisen since 1990 to convert rubles into dollars at market rates at auctions and foreign currency exchanges and by direct deals with other companies or banks. Many joint ventures now prefer to accumulate ruble earnings and then to invest them in real estate (such as apartments and houses), possibly other fixed assets in the future, and sooner or later, land. Following the latest liberalization in foreign exchange regulations, joint ventures may now sell and buy rubles for hard currencies. In 1991, many joint ventures actually preferred to buy rubles; the government had to impose restrictions on the exchange rate.

There are a number of ways to approach the problem of nonconvertibility of the ruble (Table 4-1), as joint ventures that already have gained experience in the Soviet Union usually find.

Three methods most commonly are preferred by joint ventures as well as by other Soviet companies.

1. *Barter.* Bartering has become especially popular since the government decided in December 1990 to impose mandatory foreign currency sales (earned through exports) on Soviet companies. The key in this case is to obtain permis-

Table 4-1
WAYS OF OVERCOMING THE NONCONVERTIBLE RUBLE

- Help your partner earn dollars.
- Barter.
- Purchase commodities for rubles and export them.
- Countertrade.
- Sell dollars in the Soviet market.
- Make rubles-commodities-dollars deals.
- Buy dollars for rubles at market rates.
- Reinvest your rubles.

sion to barter, which is licensed. The growing decentralization of foreign economic regulations broadens these possibilities.

2. *Foreign currency.* Goods-rubles-foreign currency deals can be made. The key is to "play" on the differences in direct market exchange rate of the ruble and those attainable through imports of specific goods. For example, R35,000 are converted into $1,000 (exchange rate 1:35), and 2,000 audiocassettes are purchased at $.50 each. They are sold at R25 each, which brings a gross revenue of R50,000. The rubles then are converted into dollars in the market at 1:35 and bring $1,429. As the profit margin shows, these deals are very popular with many companies, including joint ventures. The basic pattern has many variations (for example, commodities are purchased in the Soviet market for rubles and exported, and so forth). Such deals, however, are impeded by governmental controls, ruble instability, and growing (often unfair) competition.

3. *"Goods transfers."* A new invention born of foreign currency earning restrictions provides exchange of goods between Soviet and foreign partners, through two different export and import contracts. The key is that export contract prices are 15% to 20% lower than they should be. Import contract prices, on the contrary, are higher than they should be. The differences are accumulated in "secret" accounts of Soviet companies abroad and are not taxed. Confidential relations with the foreign partner are a prerequisite for such deals.

The transition to a convertible ruble in the near future may be economically difficult, so several issues must be addressed in the contracts of joint ventures: (1) how to evaluate fairly the partners' investments in the statutory fund, considering that the investments involve different currencies and other kinds of property; (2) how to value and record business transactions; (3) how to value and record business transactions that require payments after the approval of annual balance sheets; (4) how to convert and finance profit in foreign currency; (5) how to minimize the effect of foreign currency fluctuations on the results of operations and the financial statements; and (6) how to discourage speculation based on currency fluctuations. It must be stressed here that if these differences are not addressed in Soviet financial legislation (as is the current situation), the partners to a joint venture must address them in their contract.

Negotiating and Establishing a Joint Venture

Starting the Negotiations

The process of establishing a joint venture usually begins when potential partners find they have a common ground of interest and try to work out a form for cooperation. Sometimes a special feasibility study is necessary to choose the most appropriate form of cooperation.

When the parties reach the basic decision to form a joint venture, they usually have to discuss at least the three key items listed below.

- Statutory purposes and activities of the joint venture,
- The approximate amount and composition of the statutory fund and distribution,
- Possible ways of securing the earning of profits in hard currency for the foreign partners.

The next step in the negotiating process between potential partners often is signing the statement of intent. This document, in accordance with Soviet law, is not binding and implies no material commitments. Still, it is recommended that the potential partners include text in the statement of intent that shows the parties are interested in reaching an agreement and that states the results already achieved.

The statement is more limited in content than the agreement (see below) and covers only some of the major items that are usually further negotiable. The other purpose of the statement of intent is to furnish information to the regulatory authorities along with preliminary inquiries about obtaining registration for the joint venture in the future. Further negotiation normally leads to an agreement between the parties.

Founding Documents

Agreement Between the Parties

Joint ventures in the Soviet Union are established by agreement between the parties. Each joint venture also must have its statute. As both agreement and statute are necessary for establishing a joint venture, they usually are referred to as "founding documents." (This term is also the one used in Soviet laws.)

The agreement between the parties usually consists of 20 to 25 articles. Several standard forms of contracts, not very different from each other, are circulating throughout the country and are used widely by joint venture partners. It is highly recommended that the parties use a standard Soviet form for such a contract because it will ease the process of obtaining permission and registration.

The main articles of a joint venture agreement are the following:

1. *Preamble.* The preamble usually states the fact of establishment and the name of the joint venture, names of partners, and location of the joint venture.

2. *The main goals and principal activities of the enterprise.* The regulatory bodies usually want to ensure that a joint venture's goals do not contradict current legislation, specifically if it concerns foreign trade transactions. Joint ventures in trade (trade agents) usually are treated with a certain degree of suspicion because under Decree No. 203 of March 7, 1989, of the Council of Ministers, they may act as agents in foreign trade only with permission of the Ministry of Foreign Economic Relations. Usually manufacturing joint ventures include trading operations, marketing, and research among their statutory

activities. Very often the following formula is used: "The joint venture will engage in other operations consistent with its main goals and Soviet laws and regulations." Establishing trading operations as the main statutory activity of a joint venture is not recommended.

3. *Rights and obligations of partners.* Both rights and obligations can be bilateral and unilateral.

- Bilateral (or multilateral) rights may include obtaining all information relevant to the joint venture's operations, proposing items for the agenda of board meetings, and participating in decision making on all crucial matters relating to the joint venture's activities.
- Unilateral rights for the foreign partner may include the exclusive right both to promote and sell the joint venture's production in certain third-world countries and to purchase part of the joint venture's production for its own needs.
- Bilateral obligations include, among others, the obligation to input assets into the statutory fund according to the schedule, to assist the joint venture in achieving its goals, to supply it with relevant materials, and to help in obtaining loans from Soviet or foreign banks.
- Unilateral obligations of the Soviet partner(s) usually include assisting in preparing the documents and following all the procedures of registration; making necessary arrangements for water, electricity, and gas supply; setting up a communications network and other infrastructure; and providing or assisting foreign employees with housing and transportation.
- Unilateral obligations for foreign partner(s) include providing know-how and expertise, training Soviet personnel, and securing the sale of a specified percentage of production abroad.

4. *Legal status.* The joint venture becomes a legal person under Soviet law from the moment of registration; consequently, it has all the rights and obligations of Soviet legal persons.

5. *Statutory fund* (amount, shares, composition, schedule of replenishment, transition of shares to other partners or third parties). The Ministry of Finance usually is interested in the amount and structure of tangible assets, especially cash the foreign partner will bring. The time schedule of contributions to the statutory fund also often is scrutinized closely. The valuation of shares may be either in rubles or in a foreign currency, and the official exchange rate in the Soviet Union for commercial transactions is used for translations.

6. *Credit and loans.* This is a statement of credit and loans, if any, and the manner of their payment.

7. *Self-support in foreign currency.* The article concerning self-support in foreign currency sometimes is combined with a sales clause, which specifies a minimum share of export sales. Frequently, the foreign partner takes the responsibility for promoting these sales in foreign markets.

8. *Profits and losses.* The article concerning profits and losses states the manner of distribution of profits, including the guarantees to the foreign partner to repatriate profits. Regarding profits in foreign currency, the usual scheme can be illustrated in the following way: Suppose the shares are divided 50-50 between a Soviet and a foreign partner and 70% of the joint venture's net revenue is in foreign currency because of foreign sales. In this case, the foreign partner will receive its entire profit of 50 units in foreign currency. If the partner decides to repatriate them, it will have to pay a 20% tax (10 units). The Soviet partner will get 30 units in rubles and 20 units in foreign currency.

9. *Funds.* A reserve fund is mandatory and must be at least 25% of the statutory fund. The partners decide the length of the period of allocations to this fund. Soviet regulations do not specify other restrictions on this fund. The creation of other funds such as production development, social welfare, and economic stimulation, is at the board's discretion. If these funds are created, their amount (as a percentage, say, of net profit) and the schedule of allocations are to be specified.

Under Decree No. 49, joint ventures have the authority to choose specific depreciation policies relevant to their needs, which may be different from the usual straight-line method. In this case, an appropriate explanation of these policies must be included in the agreement. Otherwise, the joint venture's depreciation automatically falls under ordinary Soviet regulations, providing strict straight-line depreciation at government fixed rates.

10. *The governing bodies of the joint venture.* Usually the bodies are: (a) the board of directors, (b) the management, and (c) the auditing commission. The statute (see page 93) should specify their functions in detail. The agreement between parties raises only some of the major issues, that is, the division of competence, the distribution of chief positions between partners, and the method of their rotation.

11. *Financial, accounting, reporting, and auditing issues.* Usually a statement is included indicating that relevant Soviet regulations govern the financial, accounting, reporting, and auditing issues. However, the partners may specify the procedures the joint venture should follow in reporting to them or in conducting internal auditing (usually in the latter case a reference is made to the statute).

12. *Property rights, including intellectual property issues.* It is common for one of the partners to make an input to the statutory fund in the form of an intangible asset, such as know-how or a trademark. If that occurs, reference is made to paragraph 17 of Decree No. 49, either about the protection of industry rights under Soviet law or about different issues related to the partner's transfer of property rights to the joint venture.

13. *Insurance.* Usually a reference is made to relevant regulations concerning joint ventures in the USSR.

14. *Employment and personnel: relations between management and employees.* Decree No. 1405 of December 2, 1988, lifted all restrictions on hiring and

firing of employees, as well as on their salaries. It is common practice, however, for the agreement to include an article binding the management to sign a formal agreement with the employees' union to be created by the joint venture. Under Soviet law, the article regulates all aspects of the union's relationship with the employer.

15. *Responsibility.* Any nonfulfillment or unsatisfactory fulfillment of obligations by one partner usually leads to compensation to the other partner(s) for relevant damages.

16. *Force majeure.* As a rule, all the contingencies that lift any responsibility from the parties are enumerated. These circumstances usually include natural disasters, governmental decisions, international conflicts, and internal crises, including strikes. All other issues relating to force majeure circumstances and their implications for the partners should be defined.

17. *Confidentiality.* Under this article each partner assumes an obligation not to disclose any technical, financial, commercial, or other information provided by another party or parties and to take all necessary measures to prevent the leakage of the information available. It is recommended that the parties include a clause granting the board authority to determine the terms, scope, and limits of applying the confidentiality principle.

18. *Settlement of disputes.* Usually the parties agree that if they cannot settle a dispute themselves, they will submit it to an arbitration court. If the agreement contains no arbitration clause, the settlement of disputes automatically must take place in a Soviet court.

It is common practice to refer to an ad hoc arbitration court in a third country (most often in Stockholm, Sweden) and to use the laws of that country as the basis for settling disputes. Sometimes parties agree to resolve their disputes in the Arbitration Court of the USSR Chamber of Commerce and Industry, in which case the cost will be much lower. It also is recommended that arbitration be based on the UNCITRAL 1976 Regulations. The United Nations Commission on International Trade Law worked out this set of rules, and it is widely considered a very well balanced document that satisfies the needs of both Western and Eastern partners.

19. *Termination.* The article about termination usually discloses the most probable reasons for that action (such as expiration of the term of the agreement if at least one of the partners confirms in writing its intention not to renew the agreement, permanent violation of the agreement by one or more partners, and governmental decisions). The parties agree in case of termination to set up a so-called liquidation commission, whose main purpose is to determine the residual value of the joint venture's assets and to prepare a liquidation balance sheet. The distribution of net residual assets according to the liquidation balance sheet is in proportion to the partners' shares in the statutory fund. It is common to introduce a clause under which the distribution of residual assets will take into account the contributions in hard currency (or the equivalent) by the foreign partner(s).

Statute

In many respects, the statute follows the agreement, and the provisions of the agreement generally have more weight than the statute provisions. The statute usually deals in more detail with issues related to the operations of the joint venture. Special attention should be paid to articles dealing with the areas described below.

1. The composition of the board of directors and the division of offices among the partners is outlined. Since Decree No. 1405 of December 2, 1988, has been in effect, it has been very common to rotate the chief executive positions in a joint venture. For example, during the first three years the president of the board and the deputy general manager will be Soviet citizens, while the general manager will be a foreign citizen; during the next three years, the opposite will hold true.

2. The detailed list of issues requiring unanimous vote by the board usually comprises from 10 to 15 items, including the following:

- Amending the statute,
- Introducing or replacing members,
- Changing the amount of the statutory fund,
- Using the reserve and other funds,
- Distributing and allocating profits,
- Obtaining long-term loans,
- Establishing branches, offices, or affiliates,
- Appointing the general manager and that person's deputies.

This important article gives the minor partners the right of joint control of the company. In addition, it enumerates any other issues that require a majority vote.

3. This article details the procedure for conducting the meetings of the board, informing its members, voting, and carrying out the board's decisions.

4. The functions of the general manager and that person's deputy or deputies are outlined, as is the relationship between the board and the management, including the delegation of responsibilities.

5. The composition and rules relating to the commission for revision, whose purpose is to perform internal audits, are set out (see "Auditing" on page 122 for more detail).

All other items usually follow relevant articles of the agreement and are sometimes more detailed.

Feasibility Study

Feasibility studies are not, strictly speaking, part of the founding documents, but normally one should be included in the set of papers submitted to the regulatory authorities and the Ministry of Finance for permission and registration procedures. The data in the feasibility study may be used by the authorities to make their decision and may well serve as a reason for possible refusal. Therefore, a distinction should be made between a feasibility study for the peculiar needs of partners (or a partner) and the "official" feasibility study to be submitted to the Soviet authorities.

The latter should follow a certain standard form worked out at the Research Institute for Foreign Economic Relations in Moscow. The Soviet partners normally hire a group of specialists to prepare a carefully crafted feasibility study that will satisfy the authorities, and the Western partners usually agree with this practice.

Preparing feasibility studies as well as founding documents for joint venture registration purposes is a growing business in the Soviet Union, and the competition is high. Regulatory bodies at the local or ministerial levels also tend to participate in an indirect way in this kind of service, another example of how the bureaucracy does its best to maintain control over the economy in the new business environment.

Usually, the official feasibility study contains the following provisions:

1. Description of the goals of the joint venture;
2. Major technical data relating to the project;
3. Comparisons to existing Soviet and/or foreign practice in the relevant field;
4. List of benefits the joint venture will provide both to the partners and to the Soviet state;
5. Description of the statutory fund with detailed composition and schedule of contributions;
6. Statement of the expected number and salaries of personnel;
7. Description of the formulae used to calculate the profits and other financial statistics of joint venture operations;
8. The so-called basic initial data of the joint venture that are used for further calculation and estimates;
9. Different measures of the expected financial and economic performance of the joint venture, which, basically, include the following:

- The rate of return on investments discounted on the "time value of money" basis for the joint venture as a whole and for each individual partner;
- The so-called "general economic effect" of creation of a joint venture expressed in monetary terms, which represents a combined cash flow created by the joint venture both for a Soviet partner and for the Soviet government;
- The estimate of conditions of self-support in foreign currencies; this estimate represents a balance of the joint venture's revenues and expenditures in foreign currencies at the end of a statutory term of duration of the joint venture agreement;

10. The overall summary and conclusions.

The main purpose of a feasibility study is to convince the regulatory bodies and, if necessary, the Ministry of Finance that the joint venture will bring material benefits not only to the partners but also to the Soviet state and that it will be self-supporting in foreign currency. Obviously, feasibility studies that do not meet these requirements are not submitted to the regulatory bodies. It is, therefore, no secret that the studies tend to overestimate the prospects of a joint venture project (though sometimes the estimated profits are so high that it is reasonable to cut them in the feasibility study). Since such feasibility studies became irrelevant, the governments in the republics tend to pay less attention to them or even do not ask for them.

Registration Procedures

Registration procedures have been liberalized greatly since 1987, when the first joint ventures emerged. Until then, permission to establish a joint venture was granted by no less than the Soviet Council of Ministers. Before being registered by Minfin, joint venture partners had to seek permission either from a local or republic-level administration or from a superior governmental sectorial agency (ministry) of the Soviet partner. Registration procedures were described very loosely in Minfin's ordinances and left much ground for bureaucratic "creativity." Thus, the process of obtaining permission and, later, registration by Minfin could last months and months.

Enterprise and foreign investment laws passed in 1991 established a sufficiently clear procedure to limit (but not totally eliminate) the scope of red-tape maneuvers of bureaucrats. Again, the procedure for establishing a joint venture consists normally of two stages.

The first stage involves registration of a joint venture as a business entity in conformity with general enterprise and company laws. Such registration requires the availability of founding documents and a legal address and payment of an incorporation fee. The maximum time for registration is 30 days (in some cases two weeks), and it may be refused only if the joint venture's bylaws do not conform to acting legislation.

The second stage includes registration at the Ministry of Finance, according to Russian law on foreign investments. The documents to be submitted for registration by joint ventures are:

- Written application of partners;
- Two copies of the founding documents certified by a notary;
- A document confirming the solvency and credibility of the foreign partner issued by its bank or other financial institution, with certified translation into Russian;
- A certificate (statements from the trade register or any other document

certifying the incorporation of the foreign partner or its legal status in the home country), also with certified translation;
- Experts' conclusions in cases required by law;
- For Soviet legal persons, a copy certified by a notary of the decision of the owner of its property to establish a joint venture (for state-owned enterprises this step may still remain the major time-consuming obstacle before creating a joint venture—foreign partners should always take this delay into consideration); also, certified copies of their founding documents.

When wholly owned subsidiaries are created, some documents must be submitted to Minfin, except those in the final item above.

All further amendments to a joint venture's bylaws require additional registration with Minfin. Such amendments must be submitted within 30 days after adoption by the joint venture's board of directors. They are not valid prior to registration.

The established term for registration (or notification of reasons for refusal) is 21 days. Registered joint ventures obtain a certificate and then become legal persons by Russian law. Minfin is required to inform the local administration of registration and to secure publication of such information. For the refusal of registration, Minfin may be sued in court by joint venture partners.

Legal and Other Requirements for Joint Ventures

The uncertainty of the legal environment for joint venture operations is the natural result of the dramatic transition period (especially after August 1991) of the "post-Soviet" economy from central plan to market. New laws are being passed in Russia and other republics (the Soviet federal parliament that was quite productive has ceased to exist as a legislative body), but they do not cover many crucial aspects and often lag behind events. Under these conditions, inefficient laws continue to be "interpreted" or even replaced by administrative regulations, including those of the late Soviet government. This is true in all cases that are not *directly* regulated by new laws.

Despite this unavoidable uncertainty and unpredictability, even a very brief look at developments between 1987 and 1991 reveals substantial improvements in the legalistic climate for foreign business in the former USSR. The law on foreign investments in Russia and other former Soviet republics creates a favorable basis for international business. Joint ventures and other companies with foreign participation are treated as well as national companies are—in many cases, more favorably.

Joint ventures are free to engage in any kind of business activities except those prohibited by law. Insurance business and financial investment services require a license from Minfin, while banking activities need a license from Russia's Central Bank. The Council of Ministers may determine other kinds of business activities that require licenses for companies with foreign participation.

Joint ventures are not restricted in establishing prices for their business operations and may use rubles to pay for goods, services, and rent. Actually, the agony of the ruble in 1991 created exclusive opportunities for joint ventures and other foreign companies to benefit in their transactions from the falling exchange rate of the ruble to the dollar.

Certain important legalistic aspects of joint venture operations in Russia (those not mentioned specifically largely fall in line with typical requirements for domestic companies) are described below in more detail.

Customs Duties and Foreign Trade

Customs and foreign trade regulations for Soviet joint ventures generally are more liberal than for regular enterprises. A governmental decree of March 1989 imposed some restrictions on joint ventures' foreign operations. The most important was the prohibition of sales of purchased goods (such sales were possible only for equipment or materials previously acquired for use at the joint venture). Other restrictions included licensing of certain exports and imports and taxation of imports.

The present Russian law exempts joint ventures with foreign participation from customs duties and import taxes only for property brought into Russia as input to the statutory fund or intended for the venture's own production development. This exemption is valid only for those inputs to the statutory fund that fall within the schedule established in the founding documents. For example, if the agreement between parties to form a joint venture provides for foreign inputs of cash within the first six months after registration, equipment within 12 months, and materials and parts within two years, these inputs will not be subject to customs duties nor taxed during these periods. If the joint venture later proves that further imports are intended for its own production development, it will pay no taxes or duties either.

Personal belongings of expatriate joint venture personnel are not subject to customs duties if they are intended strictly for private use. The regulation of exports and imports differs for joint ventures with foreign participation of above 30%, and for those with 30% or below foreign participation. The former are allowed to export their own products and import goods for their own production needs without licenses. The exports and imports of the latter are licensed in the same manner as those of regular Soviet enterprises (at present most Soviet exports are licensed). The rules to determine an enterprise's own production and production for its own needs are established by the Council of Ministers in accordance with international practice of determining products' origin.

The proceeds from exports of joint ventures with foreign participation above 30% are not subject to compulsory exchange into rubles at the official exchange rate of the dollar to the ruble. Other types of joint ventures, like regular Soviet enterprises, may have up to 85% of their foreign currency export revenues changed by Gosbank at the unfavorable exchange rate.

Insurance

According to the Law on Foreign Investments, all property and property interests of joint ventures and their branches and affiliates on Soviet territory are subject to insurance at their own discretion with unspecified exceptions deriving from other Russian laws. Normally, however, the obligatory insurance agreements apply to the following:

1. Long-term assets, either owned or rented by the joint venture, (a) during the construction period, for all risks of construction of buildings and setting up of equipment; and (b) after the construction of equipment, for fire and other natural disasters.
2. Inventories, including semifinished goods of the joint venture's own production, for fire and natural disasters.
3. Losses caused by stoppages in economic and industrial activities due to fire.
4. Civil responsibilities of the joint venture: (a) for damage to health or property of employees of the joint venture during their employment, (b) for pollution of the environment, (c) for damage to health and property of third parties, and (d) for damage due to the use of transportation vehicles owned by the joint venture.

To arrange for insurance policies with Ingosstrakh (the state-owned insurance agency), joint ventures must observe the following schedule for submitting documents, depending on the types of insurance (described in the preceding paragraph):

- Paragraph 1(a): one month before construction begins;
- Paragraphs 1(b), 2, 3, and 4(b): one month before operations begin;
- Paragraph 4(d): not later than three days before the use of transportation vehicles;
- Paragraphs 4(a) and 4(c): within one month after the registration of a joint venture or its affiliates.

In addition, insurance can apply to the following property losses:

1. Accidental damage to equipment and machinery and losses incurred due to stoppages in production caused by accidents,
2. Loss of merchandise during delivery,
3. Theft of inventories and other properties,
4. Loss of electronic equipment,
5. Loss of animals,
6. Losses from risks peculiar to the joint venture's activities.

Insurance policies are arranged in accordance with Soviet formats. Ingosstrakh requires all necessary information relevant to the evaluation of risks to the joint venture's property. Ingosstrakh works out the draft insurance policy within 14 days after all the documents have been obtained and then submits it to the joint venture, which has 30 days for evaluation. When the policy is signed, the insurance agreement is considered in effect. Compensation is paid in the currency named in the insurance agreement and in which insurance fees were paid.

Intellectual Property Rights

Protection of intellectual property rights did not really exist in the USSR prior to 1990 when it was mentioned for the first time in the Soviet property law of February 1990. The legislation on property rights still remains somewhat vague. Russia's foreign investment law refers to legislation of a more general character valid in Russian territory.

Specifically, the foreign investment law makes the following points: Joint ventures reach an agreement with their employees defining the rights to different kinds of intellectual property. They may register trademarks or patents only after the agreement is drawn up. The agreement, besides granting the enterprise the right to a patent, establishes the enterprise's responsibilities for the employee's working conditions. If the enterprise fails to sign such an agreement, then the patent is given to the employee-author of the intellectual property. Joint ventures are free to make decisions themselves as to patenting abroad.

Labor and Social Insurance Issues

All labor relations of joint ventures, including hiring and firing, conditions of work and leave, wages and salaries, and guarantees and compensation are regulated by a collective agreement between the administration and all employees or by individual contracts. The social and working conditions of employees established by such agreements and contracts may not be less favorable than conditions established by Russian legislation.

Expatriates may be both employees and members of administration or governing bodies. Their working conditions are specified in individual contracts. Salaries in foreign currencies may be transferred abroad after payment of individual income tax (which at present is in rubles).

Unions may be created at joint ventures in accordance with Russian legislation.

Allocations to pension funds are transferred by the joint venture expatriate employees to their native countries in the currency of their country. On the other hand, joint ventures are subject to allocations for social insurance for all employees and pension allocations for Soviet employees in accordance with current Soviet legislation.

Banking Operations

Before the second half of 1991, bank restrictions on joint venture operations used to be very tight, as reflected in Decree 49, which provided the following regulations:

1. Joint ventures may take credits in foreign currency from Vneshekonombank or from banks or companies under license from it. Credits in rubles can be obtained from Gosbank or Vneshekonombank. Both banks have the right to exercise control over the use and payment of credits.

2. Cash earned by joint ventures may be kept either in rubles in Gosbank or in foreign currency accounts in Vneshekonombank. Currency accounts may be kept with a foreign bank with permission from Vneshekonombank. Interest paid on foreign currency accounts depends on international monetary rates; interest on ruble accounts is determined by Gosbank. Usually, Soviet enterprises are not paid interest on their current accounts. Gosbank pays 0.5% annual interest on joint ventures' current accounts.

Gosbank has issued more detailed credit regulations. Short-term loans can be obtained from the bank after agreement about the opening of special credit accounts. Loans must be secured by inventories (or by sellers' invoices for inventories), deferred expenses, goods delivered to Soviet buyers before the due date, and documentary credits. A limit on the credit account must be agreed upon by the bank and the joint venture. Monthly reports on the security of loans must be submitted to the bank.

Long-term loans in rubles also can be obtained by the joint venture to finance new construction (including so-called social objects), after permission has been obtained from the Gosstroi (State Committee for Construction). The joint venture and the bank sign credit agreements; the maximum term for credit is six years.

Short-term credit (up to two years) in foreign currency can be obtained for purchases of raw materials and other inventories abroad. Medium- or long-term credit can be obtained for purchases of equipment, machinery, licenses, and so forth. To obtain credit from the Vneshekonombank, joint ventures must submit applications with detailed explanations of the purposes of the credit, the goods to be purchased, the economic effect of the purchase, and the schedule of payment of debt.

The rapid growth of the non-state-owned banking sector and the development of commercial banking give joint ventures more flexible choices in their banking operations.

Distribution of Profits and Taxation

Before outlining the taxation procedures for joint ventures, we must explain the notion of "pretax profits" as it is defined for joint ventures in the USSR. Table 4-2 is the simplified first part of the Standard Income Statement form for joint ventures; the figures displayed are exclusively for the purpose of illustration.

As shown in Tables 4-2 and 4-3, the taxable income is a deduction of miscellaneous tax exemptions and allocations to reserve and development funds from the balance of profits. The usual tax since Decree No. 49 is 30% of the pretax

Table 4-2
SIMPLIFIED STANDARD INCOME STATEMENT FORM

	Profits	Losses
1. Revenue from sales	100	X
2. Expenses	X	60
[Including cost of production and selling overheads]	<- X -> <- X ->	<- [50] -> <- [10] ->
3. Profit (loss) from sales (1-2)	40	
4. Profit from other sales	5	
5. Other profits and losses	6	3
6. Total profits and losses (3 + 4 + 5)	51	
7. Balance of profits (or losses)	48	

NOTES:

1. Revenues from sales are determined in two different ways depending on the nature of the joint venture.

(a) For manufacturing joint ventures--revenue from sales of goods and rendering of services produced in accordance with the provisions of the statute of the joint venture. The amount of revenues is the sum of cash obtained from customers in the bank accounts and of accounts receivable from <u>exporting operations</u> after invoices have been submitted to banks for further collection;

(b) For joint ventures in the trade and the "public meals" industry, the revenue is calculated as a difference between purchases and sales of goods.

2. For joint ventures in the trade and the "public meals" industry, expenses include only the overheads related to goods sold and services rendered.

3. Sales as part of nonstatutory activities.

The bottom-line result of operations represents the so-called balance of profits, which is the starting point for further allocation and calculation of tax (see Table 4-3).

profits. The amount of tax is determined and accrued in accordance with the joint venture's budget for the current fiscal year. (The January 1 to December 31 fiscal year is mandatory for joint ventures as well as for all Soviet enterprises.) The statement of amounts of taxable profit and the schedule of payments of tax due for the current year are to be conveyed to the tax inspector not later than January 15.

Table 4-3
CALCULATING PROFITS

7. Balance of profits (from Table 4-2)	48
8. Allocation to the reserve fund (until it reaches 25% of the statutory fund)	10
9. Allocations to production and technology development funds (for example, 16% of the balance of the profits)	8
10. Pretax profit (7-8-9)	30
11. Profits tax (30% of 30) beginning two years after profits have been declared by the joint venture	9
12. Profits after tax (10-11)	21
13. Net profit* (7-11)	39
14. Allocations to economic stimulation, social welfare, and other funds not related to production development (for example, 12.5% of the balance of profits)	6
15. Profit for distribution to the partners (12-14)	15
16. Share of profits of the foreign partner (50%) to be repatriated in foreign currency	7.5
17. Tax on profits for repatriation (7.5 x 20%)	1.5
18. Net repatriated profit of the foreign partner (16-17)	6

*Often used to calculate returns on investment in the feasibility studies.

Payments are made four times per year, in equal parts, not later than March 15, June 15, September 15, and December 15. The calculation of tax on profit due for the fiscal year should be made no later than March 15 of the following year. By this date, the financial statements of the joint venture, together with the tax calculation statement, must be audited and submitted to the local tax inspection department of the Ministry of Finance. Differences between the accrued and actual amounts of tax are to be paid within five days after the date of application, either by the tax authority or by the joint venture.

The tax is paid in rubles. In order to obtain a reduction of the tax rate, a joint venture must apply to the Ministry of Finance stating the reasons for the application.

In June 1990, the Soviet parliament passed a new law on taxation of enterprises and organizations. The law significantly restructured the taxation system and introduced certain changes regarding joint venture operations. These provisions were by and large included in the similar Russian law passed in December of the same year.

First of all, certain tax benefits granted to joint ventures are now valid only for those joint ventures in which the foreign partner's share in the statutory fund exceeds 30%.

Second, several changes concern the determination of pretax profits and profit distribution:

1. Deducted from the taxable income, in addition to the items mentioned above, are: (a) dividends on shares of stock and securities owned by the joint venture, (b) income from participation in other joint ventures, (c) interest paid on long-term loans with the exception of overdue and deferred credits, and (d) profits allocated to ecological investments. Items (a) and (b) are also valid for all Soviet enterprises.

2. Losses on the balance sheet can be deferred for a five-year term, and relevant future profits are tax exempt in case the reserve fund is not sufficient to cover the loss.

3. If the joint venture is terminated, the part of the statutory fund that was not used is taxed.

4. If termination occurs before the end of the two-year tax holiday, all profits disclosed on the balance sheet during that period are fully taxed.

5. The tax on transferred profits of foreign partners has been reduced to 15% (and is paid in the currency of transfer).

Incidentally, income earned by Soviet partners from participation in joint ventures now also is taxed at the rate of 15%, which lessens the benefits derived from items 1(a) and 1(b).

The taxation climate for joint ventures in the former USSR generally remains much more favorable than that for most other Soviet legal persons. In the case of joint ventures including foreign participation of less than 30%, however, all tax regulations are the same as for Soviet enterprises, creating a rather unattractive situation for foreign investors.

The basic features of the new taxation system for Soviet enterprises include two major disincentives for entrepreneurs:

1. The regular tax was established at the rate of 45%. In the spring of 1991 the government, under pressure, reduced it to 35%.

2. The increase of overall payments to personnel (including salaries, bonuses, and dividends) over the adjusted amounts of the previous year is taxed at a rate determined annually by the Supreme Soviet. For the years 1991 and 1992, the rate varies from 50% to 66.7%, depending on the increase in overall income of personnel.

Moreover, three innovations in the taxation system affect both Soviet enterprises and joint ventures, independent of the share of foreign participation:

1. The so-called marginal profitability, a major killer of profit and incentive, has been introduced. It means that all profits earned beyond a limit of approximately 30% of the rate of return are taxed at the rate of 80% or even 90%.

2. Monthly bonuses to personnel now are included in the salaries expense and make up part of the cost, but, at the same time, the average salary is limited to a basic amount of 480 rubles and any increase is linked to the growth of sales or revenues of the enterprise.

3. Most imported goods are taxed at excessively high rates, ranging from 130% to 2090% of their contract prices.

In December 1990, Minfin issued a lengthy regulation, No. 146, on taxation of profits of joint ventures. This regulation is based on the provision of the June 1990 law on taxation discussed above. It contains detailed procedures for calculation of taxable income and tax payments:

1. For joint ventures with foreign participation of 30% or less;

2. For joint ventures with foreign participation exceeding 30%; and

3. For both categories of joint ventures: (a) taxation of partners' dividends, (b) taxation on liquidation of a joint venture, (c) responsibilities of taxpayers, (d) returns on amounts paid erratically, and (e) control by tax authorities.

The practical examples provided by the regulation cover the following issues:

- Computation of wages of joint venture personnel subject to taxation,
- Taxation of "super-profits" exceeding the ceiling of return on investment,
- Carrying forward of losses for taxation purposes, and
- Eliminations and adjustments resulting from double-taxation arrangements.

Decree No. 815 of August 13, 1990, introduced a new sales tax for joint ventures on the goods they produced and then sold in the Soviet market. The tax ranges from 20% on tissues and plastics to 90% on liquors. In January 1991, the USSR Council of Ministers issued a decree (to replace a similar one dated August 1990) establishing new turnover tax rates for joint ventures. The turnover tax applies to joint venture-produced goods at retail prices net of trade discounts and transportation costs.

The decree specifies nine categories of taxed products. Those categories and their respective tax rates are as follows:

1. Computers—10%,
2. Cotton and woolen cloth, plastics—20%,
3. Footwear, textiles, jewelry, fish and seafood—25%,
4. Refrigerators, watches, perfumes and cosmetics, chinaware—30%,
5. Silk (artificial) cloth, beer—40%,
6. Rugs, artificial fur, video and audio cassettes, cars, crystal, socks and hose, silver jewelry, caviar, sparkling wines, cognacs—50%,
7. Gold jewelry with precious stones—70%,
8. Liquors and vodka—90%,
9. Other products subject to turnover taxes payable by Soviet enterprises—15%.

As said above, current Russian (and other republics) financial and tax regulations are largely inherited from the Soviet parliament and government. The reforms launched in Russia will inevitably require changes in such regulations. However, for mere technical reasons, such tax regulations for foreign investments will be adopted in 1992 or early 1993.

The following section shows the detailed tax computation required for joint ventures according to Regulation No.146.

Tax Computation Format for Joint Ventures

Supplement 8 to Regulation 146 presents a detailed format of income tax computation that joint ventures must present to local tax authorities:

Seal of the
joint venture

To: The state tax authority of . . .

COMPUTATION OF INCOME TAX
by_____

for the year of 19__

Indicator	Planned by the Joint Venture	Actual	
		Taxpayer's Data	Tax Authority Data
1	2	3	4

1. Statutory fund[1]
   (as of 1/1/19_)

2 Partners' inputs:
   Soviet
     Total
       Total share, %
   Foreign
     Total
       Total share, %

3. Reserve fund

4. Accrued amount of reserve fund
    (1, col. 3, x 25%) for taxation purposes

5. Balance sheet profit, total
    including:
    (a) profit from sales of products
        (services) and other material values
    (b) income from operations not related to
        sales reduced by costs of such
        operations

6. Excess (deficiency) of actual main
    labor costs compared to standard
    (normal)*

7. Balance sheet profit adjusted
    by (6) [(5) + (6)]*

Indicator	Planned by the Joint Venture	Actual	
		Taxpayer's Data	Tax Authority Data
1	2	3	4

8. Profit from sales as basis for
   computation of profitability
   [(5a) - rental payments]

9. Computation of profit exceeding
   the "ceiling level of profitability":
   9.1 Cost of sales
   9.2 Profitability of sales
       [(8) ÷ (9.1) x 100], %
   9.3 Average profitability ratio,
       by branch, %
   9.4 "Ceiling" level of profitability [(9.3) x 2], %
   9.5 Profitability in excess of
       "ceiling" level [(9.2) - (9.4)], %
   9.6 Profit corresponding to excess of
       profitability [(8) ÷ (9.2) x (9.5)],
       total
       (a) 10 points and below
       (b) above 10 points

10. Tax on profit exceeding "ceiling"
    profitability level
    (a) 10 points and below
        [(9.6.a) x 80%]
    (b) above 10 points
        [(9.6.b) x 90%]
        Total of line 10

11. Tax on profit exceeding "ceiling"
    profitability level, payable to:
    (a) federal budget
        [(10) x 50%]
    (b) republic's budget
        [(10) x 50%]

12. Balance sheet profit below the
    "ceiling" profitability level:
    [(5) - (9.6)], total **
    [(7) - (9.6)], total *

13. Adjustment of the amount of
    balance sheet profit subject to
    taxation at normal (fixed) rate (12):
    (a) minus rental payments
    (b) minus allocation to reserve
        fund (9)

| | | Actual | |
| | Planned by the Joint Venture | Taxpayer's Data | Tax Authority Data |
Indicator			
1	2	3	4

(c) minus dividends on stock
(d) minus premium on bond and
    other securities
(e) minus dividends on participa-
    tion in other joint ventures
      Total of line 13
      [(12) - (13a, b, c, d, e)]

14. Tax benefits, total
    14.1 Profit allocated to
          production development
      14.2 Profit utilized for R&D:
          (a) full amount**
          (b) 30% of actual expenditures*
      14.3 Profit utilized for interest
          expense on bank long-term
          loans**
      14.4 Profit allocated to maintenance
          of nonproductive assets
          (according to rates, fixed by
          local soviets)
      14.5 Profit allocated to
          environmental protection:
          (a) full amount**
          (b) 30% of actual expenditures
      14.6 Profit allocated to charity not
          more than 1% of taxable profit
          [not more than (13) x 1%]
      14.7 Project utilized to cover losses
          of the years**:
          19_
          19_
          19_
      14.8 Other benefits reducing the
          taxable profit

15.   Taxable profit below "ceiling"
     profitability level [(13) - (14)].

16.   Tax on profit below "ceiling"
     profitability level, at rates:
     16.1 30%, including tax
          allocated to:
          (a) federal budget
            [(15) x 30% x 50%]
          (b) republic's budget
            [(15) x 30% x 50%]

		Actual	
Indicator	Planned by the Joint Venture	Taxpayer's Data	Tax Authority Data
1	2	3	4

16.2 Up to 45% including tax
allocated to:
(a) federal budget
  [(15) x 22%]
(b) republic's budget
  (15 x rate established by a
  republic)

17. Tax on profit [(10) + (16)], total

18. Accrued amounts of income taxes
paid abroad

19. Computed tax payable [(17) - (18)].

20. Tax payable taking into account
advance payments of tax
[(19) - advance payment]

21. Additional payment
[if (20) is positive]

22. Return [if (20) is negative]

———

Notes:
¹The amount of the statutory fund is recorded as of January 1 of the year next after reporting year. The initial amount of the statutory fund is entered in column 2.
˙Filled in only by joint ventures with foreign participation of 30% or less.
˙˙Filled in by joint ventures with foreign participation of more than 30%.

GENERAL DIRECTOR OF THE JOINT VENTURE (signature)

CONTROLLER (signature)

(SEAL)

"COMPUTATION ACCEPTED"
TAX INSPECTOR (signature)

The income tax computation pattern provides a good illustration of Soviet joint venture taxation peculiarities. These features can be summarized as follows:

First, the amount of reported profit for the year is subject to significant adjustments for taxation purposes. These adjustments fall into two main groups:

- Tax exemptions (rental payments, reserve fund replenishments, and dividends and premiums on stock participation and securities);
- Profit allocation benefits (production development, research and development, interest on long-term loans, environmental protection, charity, and coverage of losses of previous years).

Second, tax treatment of joint ventures with foreign participation below and above 30% is significantly different. The above 30% joint ventures enjoy incentives such as:

- No tax on wages and salaries fund increase;
- No tax on profits utilized for production development, and interest on long-term bank loans, offsetting previous years' losses;
- Full tax exemption for research and development and environmental profit allocations.

The below 30% joint ventures receive the same basic tax treatment as Soviet enterprises.

The third feature is that, despite gradual harmonization with international accounting standards, Soviet reporting and taxation principles still remain different in aspects such as:

- Utilization of profits;
- Interest on credits and losses;
- Premiums and bonuses to employees;
- Rent expenses.

The Soviet joint venture taxation pattern can be summarized in the chart shown in Figure 4-1 (numbers correspond to the lines in the foregoing Supplement 8, Regulation No. 146).

Figure 4-1
JOINT VENTURE TAXATION CHART

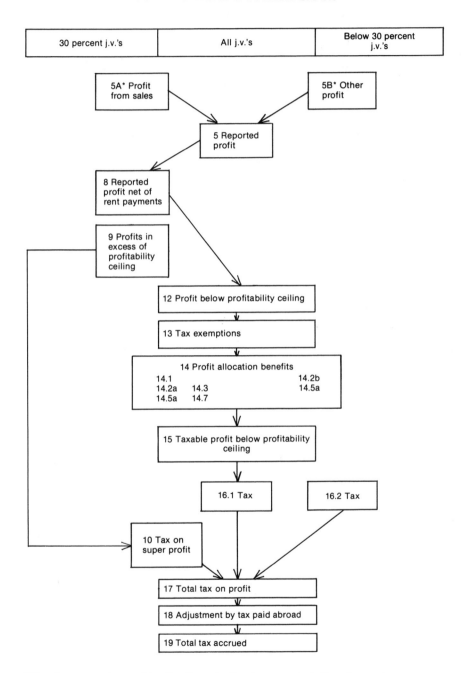

| 30 percent j.v.'s | All j.v.'s | Below 30 percent j.v.'s |

*Numbers correspond to the lines in the tax computation form above.

Chapter 5

Accounting by and for
Joint Ventures in the Soviet Union

Many of the Soviet accounting and reporting practices may seem cumbersome, or at least unusual, to Westerners. Joint ventures in the Soviet Union are supposed to engage in market relations, and they are created to make profits, not to fulfill plans. Still, even now, they operate in a centrally planned environment, as will be the case for at least several years during the transition period toward a market-oriented economy.

The basic differences between a market economy and a centrally planned economy have a major impact on the position and behavior of individual enterprises—and on their accounting systems. Joint ventures could not be pulled out of this system immediately in 1987. Table 5-1, though subject to the limitations of such a scheme, provides major keys to understanding differences between the two accounting systems.

Accounting Requirements Peculiar to Joint Ventures

Initially, according to Decree No. 49, accounting by joint ventures had to follow the principles that were observed by Soviet enterprises. Between 1988 and 1991, the Ministry of Finance gradually introduced exemptions to this rule. The major special features of accounting set up for joint ventures are discussed below.

1. Joint ventures have the right to adopt their own accounting procedures and techniques. Ordinary Soviet enterprises are limited to a choice of three basic techniques of recording operations and maintaining the accounts. As a result, Soviet accounting practice is much more standardized and uniform than Western accounting practice. The most commonly used paper-based procedure (in Russian terminology, form of accounting) is called the "journal-order form." Journal orders are a certain type of register that combines chronological and systematic records. Registers are opened for all major accounts. Actually, this register is somewhat similar in structure to the sales journal that American companies use.

Table 5-1
DIFFERENCES BETWEEN THE TWO ACCOUNTING SYSTEMS

	Type of Economy	
	Market	Centrally Planned
I. Ultimate goal of a business	Make a profit.	Fulfill the plan.
II. Main purpose of accounting	Measure profit against capital; evaluate the net worth of a business.	Control the process of fulfillment of plan and the use of state property.
III. Basic principles of accounting	Generally accepted accounting principles (GAAP), dealing mostly with financial accounting and worked out by the accounting profession under the general supervision of a regulatory agency such as FASB or SEC.	Mandatory accounting principles (MAP) covering the whole accounting cycle of an enterprise, including minor details, set up by the Ministry of Finance after consultation with the accounting profession. You may not accept these principles but you have to follow them.
IV. Accounting procedures	Many options in internal accounting techniques. Use of the worksheet as a tool for preparation of financial reports.	Three main accounting techniques for forms of accounting in Russian terminology are used by Soviet enterprises. The most widely used is the "journal order form" technique. All accounting formats are statistics oriented.
V. Financial accounting	The balance sheet-- classification has at least two main goals: (1) to classify assets according to their liquidity and liabilities by the time they have to be met; (2) to measure the net worth of a business.	The main goals are: (1) to show the structure of means in possession of an enterprise that are used to fulfill the plan; (2) to show whether these assets initially provided by the state are used in a proper and rational way so as to fulfill plans and assure that state property is not stolen or wasted.

Certain liberties are granted to joint ventures regarding their internal accounting procedures, but in practical terms, these liberties are very much restricted by the fact that Western techniques do not meet Soviet reporting needs. The worksheet hardly matches formal Soviet financial reporting. Another problem is that Soviet accountants have not learned Western procedures.

2. Joint ventures have the right to introduce first-level accounts into the chart of accounts upon consultation with the Ministry of Finance and the right to introduce, on their own initiative, new, second-level accounts or to combine existing ones. While the latter right seems obvious, the former can hardly be enjoyed because: (a) there are practically no free spaces in the existing chart of accounts and (b) "consultation" with the Ministry of Finance means asking for permission, which normally is not granted. (Even though the number of free spaces in the chart of accounts increased after December 1991, joint ventures can hardly use them as they wish because all accounts are grouped in sections.)

3. Accounting and reporting will be in Russian, the official language. Parallel entries can be made in statutory foreign languages.

4. All the accounts must be kept in rubles. At the same time, parallel entries can be made in foreign currencies for receivables, payables, and banking operations. Granting these rights to a joint venture is analogous to allowing foreign employees to speak their own language among themselves.

5. Property, plant, and equipment, as contributions to the statutory fund, are accounted for at historical cost, including transportation costs. This formula is standard for Soviet accounting, but its implications for joint ventures are different. For a Soviet enterprise, historical cost in most cases means the value of an asset determined on the basis of state-fixed prices. Historical cost of fixed assets contributed by the partners to the statutory fund of a joint venture is based on the market value or a value agreed on between partners.

The question arises, How should one account for assets not contributed to the statutory fund but purchased later in the course of operation? According to Soviet accounting practice, all fixed assets, at the time they appear on the balance sheet, should increase the statutory fund on the liabilities side. This practice can be justified under the circumstances of a rigid, centrally planned economy in which the state usually provides all enterprises with the means of production, namely, fixed assets. In this case, all the assets of an enterprise emerge from three main sources or funds: state funds, loan funds, and the enterprise's own funds. But this practice leads to great confusion when an enterprise engages in market relations, because amounts relevant to the new assets must be credited twice, including one credit to the statutory fund account. Therefore, the Ministry of Finance provides the possibility of accounting for fixed assets at historical cost based on market prices but also permits the joint venture to decide how to account for fixed assets.

6. Property rights, including lending rights, intellectual rights, and other property rights, as contributed to the statutory fund, are accounted for at historical cost in the newly established first-level account called Nonmaterial

Assets. This account is the major concession to market orientation in the letter of the Ministry of Finance of May 3, 1988. Again, as in the case of fixed assets, the partners determine the cost. No mention of goodwill is made, but the formula "other property rights" is broad enough to cover all kinds of intangibles. A joint venture's rights in rented facilities, including land and buildings, are treated as nonmaterial assets contributed by the Soviet partners to the statutory fund. The regulation did not mention any provision for amortization of the nonmaterial assets, but paragraph 33 of Decree No. 49 practically already gave a free hand to joint ventures in their depreciation and amortization policies when the founding documents have set out these policies. Amortization of intangibles was later legalized in 1990.

7. Several new first-level (e.g., foreign currency) accounts are introduced in the chart of accounts. Obviously, current regulations on joint venture accounting are still inadequate to meet those needs of joint ventures that result from their being profit oriented. The vagueness of many aspects of joint venture accounting regulations (for example, those concerning depreciation, intangibles, securities, and investments) reflects the difficulties that regulatory agencies encounter in classifying all the emerging market "novelties" into the usual rigid accounting scheme. Broad liberalization of accounting regulations on the basis of a significantly new set of generally accepted accounting principles would seem to be the only solution.

New Accounting Regulations

Later developments in the joint venture accounting regulations confirmed the trend toward change. Minfin's Instruction No. 74, dated June 6, 1990, and effective on July 1, adopted a number of international accounting principles for joint ventures. These concessions are much more far-reaching than the previous ones. A major discussion of a new internationally oriented chart of accounts was launched in April 1990, and a joint task force with the United Nations on creating new accounting standards for joint ventures began its work in Moscow in June. The work of the task force largely contributed to the adoption of new joint venture reporting formats (August 1991), and finally the new national chart of accounts (October 1991).

The new accounting regulations for joint ventures cover the issues described below.

Depreciation of Assets

Amortization of intangible assets is allowed provided it is regulated by the founding documents.

Depreciation is debited directly to cost and expense accounts and credited to a contra assets Account 02, Depreciation (Amortization) of Property, which is disclosed on the assets and not, as previously, on the liabilities side of the balance sheet. Because Account 86, Amortization Fund, has been abolished, depreciation in joint ventures no longer has to be accounted for twice.

Investments for New Construction and Development

The cost of new plant and buildings is accumulated in Account 30, Investments, until construction is finished; then it is debited to Account 01, Tangible Fixed Assets. The accounts credited are Accounts 51, Cash; 52, Foreign Currency; or 92, Long-Term Credits, depending on the source from which new construction is financed. At the same time, the statutory fund is increased (Account 83 credited), and relevant retained earnings accounts, previously allocated to funds such as Account 88, Special-Purpose Funds, are debited. No special entries are made when new construction is financed with current assets, including cash from depreciation.

Sales

Finally, the major shift from the cash basis to the accrual basis has been made in joint venture accounting. Revenues from sales are accrued after invoices and other documents confirming delivery are given directly to the customer or to a bank for collection. The cost of goods sold now is debited directly to Account 46, Sales. The price of the goods sold, according to the invoice, is credited to Account 46 and debited to Account 62, Accounts Receivable (Settlements with Buyers). Account 45, Goods Delivered, Services Rendered (Sales), now is used only for exported merchandise until the title passes to the foreign customer.

Financial Investments

See "Accounting for Investments in Joint Ventures" on next page.

Exchange Rate Differences

See "Foreign Currency Issues," on page 139.

Lease of Property

Although mentioned specifically for the first time in Soviet joint venture accounting regulations, the treatment of property leasing is not much different from the usual Soviet accounting rules. The only distinction is that property leased by joint ventures to other entities is depreciated according to the rules described above.

Allowances for Bad (Doubtful) Debts

According to the new regulation, debts (accounts receivable) are considered to be doubtful when they are overdue and not secured. Allowances (reserves) are made at the end of every year by debiting Account 80, Profit and Loss, and crediting Account 88, Special-Purpose Funds. Unlike depreciation since August 1991, allowances for bad debts are not deductible from total receivables on the assets side and are accounted for on the liabilities side. At the end of the year, after allowances have been made, the amount of the unused reserves is added to the amount of profit for that year (debit to Account 88, credit to Account 80).

Retained Earnings

The August 1991 reporting format allowed joint ventures to record retained earnings. The previous traditional Soviet practice was to disclose "profit utilization." This meant that every ruble of the enterprise's net income had to be allocated for a specific purpose: either tax or reserve or a development fund.

Accounting for Investments in Joint Ventures

The practice of accounting for investments in other business entities did not exist in the Soviet Union until the process of establishing joint ventures began. It still is practically unregulated in the usual Soviet sense; that is, no instruction has yet been provided about how to do it. In the meantime, different points of view are being expressed. The dominant one is that the investments of Soviet partners in joint ventures should be treated as so-called put-aside assets.

In Soviet accounting terminology, put-aside assets represent items that cannot be classified as fixed or current assets and that are put aside in a figurative sense to be used later for special purposes. These purposes normally include provision for taxation and interest on short-term loans and allocations to funds. The put-aside items normally represent cash earned from sales and other sources, but they are accounted for separately because of their special-purpose designation.

Actually, they are not real assets but a second recording of certain amounts of cash that already have been entered into the balance sheet. Put-aside assets are recorded solely for the purpose of control, and, unlike investments, they overvalue the actual total assets.

The put-aside items normally are recorded in the process of distribution of profits, which also makes them very different from investments in joint ventures. The not very convincing attempts to account for investments as put-aside items reflect the difficulties the Soviet accounting system encounters in the face of new market realities. Actually, there is even less reason to consider investments as fixed or current assets, but the established Soviet classification of assets provides no other variants.

As a practical matter, according to Ministry of Finance Letter No. 97/8-07 of August 8, 1989, investments initially had to be accounted for at their historical cost as a separate item. The 1991 innovations have finally established the current procedure.

- "Long-term financial investments" are disclosed in the fixed assets section (including investments in joint ventures).
- Short-term financial investments such as marketable securities are disclosed in the cash section.

Action that needs to be taken in the future includes: (1) determining when the equity method and proportionate consolidation should be applied to accounting for investments in joint ventures and other entities and (2) classifying investments as such in a separate section of the balance sheet.

According to Minfin's regulation of June 6, 1990, equity investments in other business entities, as well as shares of stocks and securities, are accounted for in a new Account 58, Short-Term Financial Investments. At that time, Account 58 is debited and related assets are credited. Profits earned from financial investments are credited to Account 80, Profits and Losses, and debited to Accounts 51, Cash, or 52, Foreign Currency.

Reporting

Initially, joint ventures were to submit financial statements in the same format as Soviet enterprises. Annual reports are to be submitted to the local agencies of the Ministry of Finance no later than March 15 of the year following the accounting year.

Reports also are to be submitted to each partner, to banks providing loans to joint ventures, and to statistical committees. Soviet partners should supply joint ventures with appropriate accounting forms and blanks. All reports should be signed by the general manager and the chief accountant and bear the seal of the joint venture.

Detailed accounting procedures applicable to foreign joint ventures (see page 148) were issued in June 1990. These guidelines generally also are valid for the new format of August 1991.

The first regulation concerning the submission of annual reports to the agencies of the Ministry of Finance was approved on August 8, 1989. In August 1991 the Ministry of Finance prescribed a new Annual Financial Report of Joint Ventures with Foreign Investments (Decree No. 50). This latest format also has been adopted by the Russian Federation. The Annual Financial Report of Joint Ventures is presented at the end of this chapter, on page 152. It includes the balance sheet, the income statement (profit and loss statement), and the supplements to the balance sheet (Annex 3-SP).

The supplements to the balance sheet include the following:

- The statement of funds flow, reserve fund, other funds established by founding documents, and the retained earnings;
- The statement of intangible assets;
- The statement of changes in long-term assets;

- The composition of long-term assets, including buildings and structures, machinery and equipment, vehicles, tools, and other long-term assets;
- The structure of financial investments;
- The statement of cash flow in foreign currencies; and
- Investments in new construction (capital investments) from different sources.

In addition, a statement of securities issued and accepted must be provided.

The two major financial statements of joint ventures—the balance sheet and the income statement—though changed and cut, still in many respects follow the centrally planned model. Western accountants and managers not familiar with this model need to use special "transition keys" to evaluate the financial position and financial results of a Soviet-based joint venture. Table 5-2 shows a U.S. format balance sheet.

As previously stated, in October 1990 Minfin issued Regulation 122 imposing a quarterly reporting format on all Soviet business entities. The quarterly balance sheet format does not include the same items as the annual format, which creates a certain confusion. To make things even more complex, the slightly different June 1991 format for regular Soviet enterprises informally applies to joint venture quarterly statements. Such confusion is sometimes discouraging. However, frequent changes in reporting requirements are inevitable in this transition period, and one can also see the positive trend of increasing comparability with Western standards.

In its Regulation 142 of December 29, 1990, Minfin established new rules of accounting for so-called profit utilization by joint ventures. According to traditional Soviet methodology, all profits of a joint venture allocated to different purposes (production and social development funds and other allocations) are debited to Account 81, Profit Utilization, which, as indicated above, is a purely fictitious account with no real assets behind it. Account 88, Special-Purpose Funds, is credited at the same time. The innovation is that in joint venture accounting Account 88 becomes a prototype, Retained Earnings.

Contrary to usual Soviet accounting procedures, joint ventures are required to maintain their statutory fund (Account 85) at the level determined by initial output according to the founding documents. All accumulated profits, including capitalization, are credited to Accounts 87 and 88 (Soviet enterprises credit Account 83). This method differs from American practice in that all offsetting debits (actual profit allocations) are possible only: (1) as construction of new plant and equipment (Account 01), (2) as acquisition of intangible assets (Account 04), and (3) as investments in securities (Accounts 06 and 58). (Theoretically, allocations of profit in assets other than cash are possible. However, because such allocations are not specified by Minfin, they usually lead to disputes with local financial inspectors.) Unallocated retained earnings therefore are not permitted. All utilizations of profits that do not increase the joint venture's property (assets in Accounts 01, 04, 58) are considered expenses.

Table 5-2
JOINT VENTURE BALANCE SHEET

ASSETS

I. Current assets

	1.1 Cash	10.0
	1.2 Marketable securities	3.0
	1.3 Receivables, net of bad debts = 0.5	14.3
	1.4 Deferred expenses	2.7
	1.5 Inventories	21.0
	TOTAL CURRENT ASSETS	**51.0**

II.	Investments and long-term receivables	4.2
III.	Property, plant, and equipment, less allowance = 11	22.0
IV.	Intangible assets, less amortization - 1	4.0
	TOTAL ASSETS	**81.2**

LIABILITIES AND PARTNERS' EQUITY

I. Current liabilities

		:
	1.1 Short-term borrowings	6.0
	1.2 Current portion of long-term debt	0.5
	1.3 Payables	3.7
	1.4 Accrued expenses	3.8
	TOTAL CURRENT LIABILITIES	**14.0**

II.	Long-term loans	8.0
III.	Deferred income	0.5
IV.	Equity	

		:
	4.1 Capital	25.0
	4.2 Retained earnings	34.0
	TOTAL PARTNERS' EQUITY	**67.5**
	TOTAL LIABILITIES AND PARTNERS' EQUITY	**81.2**

Thus, Regulation 142 brought Soviet joint venture accounting slightly closer to international standards; however, the traditional Soviet principle of mandatory "utilization of profit" still is applied. Therefore, some "dual accounting" will be required from joint ventures that wish to maintain free control over retained earnings and their utilization.

Various profit utilization entries are illustrated in Table 5-3.

Auditing

Auditing practices for joint ventures in the Soviet Union originally established by Decree No. 49 were to some extent a departure from the traditional "revision." But, in general, they were still very far from the usual Western procedures.

Internal Auditing

Decree No. 49 provides that partners must specify in the statute how often and in what way internal audits of the joint venture will be performed for purposes of control and how relevant information is to be conveyed to partners. Usually, a clause is introduced in the statutes providing that a partner or partners may at any time ask for any information concerning the joint venture's operations and financial position.

Auditing commissions appointed by the board of directors make yearly internal audits. The commissions normally include representatives of all the partners. Contrary to the usual Soviet practice, participation of ministerial officials in the auditing commissions is not obligatory. Partners also hire professional accountants to perform internal auditing. The reports of the auditing commission must be submitted to and approved by the board.

External Auditing

The auditing for joint ventures introduced in 1987 was supposed to conform to Western practice in that audits must be performed by independent auditors, that is, "by a commercial Soviet auditing organization for a fee" (Decree No. 49). The goals of auditing of joint ventures are different from the goals of revision. The former are tax oriented, and the latter are antifraud oriented.

Auditing at present is performed by a specialized organization, Inaudit, controlled by the Ministry of Finance, to assure that no profits are hidden from taxation.

The audits must be completed and the auditors' opinion must be issued before March 15, the date when financial reports must be submitted to the Ministry of Finance. But because auditors from Inaudit usually cannot possibly complete audits of all of the joint ventures by that time, the joint ventures often submit a letter confirming that their financial statements conform to Soviet laws and regulations.

Table 5-3
PROFIT UTILIZATION ENTRIES

(1) Profit of the year, not distributable

88 Special Funds		81 Utilization of Profits	
	(1) 100,000	(1) 100,000	

(2) New machinery purchased - R50,000

51 Cash in Bank		33 Capital Investments	
Bal. 200,000	(2) 50,000	(2) 50,000	

(3) Machinery installed (ready to work) - R30,000

33 Capital Investments		01 Fixed Assets	
(2) 50,000	(3) 30,000	(3) 30,000	

(4) Stocks and bonds purchased - R30,000

51 Cash in Bank		58 Financial Investments	
Bal. 200,000	(2) 50,000	(4) 30,000	
	(4) 30,000		

(5) Consumer goods purchased for the individual needs of the joint venture's employees - R20,000

51 Cash in Bank		26 General Expense	
Bal. 200,000	(2) 50,000	(5) 20,000 *	
	(4) 30,000		
	(5) 20,000		

* Note: This general expense is not included in costs (and is tax exempt).

(6) General expense of R20,000 (entry 5) is debited to account 88

26 General Expense		88 Special Funds	
(5) 20,000	(6) 20,000	(6) 20,000	(1) 100,000

(7) Profit Utilization account is offset against Profit and Loss - R100,000

81 Profit Utilization		80 Profit and Loss	
(1) 100,000	(7) 100,000	(7) 100,000	Bal. 100,000

(8) The balance of Statutory Fund exceeding initial amount (R300,000) is credited to Special Funds to show accumulated profit - R50,000

88 Special Funds		85 Statutory Fund	
(6) 20,000	(1) 100,000	(8) 50,000	Bal. 350,000
	(8) 50,000		

The result of these entries is that R80,000 were accumulated as "retained earnings" during the year in addition to R50,000 accumulated in the previous periods (and initially posted to the statutory fund).

Joint ventures and other Soviet business entities are no longer legally obligated to have Inaudit perform their audits, so dozens of auditing firms offering such services have sprung up throughout the country. Some of them have gained substantial expertise, especially those that are in some way associated with international accounting firms. However, until recently they could not seriously compete with Inaudit, primarily because of the latter's connection to Minfin.

Early in 1991, the Chamber of Auditors was organized in Moscow. One of its duties is supposed to be the certification of auditors, or public accountants. (Earlier, the Soviet Association of Accountants, established in December 1989, also assigned itself such a function.)

Some important developments took place in 1991. First, the Russian government has granted some major accounting firms already at work in Moscow the right to perform full-scale audits—not only of joint ventures but also of Russian companies. For example, Russia's Central Bank authorized Arthur Andersen to audit banks. Second, the laws on auditing are to be passed in 1992 by Russia, and later by Ukraine and other states, establishing main independent auditing procedures and passing the certification authority to the respective chambers of auditors. This will create a totally new auditing environment that most certainly will be dominated by big international accounting firms.

The Joint Venture Balance Sheet

The balance sheet format (see page 152) provides all necessary items for reporting purposes. When there is no need for a certain item, the relevant position in the statement is marked with a dash (—). Before submitting the annual report, an organization must take inventory and adjust all items. Balances of analytical and general ledger accounts, as well as bank statements, must be reconciled. The balance sheet must contain information for both the last accounting year and the preceding year (from previous audited reports).

Assets (Aktiv)

Fixed Assets and Other Noncurrent Assets

In the past, fixed assets were treated differently in Soviet and Western accounting. The principal differences included the following:

- Accumulated depreciation was disclosed on the liabilities side and not deducted from cost.
- Intangibles and amortization of intangibles were not accounted for.
- So-called "put-aside" assets, or "profit allocation," were disclosed under this section, which, for purposes of control, represented the net earnings of the

year distributed among different funds and therefore put aside from the regular operations of an enterprise. This item was artificial and without actual value.

- Losses also were disclosed in this section.

As a result of changes between 1988 and 1991, these differences gradually have been removed. At present, the 1-SP format of the balance sheet, approved by Minfin in Letter No. 50 of August 1991, is oriented much more closely to international standards. The main items are described below.

Fixed (tangible) assets include plant and equipment, both used in the process of production and kept for future use. This item includes capital improvements of land and expenditures for leased assets. Each group of similar items is disclosed separately in the annex to the balance sheet (Annex 3-SP, Section IV—see page 160). Fixed tangible assets are reported at historic cost and at net value less accumulated depreciation.

Unfinished capital construction and investments include the cost of unfinished buildings and installations and of equipment to be installed and specially purchased for new construction. This item was included in the section on fixed assets only recently (by Minfin's letter No. 50). Previously it was classified under a separate section in the balance sheet.

Intangible (nonmaterial) assets include various property rights brought by the partners to the statutory fund or acquired by the joint venture in the process of operations. They include rights to use land, water, and other natural resources, buildings, installations, know-how, technologies, and so on. The costs of renting facilities are treated as intangible assets, rather than deferred expenses. Actually, any right to use rented buildings and the like is purchased initially by the Soviet partner (as rental payment) and passed as input to the statutory fund. The joint venture theoretically can sell the right for cash to somebody else. Such prepaid expense is obviously different in its nature from intangibles such as know-how, trademarks, expertise, and, especially, goodwill.

All intangible assets must be reported separately in the annex to the balance sheet of a joint venture (format 3-SP, item II—see page 159). They also must be disclosed separately at cost and at net value less accumulated amortization (actually, in Russian terminology, the word *iznos*, "depreciation," is used rather than "amortization").

Long-term financial investments are also new in this section. Previously they were grouped with short-term investments in the "Settlements" section of the balance sheet. Long-term financial investments include bonds (payable in a one-year period), participation in other enterprises, and long-term loans to other business entities. Soviet reporting standards do not, as yet, make any distinction between different kinds of investment depending on the degree of control over the investee (wholly owned subsidiaries, direct investment, association, participation, or joint control). Therefore, such methods of accounting for investments as proportionate consolidation and equity basis are still unknown. The composition of long-term financial investments in kind is disclosed in Annex 3-SP.

Other noncurrent assets include items not disclosed above, such as accounts receivable in the future accounting periods beyond one year. No distinction is made in this case for the current portion of a long-term receivable.

Inventory and Expenses

This section of the balance sheet is traditional to Soviet accounting. The latest amendments include different methods of valuation of certain items (see below) and exclusion from their section of prepaid expenses. However, contrary to U.S. practice, certain kinds of expenses are treated as assets and are recorded here. Another significant difference is that inventories are valued by a method somewhat similar to specific identification. Such methods as LIFO and FIFO are known, as well as the lower-of-cost-or-market (LCM) principle. However, LCM can hardly be applied now in Russia because of inflation.

Production stocks include the following items at actual cost: materials, fuel, spare parts, and other items accounted for by Soviet standards as production stocks (other than new low-value and short-life items).

Low-value and short-life items include tools and other low-value means of production, special uniforms, and footwear. Minfin's Letter No. 50 now has established that these items must be recorded both at cost and net of depreciation. The usual depreciation period is two years. Because low-value and short-life items normally are treated as expenses, their value should be deducted from the total assets if the balance sheet is translated to the U.S. format.

Work-in-process (WIP) includes cost of unfinished production or services that usually are recorded in the accounts of Section 3, "Production Cost and Expenses," of the national chart of accounts. They usually are valued at actual cost, though joint ventures are allowed to value WIP at so-called norm cost in case of scale (mass) production.

The finished products item represents the actual production cost of the balance of finished products that have passed quality control and testing, are fully equipped with parts according to contracts with customers, and conform to technical standards. Products that do not comply with the criteria above must be disclosed under WIP.

Merchandise inventory is an item reserved only for merchandise (trading) joint ventures and restaurants. It is recorded at acquisition cost and at the selling price. The trade discount (work-up, markdowns) offered by the supplier to the joint venture must be disclosed separately. The rates of trade discounts are determined according to the instruction accompanying the national chart of accounts. This requirement of the Ministry of Finance obviously is a remnant of the centralized system of financial control in the former USSR and probably will be lifted soon.

Selling overhead on ending inventory, another item reserved only for merchandise companies, includes transportation, storage, and other similar expenses falling on the ending inventory of goods that have been delivered to the customer already but have not yet been billed. According to cash basis accounting, such goods are not considered realized (sold). Restaurant joint ventures are required to add such expenses to the balance of "merchandise inventory." After delivered goods have been sold in the next accounting period, items of selling overhead are written off as expenses. Translation of the Soviet balance sheet format to the U.S. format requires deduction of this item from total assets.

Cash, Settlements, and Other Assets

Minfin's Letter No. 50 has slightly restructured this section. An attempt was made to classify the current assets according to their liquidity. Cash was placed at the end of the list, therefore, and deferred expenses were transferred to this section. This reclassification, however, was not fully consistent, as one can see from the balance sheet. The usual Russian term for assets, payables, and accounts receivable taken together is "settlements." Actually, some "analytic" settlement accounts may have either a debit or a credit balance, for example, Settlements with the State Budget or Settlements with Other Debtors and Creditors. Debit balances of such accounts must be disclosed on the asset side and credit balances on the credit side, no netting being allowed under Soviet standards. Note that analytic accounts sum up to make a summary, or first-level, account. For example, Account 71, Settlements with Accountable Persons may have two analytic accounts: Settlements with Employee A and Settlements with Employee B. If the former has a debit balance, it must be disclosed under this section of assets; if the latter has a credit balance, it will go to the relevant section of the liabilities.

Accounts receivable (which, in Russian terminology, is Settlements with Debtors) are divided into three groups:

- Accounts receivable for goods and services, which are accrued at the moment when invoices are presented by the joint venture with further payment by the debtor in cash or from a letter of credit. Goods may be sold (or services rendered) on open account or interest-bearing credit. The accrual of revenues upon invoicing was made possible for joint ventures in 1990, while most Soviet enterprises still account for their sales on the cash basis.
- Notes receivable (notes overdue—not paid on time), which are disclosed separately.
- Other debtors, a term that includes debts of accountable persons, contractors, tax agencies (because of recalculations of payable taxes), and receivables resulting from settlements with different contractors due to losses and damage to received (purchased) assets. Penalties and fines imposed on the joint venture by court or arbitration decision are accrued under this item as well. Advance payments (actual) to suppliers and contractors are

recorded separately under this item in the case of purchases conditioned by payments of parts of the amounts in advance.

Prepaid expenses (or, in Russian terminology, Expenses of Future Periods) are generally analogous to the similar item in American accounting. They represent actual expenditure of the current period charged to production or distribution costs in future periods. Prior to 1992 this item was classified under Section II of the assets. One should remember that, according to Soviet regulations, a joint venture's rights of utilization of leased facilities are considered intangible assets. Thus, rent expense for a period of, say, two years incurred by one of the partners and contributed as input to the joint venture's statutory fund will not be recorded as prepaid expense but as an intangible asset.

Soviet rules of accounting for foreign trade transactions are somewhat cumbersome, as they may require recording of accrued interest expense as deferred expense until interest actually is paid. Translation of the Soviet joint balance sheet to the U.S. format requires relevant adjustments:

Cancel the recorded deferred expense of interest expense:

> Dr   Notes Payable (items under which the interest liability is recorded in Soviet books)
> Cr   Deferred Expense

Record the accrued interest expense:

> Dr   Retained Earnings
> Cr   Accrued Expenses

As a result, the total of the balance will be smaller by the amount of interest payable in the future periods.

Short-term financial investments include securities (such as bonds with a maturity period of less than one year), short-term loans to other business entities, and so on. Such investments must be disclosed in detail in the annex to the balance sheet (Annex 3-SP). Securities are recorded only at cost, not market (securities markets are actually embryonic in Russia).

Cash discloses the balance of various kinds of monetary assets, such as cash on hand, cash in bank (business account and other accounts, cash in foreign currencies, both on hand and in bank).

Other current assets disclose miscellaneous items not recorded above in "Inventory and Expenses" and "Cash, Settlements, and Other Assets."

Losses

Losses disclose both the financial result (negative) of the current year and the accumulated loss carried forward from the previous years in conformity with the provisions of the Tax Law of 1990.

Liabilities (Passiv)

Sources of Owned Assets

The statutory fund, according to Soviet accounting principles, is part of a business entity's own resources, along with the depreciation fund and funds created from profits. According to the rules, the statutory fund must include not only the initial contributions by partners but capitalizations made in the course of operation, additional input by partners, and increases from other sources (such as governmental financing). The initial notion of the statutory fund in a centralized economy required separate disclosure of all initial and subsequent contributions (or allocations) of the government to the enterprises and the build-up of long-term tangible assets by the enterprises themselves from their profits (which actually belong to the state).

This heritage of the centralized accounting system remains largely intact and dictates recording rules. For example, in accordance with this concept, an acquisition by a joint venture of a bulldozer will require a credit entry to the statutory fund account (and a debit to long-term assets). A parallel entry will credit cash and debit a production development or similar fund.

The reserve fund is a mandatory fund equalling 25% of the statutory fund when it is fully replenished. The rates of formation of this fund may be determined either by the founding documents or the board. The changes in the reserve fund during the year are disclosed in Annex 3-SP.

Funds for reinvestment used to be mandatory for all Soviet enterprises with rates of allocation to such funds determined by the ministries. Now, creation of such funds is fully at the discretion of the enterprises (with the exception of some state-owned sectors). However, if the founding documents of a joint venture indicate the creation of specific funds and methods of allocations to them, the enterprise is bound to follow such provisions. Besides, joint ventures must disclose all capitalization from such funds in the balance sheet and in Annex 3-SP. Donations to joint ventures also are disclosed under this item.

Funds for consumption and specific-purpose finance, again, may be created either according to the founding documents or board decision. These funds are aimed at "social development," that is, consumption other than production development. According to Soviet rules, they may not be used to create new property for an enterprise. They may be used for bonuses, purchase of consumer goods for employees, acquisition of meal tickets, subsidies for treatment in sanatoria, and other purposes. The flow of such funds is disclosed in Annex 3-SP.

Retained earnings of previous years were introduced in the Soviet joint venture balance sheet format in August 1991 for the first time. Prior to that, all Soviet enterprises, including joint ventures, were required to allocate all profits to various funds. The government tightly controlled allocations to funds in the state-owned sector. Joint ventures had two privileges:

- A share of the net income could be distributed to partners;

- No fixed percentages of allocations of profits were fixed for them by the government (with the exception of the reserve fund).

Retained profits of previous years are disclosed separately in Annex 3-SP.

Profit is the net result of all joint venture operations during the accounting period and the assessment of the balance sheet items made in accordance with the statement on financial reports and balance sheets (see previous chapters). The amount of profit is disclosed gross (as profit of the reporting year) and net (retained earnings of the reporting year). The numbers are entered only for year end.

Profit Utilization shows profits allocated during the year for payments of tax and to reserve and other funds, and other amounts put aside from regular operations during the year. The detailed description of these allocations must be provided under Section II of the 2-SP report (Profit and Loss Statement). It is interesting to note that, prior to 1992, Profit Utilization (recorded in the identical account No. 81) was disclosed under the fixed assets section of the balance sheet. As mentioned on page 125, it had no real value and was recorded there only for control purposes.

Long-Term Liabilities

Long-term bank credits show the liabilities on long-term loans (over one year). The amounts must be reconciled with the banks. Loans not paid back on time are recorded separately in line 361.

Other long-term loans are the same as the preceding but to enterprises other than banks. Other long-term liabilities show the remainder.

Settlements and Other Liabilities

Short-term bank credits and other short-term loans are similar to the two long-term liabilities above but are for loans of less than one year. Overdue short-term bank loans are recorded separately in line 401.

Accounts payable are divided into seven groups:

1. Payables for goods and services purchased. Besides goods actually purchased, this item also includes "uninvoiced" purchases, that is, goods or other assets received and documented with a receipt voucher but for which invoices have not yet been received from suppliers and contractors.

2. Notes payable (the exact Russian term is Settlements with Creditors on Notes Issued) as security for the obtained commercial credits. Overdue notes payable are recorded on line 431.

3. Accrued salaries, not yet paid, also include amounts deposited back to the bank from the cashier's desk. If a debit balance occurs in the relevant account (normally the amount is recorded under "Wage Settlements"), then it has to be recorded under "Other Debtors" in Section III of the assets.

4. Accrued social insurance expense includes social security and pension liabilities. Debit balances on the relevant account, Account 69, are recorded the same as above.

5. Property insurance liabilities include all kinds of payables on insurance.

6. Payables to the state budget include liabilities for income taxes and other amounts due to central and local governments, including taxes levied from employees' earnings. Debit balances of Account 68, Settlements with State Budgets, are recorded under "Other Debtors" in Section III of the assets).

7. Other creditors include various payables to contractors, customers, liabilities on deposits in banks (except for salaries), penalties, fines and demurrages payable according to court or arbitration decision.

Advance payment from buyers and customers is recorded under this item until final settlements upon shipment of goods or completion of work takes place. Deferred revenues include items similar to the U.S. equivalent. Provision for future payments and expenses, according to Soviet accounting rules, includes the balance of refunds reserved as part of production costs and designed to cover forthcoming payments and expenditures.

Provision for bad debts is a new item for Soviet accounting that did not exist under the former cash basis accounting. The amounts are established after verification at year end of accounts receivable.

Other short-term liabilities are others than those described above.

Bank loans, payables, and other liabilities include items listed below.

1. Short-term bank loans represent a major source of finance, especially for merchandising and exporting joint ventures. Short-term loans are obtained automatically from "special crediting accounts" with the banks under relevant credit agreements. Such items as loans secured by goods delivered, loans secured by exports, and loans not paid on time are disclosed separately.

2. Liabilities to banks on long-term loans are disclosed separately for debits in rubles and in foreign currency. The current portion, however, is not recorded separately.

3. Payables include: (a) Accounts Payable for Goods and Services, (b) Notes Payable (foreign transactions), (c) Commercial Credit Payable (foreign transactions), (d) Advance Payments Payable, (e) Wages and Security Insurance Payable, (f) Payables to the Budget, and (g) Others. Each one is disclosed separately under the Payables item. Items (b) and (c) include accrued interest expense on credits, which is to be classified on the relevant entry in the American format balance sheet.

4. Funds for credit to employees are provided either by bank loans or by the joint venture's own resources. In American format balance sheets, they have to be disclosed separately.

5. Special funds, a voluminous item, covers all funds established by joint ventures in accordance with their statutory documents and the balances of the

amortization and maintenance funds. Actually, they all represent retained earnings of the joint venture.

6. Deferred income is similar to its American equivalent with one exception: It also includes interest income for the period (actually, accrued) on notes receivable. This amount must be reclassified as retained earnings.

7. Funds for new construction are displayed separately. Like the related assets, they must be reclassified according to the American format.

Some Conclusions

A comparison of the Russian joint venture balance sheet with the American format perfectly demonstrates two ideas. First, the two accounting systems serve different purposes—measurement of profit in a market economy versus evaluation of plan fulfillment in a centrally planned economy. Second, joint ventures, which are supposed to operate in a market environment (their goal being profit making, not plan fulfillment) still account and report according to principles appropriate to the goal of plan fulfillment.

A manager of a joint venture in the USSR cannot answer questions such as these:

- What is the current ratio of the joint venture?
- What is the amount of long-term debt?
- What is its current portion?
- What is the gross profit margin?

Other crucial questions can be answered formally, but the answers will give a very distorted picture of the joint venture's financial position:

- What is the return on assets?
- What is the amount of working capital?
- What is its ratio to total assets?
- What is the cash flow against assets?
- How long is the cash cycle?

To answer these and many other questions, an accountant must perform a substantial restructuring of the Soviet prescribed financial statements. Still, some questions will remain until market instruments are introduced.

Accounting for Foreign Transactions

Basic Soviet Regulations

Regulation of foreign trade transactions in the USSR deserves a brief discussion because it is quite different from such regulation in other countries.

During the entire postwar period, practically all the foreign trade operations of the Soviet Union have been centralized within the Ministry of Foreign Trade (Minvneshtorg). About 60 specialized export/import companies have been organized under the auspices of Minvneshtorg to carry out foreign trade operations, with products specified for each company. In the 1970s and early 1980s some of these specialized foreign trade companies (in the Russian abbreviation, V/O) were transferred to the control of several branch economic ministries. For example, V/O Avtoexport (exports of cars, imports of parts, technology, and so forth) was placed under the control of the Soviet car-building ministry.

All foreign trade activities were subject to very tight planning. The manufacturers of products for export could not engage in foreign business on their own or even show any initiative in opening up foreign markets. That right was reserved chiefly for V/Os. The procedure was as follows: Once the plan was approved by the governing bodies of the USSR, including a separate plan for exports and imports and a payments balance, relevant instructions were given to the Ministry of Foreign Trade. It established its own plans for each of the V/Os according to that company's specialization. On the other hand, relevant manufacturers and suppliers of export goods and receivers of imported goods were designated centrally. Thus, the task of the V/Os was to act as trade agent, that is, to enter into contact with both Soviet exporters and importers and to match them with the foreign market. Actually, Soviet clients of V/Os often had only a very vague idea of who the foreign partner was on the other side of the deal. The government tightly regulated all the relations between V/Os and Soviet exporters and importers. The legal form of these relations was somewhat similar to a purchase order (Russian term, *zakaz-naryad*) issued by a V/O to a manufacturer of export goods.

Receiving a *zakaz-naryad* from a V/O (actually, an order from the state) to supply goods for export in most cases meant additional headaches for Soviet manufacturers, because quality, documentation, packaging, and other terms had to meet international standards. On the other hand, most exporters did not receive adequate compensation for their additional efforts.

First, all foreign currency earnings went to the state, and there was no guarantee at all that at least part of these earnings would be paid back to the manufacturer as a "limited fund" for import purposes. Second, the price in rubles received for the goods delivered was based on regular Soviet wholesale prices, and even if some additions were made, they would just cover the extra expenses incurred in the course of the exporting activities of the manufacturer.

Changes Between August 1986 and December 1988

Such a system, by and large, existed until August 1986, when the first reforms were introduced in the Soviet system of foreign economic relations. From that time until December 1988, some major changes took place, leading to decentralization of foreign business transactions and to breaking the monopoly of the

Minvneshtorg. For example, a growing number of Soviet enterprises and other legal persons (starting with 70 in 1986) have obtained permission to engage in foreign business on their own. Decree No. 1405 of December 2, 1988, theoretically gave this right to all Soviet legal persons, provided they are registered with the Ministry of Foreign Economic Relations (MVES). The MVES was formed by the merger of the Ministry of Foreign Trade and the State Committee for Foreign Economic Cooperation (created for long-term projects in the third world). At the same time, the State Commission for Foreign Economic Relations was created to administer and coordinate all kinds of international business activities of the USSR. Its chairman is a deputy prime minister.

While the number of V/Os belonging to MVES was constantly decreasing (through mergers and reorganizations), many branch ministries as well as the governments of all 15 Soviet republics created their own foreign trade companies. Since July 1988, V/Os have been able to become foreign trade agents only by agreement with potential Soviet exporters and importers, if the exporters and importers choose to use their services as middlemen for any contract. V/Os charge their Soviet customers commission fees directly (formerly, the state paid each V/O its commission).

The form of direct orders from the state for Soviet manufacturers to export certain products has changed slightly from *zakaz-naryad* to *goszakaz*, which are carried out through the intermediation of MVES and its V/Os on the basis of the so-called agreements of delivery. *Goszakaz* deal mostly with exports of raw or strategic materials.

An attempt has been made to get Soviet and international prices closer to those of goods in foreign trade. The linkage was meant to be provided by the so-called differentiated exchange rates (Russian abbreviation, DVK), introduced in early 1987 for specific products. For example, a Soviet exporter can obtain a higher price in rubles for the goods delivered abroad through a V/O than the regular Soviet wholesale price. First, this price is linked to the price of the V/O's contract with the foreign buyer. Second, the exchange rate can be more favorable than the official exchange rate of the ruble, especially in the case of exports of finished goods for hard currencies. Although the system turned out to be too cumbersome and complex, still it created certain incentives for Soviet exporters.

Soviet exporters now can control part of their revenue from exports of goods and services in foreign currencies. The total revenue in foreign currencies is taxed at fixed rates, while the remainder becomes the property of manufacturers and can be used without significant restrictions. Soviet enterprises also can obtain credits in foreign currencies from Soviet banks, under certain conditions, and earn interest on their dollar (or other) accounts.

These measures have led to significant changes in the whole process and organization of Soviet foreign trade. Numerous newcomers have emerged on the Soviet business horizon, and the effects have been controversial. On the one hand, the old Minvneshtorg bureaucratic machine has been forced to move a little faster to avoid complete loss of control over Soviet export and import operations. The newcomers have brought more dynamism, new products, and new ideas, but, on the other hand, they have brought inexperience, incompetence, and "Wild West" anarchy. This situation has led to shocking price proposals, dumping, inaccuracy (Minvneshtorg was famous for that, too!), and readiness to sell anything that could or could not normally be sold.

It is no secret that raw materials are the main Soviet export, so a sellout of different raw materials began. At the same time, the best of what remained on the Soviet consumer market started disappearing, with "specialized trade tourists" from Eastern Europe contributing substantially to its disappearance.

Decree No. 203: Licensing of Exports and Imports

Euphoria did not last long, and the Soviet authorities responded on March 7, 1989, with Decree No. 203, "One of the State Regulatory Measures of Foreign Economic Activities." It imposed a new mechanism for state control of foreign business through the measures described below.

All potential participants in foreign economic transactions must be registered with the MVES. They must obtain its permission to engage in foreign operations, and it has practically unrestricted means to delay the registration. The only exception is for joint ventures, which automatically obtain the status of "participants in foreign economic relations" as soon as they are registered by the Ministry of Finance and become legal persons.

New customs procedures have been established. A customs declaration very similar to that used in the European Community is to be filled out when goods cross the Soviet border. The customs authorities charge fees for customs procedures, both in rubles and in foreign currencies. Customs officials have the authority to stop or delay the passage of goods across the border for a large variety of reasons.

The introduction of licensing of exports and imports represents a major move of the MVES toward regaining control over Soviet foreign trade. The list of exported goods to be licensed includes all raw materials, many consumer goods, and numerous other items. The list, already long to begin with, was extended several times during 1989.

Moreover, any operations that include purchases of goods to be sold abroad or on the domestic market are strictly prohibited. Thus, joint ventures must seek special permission from the MVES. Otherwise, they can import goods only for their own needs and export only their own production.

Finally, the State Commission on Foreign Economic Relations (GVK) and the MVES have the authority to suspend the right of registered "participants in foreign economic relations" to engage in international transactions, for a term of up to one year. The number of reasons can be extended to infinity. Also, the GVK and MVES can introduce quotas on any exported or imported products. An exception is made for imports and exports of joint ventures, provided the joint ventures obtain permission from the MVES as mentioned above.

Though Decree No. 203 declares that all restrictive measures are to be carried out in the true good spirit of *glasnost*, they obviously have not made the "new Soviet exporters" very happy. Actually, regulation of foreign transactions is a sovereign right of any state and its government. However, the measures under Decree No. 203, though not at all unusual in international practice, are very far from being clearly defined. Thus, they look very much like "the good old days" of the Minvneshtorg monopoly. It must be recognized, however, that the young, aggressive lions of the new Soviet foreign trade have contributed a lot to the restrictive character of the new regulations. Actually, for joint ventures the regulations mean more difficulties in transferring profits obtained in rubles to Western partners, because free export of raw materials is no longer possible.

Foreign Transactions

After obtaining the status of participants in foreign transactions, joint ventures also are covered by all Soviet regulations, including accounting regulations, concerning foreign transactions. There is nothing like these transactions anywhere else in the world or even in the Soviet Union itself. Even after recent changes, they are still unique.

First, all Soviet legal persons engaged in foreign transactions meet two completely different systems of prices. The fact that Soviet and international prices are very different in their nature derives from the basic differences between market and centrally planned economies. A product that is to be exported has two prices, a Soviet price before the title passes to the importer and a contract price. If the former price of a commodity in rubles is 100, and the latter in dollars translated into rubles is 150, the export transactions can be shown with T-accounts as follows:

Merchandise	(1)	Sales	(2)	Accounts Receivable
	100	→	100	150	→	150	

The difference between the prices, 50 rubles, accumulated on the credit side of the Sales account, normally should constitute the gross profit of a merchandise company. Not so in the case of Soviet foreign trade. The difference until 1991 went to the state budget, but on the other hand, all the "negative" differences between manufacturing or purchasing prices and selling prices were subsidized by the Ministry of Finance. The transaction looks like this, assuming the domestic price is 100 rubles and the "external" translated price is 50 rubles:

Merchandise	(1)	Sales	(2)	Accounts Receivable	(3)
	100	→	100	50	→	50	50	→

Budget
50	

State subsidies were very common with Soviet exports because internal prices in the USSR for most export items are higher than international prices. This situation occurs largely because the official exchange rate of the ruble to hard currencies (for commercial transactions) is overvalued beyond any reasonable limit. In 1989, budget expenses for export subsidies reached almost 11 billion rubles, or 2.2% of the Soviet budget.

To complicate the situation even more, part of this sum went to finance overhead on the sale of exported goods (excluding transportation costs in Soviet territory). State subsidies for overhead on the sale of exports are provided to all Soviet participants in foreign transactions, including joint ventures.

At the same time, however, the state budget has a much larger source of income—imports. Again, differences between contract and internal Soviet prices for imported goods are conveyed to the budget. Usually, these differences make an enormous income for the state. After overhead on the sale of imports is subtracted from the "customs income" (a strange term used for the difference in prices of imported goods), the latter joins the budget revenues. In 1989, revenues from imports constituted more than 60 billion rubles, or 14% of the Soviet budget.

It is obvious that the revenues and expenditures of the Soviet budget due to foreign trade price differences have nothing to do with real values expressed in hard currencies. The process is like gambling from one pocket to another. If the Soviet government spent $1 billion to buy consumer goods in order to sell them to Soviet customers for 10 billion rubles, it certainly would be an effective way to close the gap in the budget. The time has come to bring both Soviet internal prices and the exchange rate of the ruble closer to reality.

Further Reforms in Foreign Trade Regulations

The growing contradiction between needs and factors for activating foreign trade and mounting crises in the isolated Soviet economy brought about another most dramatic and controversial round of reforms in foreign trade regulations. These measures can be classified in three groups:

1. *Taxation.* From August 1990 through January 1991, a system of export and import taxes was introduced. In February 1991, Minfin formally abolished the long-existing system of settlements between companies and the government foreign-domestic price differences (details follow).

2. *Foreign currency.* In November 1990 the Soviet government reduced by three times the official commercial exchange rate of the ruble to the dollar (from $1 = R0.6 to $1 = R1.8). In April 1991 the exchange rate for individuals, including a possibility for foreign citizens to convert rubles back into hard currencies, was brought close to market ($1 = R28.0). In June 1991 the "domestic" convertibility of the ruble was provided for 1992, earlier than the government previously had envisaged.

On the other hand, in December 1990 the government required all enterprises to sell 40% of their foreign currency revenues to the federal hard currency fund, plus roughly 30% as other obligatory disbursements. In March 1991 transactions in hard currencies in the domestic market were prohibited, and in May all Soviet enterprises were required to return all their deposits in foreign banks back to the motherland. The new government of Russia recently introduced a new approach to the determination of the exchange rate of the ruble. The artificial "official" rate was cancelled. Instead, a single market exchange rate of the Central Bank applies for all commercial transactions (in March 1992 it was $1=R90). For some groups of export items the government imposes on exporters a mandatory sale of 40% of their foreign currency revenue at a "special" rate of R55 per $1 (March 1992). The principles of establishment of exchange rates in Ukraine are similar.

3. *Decentralization.* While the federal government rushed desperately from hard-line to liberal policies and back, Soviet republics grew bolder about taking the initiative. Ukraine passed a law on foreign economic activities in which the federal government is not even mentioned. It imposed its own registration and taxation procedures, canceled the federal government's customs duties on individuals on Ukrainian soil, and claimed the Ukrainian share of hard currency assets and liabilities from the federal bank for generating new resources for future foreign currency earnings through export, with the introduction of the exports/imports tax system.

Foreign businessmen will observe significant variations in foreign trade regulations among the new states. However, the starting conditions in every republic are largely similar: They all need to attract foreign investment and earn hard currencies and, on the other hand, protect the domestic market.

Accounting Peculiarities of Foreign Trade Operations

Accounting practice for foreign transactions for many decades has represented a unique mixture of Soviet and international approaches. Certainly, the accounting principles basically remain oriented toward central planning, but for many reasons, accounting for foreign transactions was always a kind of bridge between the Soviet and Western accounting systems, long before the first joint ventures appeared in the USSR. Even today, when Russia's accounting procedures tend to harmonize with Western standards, the requirements for export/ import accounting remain as a separate block of rules. Specialized foreign trade companies still report under separate specific formats, and they use a modified chart of accounts. Some of the major peculiarities are discussed below.

1. Revenues from exports are accrued. Accounts Receivable is debited after the goods for export are delivered and the invoice with other documents is submitted to the bank for collection. The Goods Delivered account is not used.

2. Provision is made for bad debts, but the amount of the allowance is recorded on the liabilities side of the balance sheet.

3. Interest expense on commercial credit is shown on the balance sheet. However, it is displayed as a deferral on the assets side of the balance sheet until

interest is paid. This method is somewhat cumbersome insofar as interest expense normally must be accrued at the end of the accounting period by the amount due for that period. Similarly, interest income is shown as a deferred revenue on the liabilities side.

4. Notes and securities are displayed on the balance sheet as assets or liabilities.

5. The summary account, Merchandise, is used widely with up to 10 subaccounts (second-level accounts) for exports and imports, for example, Merchandise Exported in the Process of Transportation Abroad or Merchandise Exported on Consignment Abroad.

6. Because banks credit most of the purchases of exported and imported goods, a Special Credit Account for Exporting/Importing Operations plays a central role in foreign trade transactions and usually is the most important liability item of specialized foreign trade companies.

Foreign Currency Issues

For decades, all Soviet transactions in foreign currency were based on the so-called currency monopoly of the state principle. This meant that only the state through its agencies, chiefly Gosbank and Vneshekonombank, had the exclusive right to possess and operate with foreign currencies. By and large, this principle still applies. However, in early 1991 a limited number of other banks were permitted to carry out some operations with foreign currencies.

Decentralization of foreign business operations in the Soviet Union finally led to a situation in which many state enterprises and cooperatives possess their own foreign currency and have significant freedom in using it for their own needs. However, the currency monopoly principle remains in two aspects.

First, Soviet legal persons, including joint ventures, keep foreign currency accounts chiefly with the Vneshekonombank. Only a very limited number of other banks were granted the right to open foreign currency accounts for individuals. Usually the currencies earned through exports of goods or services are kept in the so-called off-balance sheet currency accounts. That is, the owner of the account possesses, and operates with, an equivalent in rubles of the foreign currency amount belonging to him or her. Any time the owner wants to use the foreign currency for imports, an equivalent sum of rubles is transferred to the bank, which, upon request of the importer, pays the foreign seller's invoice. In fact, the off-balance sheet account represents a right to use foreign currency, not the currency itself.

At the same time, Soviet companies also can have "real" accounts in foreign currency and earn interest on them. If so, they must provide equivalent coverage in rubles from their current accounts. Usually, however, they are encouraged to keep off-balance sheet accounts, and it is often convenient to do so because, in this case, their current account in rubles remains intact, as in the example below.

A Soviet manufacturer delivers goods to a V/O for export; the price of the contract with the foreign customer is $100,000, or 64,000 rubles at the official exchange rate. The V/O pays the manufacturer the "internal" price for the product using a differentiated exchange rate (DVK), which is 2—64,000 x 2 = 128,000 rubles. The foreign buyer pays the V/O for the exported goods. The 64,000 rubles in foreign currency are taxed at a rate of 50% by the state and local authorities. The remainder (32,000) belongs to the Soviet manufacturer, which has two options:

1. Account for the 32,000 rubles in hard currency off balance and keep all the rubles earned from the V/O (128,000). The manufacturer's debit cash balance will be 128,000, and at the same time the manufacturer will have the right, as an off-balance sheet account holder with Vneshekonombank, to use 32,000 for imports. In this case the manufacturer will have to transfer 32,000 rubles to the Vneshekonombank, and the latter will pay the foreign supplier in foreign currency, say, $50,000.

2. Open a foreign currency account with Vneshekonombank. Before that, the manufacturer has to transfer 32,000 in rubles to the Vneshekonombank. The manufacturer's cash position on the balance sheet will be as follows: 96,000 debit cash balance in rubles and 32,000 debit cash balance in foreign currencies. The exporter has real dollars in its account with Vneshekonombank and earns interest but has less cash in rubles for everyday operations.

Joint ventures are supposed to have "real" foreign currency in their accounts with Vneshekonombank recorded in a special Foreign Currency account on the balance sheet. Foreign currency accounts of joint ventures can be opened in foreign banks only with the permission of Vneshekonombank.

Second, all transactions with foreign currency normally must pass through the Vneshekonombank. The usual forms of settlement include cash payments, with Vneshekonombank acting as an intermediary.

Another issue concerning foreign currency that deserves attention is the fluctuation of exchange rates and translation issues. The general rule of accounting for exchange rate differences is to debit negative differences and to credit positive differences to the Profit and Loss account.

The June and December 1990 regulations of the Ministry of Finance define accounting rules for exchange rate differences more specifically. In accordance with Decree 49, the differences between the values of assets at historic date (date of recording) and date of actual payment are debited or credited to Account 80, Profit and Loss. Cash, securities, receivables, and payables in foreign currencies are to be translated into rubles at the exchange rate of the first day following the accounting period (for example, January 1). Differences in revaluation due to exchange rate changes are to be posted to Account 80. Other assets, as well as all liabilities (except payables), are recorded in the balance sheet at historical cost and at historical exchange rates.

Provisions of the June 1990 regulation have been adjusted by Minfin's Regulation 142 of the following December. It established that not only assets but also liabilities in foreign currencies are subject to similar accounting rules.

The growing inflation and weakening of the ruble (together with attempts by some republics to initiate steps toward establishing their own currencies) impelled the federal government to more active policies regarding foreign currency issues. These policies have been inconsistent, however, as the following list of the most important measures shows:

- July 1990: Soviet individuals are allowed to purchase goods for, and open accounts in, foreign currencies without being asked about the source. The government observes indifferently as a growing number of Soviet enterprises engage in transactions in dollars and other hard currencies.
- Spring-fall 1990: Foreign currency auctions by Vneshekonombank grow in number.
- October 1990: The official commercial exchange rate of the ruble is reduced by three times.
- November-December 1990: The president and the government issue decrees obliging Soviet companies (including joint ventures) to sell 40% (in reality up to 70%) of their foreign currency revenues from exports to Vneshekonombank.
- March 1991: A law on foreign currency regulation is passed by the Soviet parliament legitimizing the right of Soviet legal and actual persons to own and possess foreign currencies and prohibiting both domestic transactions for companies in foreign countries and the opening of accounts in foreign banks.
- April 1991: The "touristic" exchange rate of the ruble to the dollar is brought close to the free market rate (April 1991: $1 for R28; August 1991: $1 for R32; October 1991: $1 for R47; and December 1991: $1 for R100), and the "official" exchange rate is finally cancelled. Dozens of banks throughout the new states are given permission to open accounts and operate in foreign currencies under licenses granted by their respective central (national) banks.

These events demonstrate the difficulties and failures encountered by the former federal government in meeting the conflicting goals of: (1) liberalizing foreign currency exchange and approaching convertibility of the ruble and (2) maintaining tight control over the foreign currency flows and paying off the external debt.

So far, liberalizing measures have proved more efficient, probably to the consternation of the federal government. Soviet companies and individuals actually gained a much broader access to foreign currency deals and speculations than in 1990 and before. On the other hand, restrictive measures have proved clumsy and have had the opposite effect from what the government expected. For example, the mandatory sales of a substantial part of foreign currency revenues from exports imposed on Soviet companies led to a decrease in export volume and an increase in somewhat shady deals aimed at "covering" foreign currency earnings.

The ruble finally faced a mortal threat at the end of 1991, so the new Russian government adopted a number of measures to stabilize it—something that Soviet leaders should have done long before. These measures provided a certain stabilization of the ruble with the dollar (and an eventual change in January-March 1992 from R250 to R80 per $1). However, more austerity measures should be imposed, and other new states, such as Ukraine, are already pushing for their own currency to be introduced later this year.

Illustrations of Accounting Organization in Joint Ventures

These examples are meant to provide future investors with a true-to-life picture. The negative illustrations are not the result of the socioeconomic environment nor the lack of appropriate legislation (although this lack may be significant) but, by and large, are due to the ill will of joint venture management or, more often, to the fact that incompetent accountants were hired. The situation is even worse when both factors exist simultaneously within one company.

The cases illustrate significant violations of accounting procedures due to incompetence, which is often related to the foreign partners' inexperience in finding and hiring accounting personnel. They often rely on their Soviet partners to do this hiring, and they believe that the high salaries offered the future controllers will be a protection against accounting abuse. Both assumptions are wrong. A Soviet partner may well find an unqualified but compliant controller who will be well paid for doing what the Soviet partner wants him to do. Thus, it is a common occurrence that persons with no experience in accounting are appointed joint venture controllers or financial directors. (To be objective, we must add that this situation is also true for other positions in joint venture management and often is explained by the considerable difficulties in finding skilled professionals.) Hence, we would like to advise all foreign investors to be very careful when choosing a joint venture controller. Your Soviet partner's reliability can be measured by the skills of the controller he recommends.

Before being offered the controller's position, a candidate should undergo a thorough examination and interview by the foreign partner. As a result, the latter should gain a clear picture of the candidate's professional skills. If the foreign partner has problems in conducting such an interview, he should address an international accounting firm with offices in the USSR. (All the major international accounting firms have such offices.) Following this advice can help to avoid complications like those described below.

Case A

Company A, a joint venture in the USSR, is a shipping (cargo) company with subsidiaries in several foreign countries. During a certain period, Company A encountered difficulties in making its current payments. Foreign banks are reluctant to accept mortgages on ships because they fear the possibility that the ships will be taken to internal waters in the Soviet Union where they are not accessible through international arbitration. Therefore, foreign banks open credit lines only under the guarantee of Vneshekonombank, which generally is not available.

Hence, Company A sells the ship to its foreign subsidiary on terms of commercial credit. At the same time the subsidiary signs a charter agreement with the parent company. The first contract provides that ownership passes to the subsidiary, which must pay for the ship over a number of years. The second contract provides that Company A not only takes back the right to use the ship but also regains the property rights over the ship. The sums and the schedules of payment in both contracts are identical, but the ship now sails under a foreign flag, and foreign banks are more willing to take a mortgage. So the ship is mortgaged and the subsidiary gets the credit and makes payments to the bank. If it is not able to pay off the loan, the bankruptcy of both the parent and the subsidiary is inevitable. The loan is secured in a highly risky manner, but Company A will be able to exist due to the credit obtained from the bank. Because the Soviet partner is a state-owned enterprise, it is not concerned about the joint venture's future bankruptcy and liquidation.

The deal is recorded in a peculiar way in the joint venture's books. According to Soviet accounting methodology, the writeoff of the ship is recorded:

(1) Statutory Fund (Account 85)   Dr
      Fixed Assets (01)   Cr

The recording of the quasi-payment of the subsidiary to the parent results in the appearance of a receivable for the parent and an increase in its development fund:

(2) Receivables from Miscellaneous Debtors (76)   Dr
      Development Fund (87)   Cr

The charter agreement requires the reacquisition of the ship, which allegedly was sold, to be recorded. The joint venture's controller makes the two following entries:

(3) Fixed Assets (01)   Dr
      Long-Term Credits (92)   Cr
     Long-Term Credits (92)   Dr
      Payables to Miscellaneous Creditors (76)   Cr

Entries involving Account 92 are supposed to register the fact that a long-term loan was obtained, but they are incorrect because the credit was available to the subsidiary and not to the parent. As a result, fictitious entries artificially create both receivables and payables.

According to the schedule of debt payments, the entry is registered:

(4) Payables to Miscellaneous Creditors (76)   Dr
    Receivables from Miscellaneous Debtors (76)   Cr

This leads to more fictitious amounts in Account 76. Moreover, if entry 3 does not immediately follow entry 2, receivables are overestimated, creating a distorted picture of Company A's liquidity.

Case B

Company B is a retailer of consumer goods for convertible currencies through a network of stores throughout the USSR. The following accounting procedures for inventories and cash are used by the company.

Merchandise purchases are recorded in the so-called *invalutni* rubles (foreign-currency rubles). This means that a purchase of $1,000 worth of merchandise will be recorded at R610 value because the official exchange rate of Gosbank is $1 = R0.61.

Each item has a tag on which the price in dollars is indicated. Merchandise sold for cash is received by salespersons. Merchandise inventory is written off in dollars, and significant differences exist between the acquisition and sales prices.

Ending inventory is undervalued. Thus, an ending inventory of $3,000 will be recorded as R1,830.

Material responsibility agreements are signed between Company B and the managers of different stores, but the usual Soviet regulations on material responsibility are not applied. At the end of the business day, salespersons inform the managers of the day's cash receipts without any supporting documents. The managers count the cash and pass it (again without documentation) to the controller, who then deposits the money in the foreign currency accounts of Company B with Vneshekonombank. There is no proof that the managers surrender all cash receipts to the controllers, nor that the controller deposits the entire sum in the bank.

Merchandise inventory is recorded both in dollars and *invalutni* rubles, making it easy to steal a part of the earnings in foreign currencies. If the black market exchange rate is $1 = R20 rather than $1 = R0.61, even small amounts in dollars become substantial revenues in rubles.

The organization of accounting is very poor. No reports are prepared for operations with merchandise and cash, and there is no cash or merchandise ledger. The balance sheet is based on very rough estimates, and no general ledger exists at all.

The absence of control makes it easy for managers to purchase merchandise from unauthorized suppliers, such as cooperatives and other small private businesses, and sell them for foreign currencies. The temptation to make a profit on the high black market rate of the dollar pushes managers to withdraw a part of the stores' dollar revenues.

Receipts and sales of merchandise without documentary evidence, as well as withdrawals of cash, cause a situation in which accounting and inventory balances of merchandise never match. There are times when inventories exceed account balances (when authorized goods are sold) or vice versa (when too much cash is withdrawn).

Although there is no general ledger, the journal orders are filled in by the controller. All the records are made in *invalutni* rubles. Below are the typical entries:

(1) Merchandise (41)   Dr
    Intragroup Settlements on
      Current Operations (78)   Cr

Entries are based on receipts, invoices, or bills. Foreign currencies are translated into rubles. The credit (Account 78) shows the liability of the store to Company B's main office.

(2) Cash-Banking Account (51)   Dr
    Sales (46)   Cr

There is no accounting of cash at the cashier's desk; revenues are debited from the sales account directly to the cash-banking account.

(3) Sales (46)   Dr
    Merchandise (41)   Cr

The company's accounting practice is unusual in that the amounts in transactions (2) and (3) are the same. Therefore, Account 41, Merchandise, is a "mixed" one—the cost of merchandise is recorded on the debit side and the selling price on the credit side. Moreover, sometimes the accountant credits the revenue to Account 41 in *dollars* while the debits are in rubles.

(4) Merchandise (41)   Dr
    Profit and Loss (80)   Cr

Once a quarter, or sometimes monthly, inventories are taken. Merchandise is valued at acquisition cost, then the cost of goods sold is calculated, and the profit margin is determined and credited to the profit and loss account.

(5) Intragroup Settlement on
    Current Operations (78)   Dr
    Cash-Banking Account (51)   Cr

Part of the revenue is transferred to Company B headquarters as payment for the goods delivered.

Entries in Account 78 are inaccurate. Memoranda received from headquarters list the documents accompanying the merchandise, but the amounts in the memoranda are different from those in the source documents to which the references are made. However, cash is transferred to the company's office only according to memoranda amounts, so real flows of merchandise and cash do not match.

Note: Most of the stores controlled by joint ventures use a different method for valuation of inventories. Profit margins are determined at headquarters, and affiliated stores receive merchandise at selling prices indicated both in documents and on tags. Stores "acquire" and sell merchandise at the same value (Account 46). The sales account has the same amounts in debit and credit. The stores make no profit. Store expenses are covered by the main office according to budget. Stores are free to use funds in any way within budget limits.

Case C

Company C buys and sells goods only for foreign currencies, but it has to pay its employees' salaries in rubles. The company's management has found Firm X, which would like to purchase foreign currency. In order to make the exchange, Companies C and X sign an agreement to conduct a sociological research project for a hard currency. Another contract is signed at the same time providing C's advertising services for X to be paid for in rubles. Both contracts are, of course, fictitious. The exchange is made at the free market rate; moreover, the profit for both companies is to a large extent tax exempt.

C's records show the following entries:

(1) Selling Expenses (44)   Dr
     Foreign Currency Account (52)   Cr

The sale of foreign currency is registered:

(2) Cash-Banking Account (51)   Dr
     Sales (46)   Cr

Both operations lead to an overestimation of Company C's sales because of fictitious entries to Account 46. Therefore, some companies use Accounts 80, Profit and Loss, or 87, Development Funds, instead of the sales account. In the latter case, the amount in rubles exchanged for dollars is protected from taxation. Company X's records show the following entries:

(1) Foreign Currency Account (52)   Dr
     Sales (46)   Cr

(2) Selling Expense (44)   Dr
    Cash-Banking Account (51)   Cr

If such deals are part of long-term arrangements, relevant amounts are posted to Account 76, Miscellaneous Payables and Receivables.

Case D

Company D encounters financial problems but can easily get access to huge supplies of merchandise. Because it has insufficient funds, it cannot obtain credit to finance the purchase of merchandise. Also, the management of the company is unwilling to disclose the details of the operation to the bank.

The essence of the transaction lies in the fact that the Soviet market consists of an infinite number of local markets, and price ratios on certain goods may be as high as 1:20 in different local markets. Companies with such information try to maintain secrecy to use the information to their advantage. Moreover, certain Soviet companies have secured access to foreign markets for themselves, and they have a competitive advantage over those companies that have no such access.

Company D's management approaches the directors of Company E with the offer of a contract providing for the sale of incredible amounts of goods and values or the rendering of services that D quite obviously is unable to provide. E's management is aware of this fact but pretends not to be. After the contract is signed, E makes an advance to D that may reach 50% of the huge amount of the contract. It is normally easy enough to obtain bank credit for such a contract. D now possesses enough current assets and may proceed to carry out the planned operation.

D expects huge profits from this transaction, which will allow: (1) payment of the principal and interest to the bank and (2) return of the advance payments and a forfeit.

If the operation succeeds, all the parties involved are happy. Entries in this case are irreproachable:

(1) Cash-Banking Account (51)   Dr
    Advance Payments (61)   Cr
Advance payment is received.

(2) Cash-Banking Account (51)   Dr
    Bank Short-Term Loans (90)   Cr
Credit is obtained from bank.

(3) Bank Short-Term Loans (90)   Dr
    General Expense (26)   Dr
    Cash-Banking Account (51)   Cr
Principal and interest on bank credit are paid in cash.

(4) Advance Payments (61)	Dr	
Profit and Loss (80)	Dr	
Cash-Banking Account (51)		Cr

Advance payment is returned and forfeit paid.

Since May 28, 1990, Soviet legislation has allowed voluntary insurance against nonpayment by debtors. This regulation allows D to ensure repayment of bank credit. Expense and liability to the insurance agency are recorded. This entry is made after entry 2.

General Expenses (26)	Dr	
Insurance Payable (69)		Cr

If D's plans fail, the following entry must be recorded:

Short-Term Bank Loans (90)	Dr	
Insurance Payments (69)		Cr

After this, property rights pass to the insurance agency. D is now bankrupt, and the insurance agency will have a claim over a part of the company's liquidation assets.

Detailed Accounting Procedures for Joint Ventures

Letter No. 74 of the USSR Ministry of Finance, June 6, 1990 (Summary)

This letter applies to joint ventures on the territory of the USSR. [These guidelines generally also are valid for the new format of August 1991.][1]

1.   Accounting for the depreciation (amortization) of property

1.1   Joint ventures shall make depreciation (amortization) deductions against the following property:
- Against fixed assets (except on property which, in accordance with Soviet legislation for Soviet state enterprises, is not subject to depreciation);
- Against intangible assets, unless stated otherwise in the foundation documents;
- Against low-value and short-life items, in accordance with Soviet legislation for Soviet state enterprises;

1.2   The amount of depreciation (amortization) of fixed assets shall be the same as the amount of amortization for complete renewal.

---

[1]Account numbers may differ from those in the chart of accounts, which was revised after this letter was issued.

Joint ventures shall make amortization deductions in accordance with the instructions applying to Soviet state enterprises, unless stated otherwise in the foundation documents.

1.3 Depreciation of fixed assets shall be debited to the production cost accounts 20, 23, 24, etc. and credited to 02, Depreciation (Amortization) of Property.

1.4 A fixed asset should be depreciated over its useful life.

1.5 When fixed assets are retired from service, their initial cost shall be written off from account 01, Fixed Assets, to account 02. Any underdepreciated amount arising at retirement shall be taken to the profit and loss account.

1.6 Costs associated with retiring fixed assets, losses arising on sale, and also receipts from the sale of property, etc., shall be taken to the profit and loss account.

1.7 For the time being, the rate of depreciation (amortization) of intangible assets shall be determined by the foundation documents. The accounting entries shall be as described in points 1.3 to 1.6 above.

1.8 Depreciation of low-value and short-life items shall be determined in accordance with the rules applying to Soviet state enterprises, unless otherwise stated in the foundation documents. The chosen method must be applied consistently.

2. Accounting for capital investments

2.1 Joint ventures shall record capital investments in account 33, Capital Investments, in accordance with the procedure established for Soviet state enterprises.

2.2 Costs of constructed (ready for use) fixed assets shall be written out of account 33 at their inventory cost into account 01.

2.3 On the realization of capital investments, the payment of suppliers shall be credited to accounts 51, 52, or 54, or account 92 if they are paid by way of a long-term loan. The repayment of long-term loans shall be recorded by debiting account 92 and crediting accounts 51, 52, or 54.

2.4 The movement of sources of financing capital investments shall be accounted for as follows:

- When capital investments are realized at the expense of the resources of funds created according to the foundation documents (account 88) and other similar funds, these funds shall be debited and the charter (statutory) fund (account 85) credited at the same time account 33 is credited;
- When capital investments are realized at the expense of other (including amortization deductions), no special accounting entries shall be made.

3. Accounting for the sale of goods and services

3.1 Delivered goods shall be considered to have been realized by a joint venture when the settlement documents have been submitted to the buyer. The settlement documents shall be considered to have been submitted to the buyer at the moment that they have been presented to the bank (if settlement is being made through the bank), or when they are passed to the buyer in the agreed manner.

Exported goods shall be recorded in account 45, Delivered Goods and Services, until the moment that the rights and risks of ownership use and disposal, etc., have been transferred.

3.2. Goods sold shall be recorded in account 46, Realization. Costs of production shall be debited here and the amount invoiced to the buyer shall be credited to the same account. (Account 62, Settlements with Buyers and Customers, shall be correspondingly debited.)

3.3 Joint ventures must ensure that appropriate measures are taken for the timely and full payment of invoiced amounts.

4. Accounting for financial investments

4.1 Joint ventures shall account for financial investments in account 58, Financial Investments.

4.2 Financial investments shall be debited to account 58 and credited to those accounts that are used to acquire the investment. For example, the acquisition of securities of other enterprises would be reflected by debiting account 58 and crediting accounts 51 or 52.

4.3 Income from financial investments shall be credited to account 80, Profit and Loss (in conjunction with account 51 or 52).

If the income is wholly or in part reinvested, account 58 shall be debited and account 80 credited. At the same time, the amount that has been reinvested shall be debited to account 81, Profit Utilization, and credited to account 85.

4.4 The movement of sources of financing financial investments shall be reflected in the books in the same manner as described in point 2.4 above.

5. Accounting for exchange differences on currency accounts and foreign currency transactions

5.1 Bookkeeping entries for foreign currency transactions shall be made in Soviet rubles translated at the official USSR Gosbank ruling on the date of the bank statement (unless otherwise provided for by Soviet legislation).

5.2 In accordance with Decrees 48 and 49 of the USSR Council of Ministers, foreign currency exchange differences arising on the currency accounts of joint ventures and also on their transactions in foreign currency shall be taken to the profit and loss account.

5.3 Balances on foreign currency accounts, other monetary assets in foreign currency, and other assets due to be received or paid in foreign currency shall be recorded at an amount translated into Soviet rubles at the USSR Gosbank rate ruling on the first date following the accounting period.

Other property of the joint venture that has been acquired at the expense of foreign currency resources and is accounted for at initial cost, and also all credit items, shall be recorded at an amount translated into Soviet rubles at the USSR Gosbank ruling on the date that they were first brought into the books.

5.4   Foreign exchange differences arising out of the procedure outlined in the first paragraph of point 5.3 above shall be treated in the manner established in point 5.2 above.

6.   Accounting for leased property and lease payments

6.1   Joint ventures shall record leased property in accordance with the procedure established for Soviet state enterprises.

6.2   Depreciation of property leased out shall be deducted in the manner established in points 1.1, 1.2, and 1.3 above. The amount of depreciation shall be debited to account 80, Profits and Losses, and credited to account 02, Depreciation (Amortization) of Property.

Depreciation of leased property received shall not be recorded in the books of the lessee.

6.3   The joint venture lessor shall debit account 76, Settlements with Miscellaneous Debtors and Creditors, with the amount of the lease payment for the accounting period and credit account 80.

The joint venture lessee shall include the lease payment for the accounting period in the cost of production and record it in account 76 until it is paid.

7.   The formation, use, and accounting for the provision for doubtful debts

7.1   Doubtful debts shall be provided for and taken to the profit and loss account at the end of the accounting period.

A doubtful debt is a debt that has not been settled within the due period and that is not secured by guarantee.

7.2   The amount of the provision shall be determined separately for each doubtful debt depending on the financial situation of the debtor and the likelihood of the debt being settled in full or in part.

If the provision is not used before the end of the year following the year that the provision was created, then the unexpensed part shall be taken to profit for that year.

7.3   Doubtful debt provisions shall be recorded in a subaccount of account 88, Special-Purpose Funds.

Account 80 shall be debited with the amount of the provision, and account 88 credited. When unclaimed debts that have previously been provided for are written off the balance sheet, account 88 shall be debited and the debtor account credited. When unexpensed amounts of the doubtful debt provision are taken to profit for the year following the year that the reserve was set up, account 88 shall be debited and account 80 credited.

This letter shall come into force on July 1, 1990.

Once this letter has come into force, joint ventures shall:

1. Add the balance on account 86, Amortization Fund (subaccount 86-1), to the balance on the charter (statutory) fund;

2. Write the full actual cost of production of delivered goods and services out of accounts 45 and 43 into account 46, Realization; at the same time, the amount at which buyers have been invoiced for goods delivered etc. shall be debited to account 62 and credited to account 46. The resultant balance on account 46 shall be taken to the profit and loss account.

Deputy Minister of Finance of the USSR
V.V. Sitnin

Head of Department for the Methodology and
Organization of Bookkeeping and Accounting
N. V. Panteleev

Format of the Annual Financial Report of Joint Ventures with Foreign Investments*

Annex to the letter of the Ministry of Finance of the USSR of August 30, 1991, No. 50

Balance sheet of
the joint venture
on January 1, 199__

Enterprise . . . .

Sector of industry . . . . . .

Unit of measurement: thousands of rubles

	CODES
Format No. 1-SP	
per OKUD	0775101
Date (year)	
per OKPO	
per OKONH	
Control total	

Address _____

Date of dispatch	
Date of receipt	
Term of submission	

*_____

Note: The new balance sheet of joint ventures will become similar to the new Russian balance sheet, undoubtedly greatly alleviating the existing confusion.

ASSETS (*AKTIV*)	Code of the Line	Beginning of Year	At Year End
1	2	3	4
I Fixed assets and other noncurrent assets			
Intangible assets:	010		
at cost			
amortization	011		
net	012		
Fixed tangible assets:			
at cost	020		
depreciation	021		
net	022		
Unfinished capital construction			
and investments	030		
Long-term financial investments	040		
Other noncurrent assets	050		
Total of Section I	060		
II Inventory and Expenses			
Production stocks	070		
Low-value and short-life assets:			
at cost	080		
depreciation	081		
net	082		
Work-in-process	090		
Finished products	100		
Merchandise inventory:			
selling price	110		
trade discount (markdown, markup)	111		
acquisition cost	112		
Selling overheads on ending			
merchandise inventory	120		
Total of Section II	130		

ASSETS (*AKTIV*), Cont'd	Code of the Line	Beginning of Year	At Year End
1	2	3	4
III Cash, Settlements, and Other Assets			
Accounts receivable (settlements with debtors):			
for goods and services	140		
notes receivable	150		
other debtors	160		
Advances to suppliers and contractors	170		
Prepaid expenses	180		
Short-term financial investments	190		
Cash:			
in hand	200		
in bank (business account)	210		
foreign currencies in bank	220		
other cash	230		
Other current assets	240		
Total of Section III	250		
Losses:			
previous years	260		
reporting year	270		
Total assets (sum of lines 060, 130, 250 260, and 270)	280		

LIABILITIES (*PASSIV*)	Code of the Line	Beginning of Year	At Year End
1	2	3	4
I Sources of Owned Assets			
Statutory fund	290		
Reserve fund	300		
Funds for reinvestment	310		
Funds for consumption and special-purpose financing	320		
Retained earnings of previous years	330		
Profit:			
of reporting year*	340		
utilized*	341		
retained earnings of reporting year	342		
Total of Section I	350		
II Long-Term Liabilities			
Long-term bank credits	360		
Other long-term loans	370		
Other long-term liabilities	380		
Total of Section II	390		
III Settlements and Other Liabilities			
Short-term bank credits	400		
Other short-term loans	410		
Accounts payable (settlements with creditors):			
for goods and services	420		
notes payable	430		
accrued salaries	440		
accrued social insurance expense	450		
for property insurance	460		
to the state budget	470		
other creditors	480		
Advances from buyers and customers	490		
Deferred revenues	500		

*Numbers in these lines are not totalled.

LIABILITIES (*PASSIV*)	Code of the Line	Beginning of Year	At Year End
1	2	3	4
Provisions for future payments and expenses	510		
Provisions for bad debts	520		
Other short-term liabilities	530		
Total of Section III	540		
Total liabilities (sum of lines 350, 390, and 540)	550		

INFORMATION			
Name of Item 1	2	3	4
Securities (guarantees): received	560		
issued	570		
Partner's liability for payments to statutory fund—total	580		

GENERAL DIRECTOR (signature)

CHIEF ACCOUNTANT (signature)

Profit and Loss Statement

for the year 199___

Format 2-SP
per OKUD
Date (year)
per OKPO
per OKONH
Control total

CODES
0775102

I FINANCIAL RESULTS

Name of Item	Code of the Line	Profits (incomes)	Losses (expenses)
1	2	3	4
Revenue (gross income)* from sales	010		
Sales tax	020		
Turnover tax	030		
. . . .	031		
Production (distribution) costs including:	040		
cost of production	041		
nonproduction expenses	042		
Profit (loss) from sales	050		
Profit (loss) from other sales	060		
Nonoperational revenues and expenses including:	070		
income from securities and participations	071		
income and loss from exchange rate fluctuations	072		
Total of profits and losses	080		
Profit (loss) of the reporting year	090		

*For merchandise enterprises and restaurants.

II UTILIZATION OF PROFIT

Name of Item	Code of the line	At end of period
1	2	3
Payments to the state budget	100	
Allocations to the reserve fund	110	
Utilized for:		
production development	120	
social development	130	
incentives	140	
charity and sponsorship	150	
other purposes	160	

III PAYMENTS TO THE STATE BUDGET

Name of Item	Code of the line	Accrued	Actually Paid
1	2	3	4
Rental payments	200		
Income	210		
Allocations for utilization of natural resources and damage to the environment	220		
Turnover tax	230		
Sales tax	240		
Export tax	250		
Import tax	260		
Tax on revenues	270		
Individual income tax and tax on single persons	280		
Other tax	290		
Economic sanctions	300		

GENERAL DIRECTOR (signature)

CHIEF ACCOUNTANT (signature)

Annex to the Balance Sheet
of Joint Ventures

as of January 1, 199___   Format 3-SP
                                 per OKUD

Enterprise   Date (YY, MM, DD)
Sector of industry   per OKPO
Unit of measurement: per OKONH
   thousands of rubles   Control total

CODES
0775122

I FUNDS FLOW					
Name of Item	Code of the line	Balance at period beginning	Accumulated during reporting year	Utilized during accounting year	Balance at period end
1	2	3	4	5	6
Reserve fund	010				
Retained earnings of previous years	020				
Funds for reinvestment— total	030				
. . . .	031*				
. . . .	039				
Funds for consumption— total	040				
. . . .	041*				
. . . .	049				

*Lines 031 to 039 and 041 to 049 disclose funds specified in foundation documents.

II COMPOSITION OF INTANGIBLE ASSETS AT YEAR END		
Name of Item	Code of the Line	Total
1	2	3
Rights on inventions and similar objects	050	
Rights on utilization of natural resources	060	
Start-up costs	070	
Other	080	

III AVAILABILITY AND FLOW OF TANGIBLE FIXED ASSETS

Name of Item	Code	Total	Including	
			Productive	Nonproductive
1	2	3	4	5
Balance at beginning of year	090			
Balance during year	100			
Disposed of during year	110			
Balance at year end—total	120			
including abroad	121			
Accumulated depreciation for improvement of fixed assets	130			

IV COMPOSITION OF TANGIBLE FIXED ASSETS AT YEAR END

Name of Item	Code of the Line	Amount
1	2	3
Buildings and installations	140	
Machinery and equipment	150	
Motor vehicles	160	
Tools, appliances and other fixed assets	170	

V FINANCIAL INVESTMENTS AT YEAR END

Type of financial investment	Code of the Line	Long-term	Short-term
1	2	3	4
Parts and stock in other enterprises	180		
Bonds and other securities	190		
Loans	200		
Other	210		

VI FLOWS OF FOREIGN CURRENCIES		
Name of Item	Code of the line	Amount
1	2	3
Balance at beginning of year	220	
Inflow—total	230	
including:		
revenue from sales	231	
loans obtained	232	
Outflow—total	240	
including:		
expenses included in production costs	241	
reinvestment in production development	242	
payment of loans, including interest	243	
dividends to partners of joint venture	244	
including—to foreign partners	245	
Balance at year end	250	

VII CAPITAL INVESTMENTS		
Name of Item	Code of the line	Account
1	2	3
Capital investments—total for reporting year	260	
including those from:		
accumulated depreciation fund	261	
reinvested profits	262	
other owned sources	263	
long-term loans	264	

GENERAL DIRECTOR (signature)

CHIEF ACCOUNTANT (signature)

Part III
An Appraisal

Chapter 6

An Appraisal of the Future of Accounting and Auditing in the CIS

Necessary Reforms and Changes

Reforms of the economic structure in the republics of the former Soviet Union, including the transition to a market-oriented economy (or to a free-market socialistic economy) are in full swing. These reforms are having a profound impact on the development of accounting and auditing in two respects. First, accounting and auditing are being called upon to solve a number of new problems, both theoretical and practical; that is, accounting and auditing must adapt to the needs of economic structure reform. Second, taking into account that both accounting and auditing play a significant role in the economic activities of the republics of the CIS, their development must contribute to economic structure reform.

A recent study on the Soviet economy,[1] carried out jointly by major international development organizations, made the following pertinent statements:

> As regards the future, it is clear that changes to both the accounting systems used in enterprises [and in government statistics] would help accelerate the transition to a market economy. Efficient decentralization of decision making will take place only if managers and investors have a full and fair view of an enterprise's financial performance. Achieving this will require the implementation of uniform accounting standards, training in these new concepts, auditing of accounts to ensure that the standards are being met, and the dissemination of audited accounts for use by shareholders, creditors, and supervisory authorities. Just as improved accounting systems are a prerequisite for efficient microeconomic decision making, so are improved macroeconomic statistics necessary for improved policy formation.

Economic structure reform in the former Soviet Union is bound to influence almost every aspect of the economy. One example is the management model.

---

[1] *A Study of the Soviet Economy*, International Monetary Fund, World Bank, Organization for Economic Cooperation and Development, European Bank for Reconstruction and Development; OECD, Paris, 1991, Volume 1, p. 133.

Single-phase administrative control by governmental agencies under the traditional structure gradually is being replaced by diversified-phase economic control emphasizing effectiveness and efficiency of economic activities. Changes will be seen in the operation of business enterprises (state or private) in a number of respects, including their organizational structure, their fund sources, their manner of operation, and their vertical and horizontal relationships with other units.

These changes inevitably will greatly influence the content, system, and methods of accounting. For instance, the accounting classification, measurement, and reporting system obviously will be modified after practitioners reconsider questions such as to whom the accounting report should be submitted, what should be reported, which salient points (key variables) should be emphasized, what kinds of accounting statements should be prepared, and what the aims and means of accounting in the new manufacturing environment are to be.

In view of the recent political and economic separation of the states (republics) that made up the Soviet Union, there may be some differentiation in the uniform accounting system that each country has adopted. The new versions are expected to combine the elements of Soviet and American (including international) accounting, however.

Stimulating state enterprises, and privatizing many of them, will be one of the important objectives of economic structure reform. The effort to revitalize enterprises centers on giving them more power and extending their right to make decisions. Then they can manage and organize their economic activities independently and not just passively carry out the centralized, mandatory plan (Gosplan) that USSR government agencies handed down. The aim of this stimulation is to make enterprises run as independent or semi-independent economic entities and assume responsibility for their own profits and losses. Under such a scheme, should an enterprise fail in operation, it will become bankrupt instead of being able to rely on the central government or republics for grants and subsidies. Thus, the need arises for ways to deal with insolvency and bankruptcy in accounting and auditing, problems that accountants and auditors in the republics have not faced before.

To be independent, enterprises must compete actively in the market, striving for survival and growth. In such a situation, accounting should direct more attention to establishing accountability (financial measurement and reporting) and to taking part in decision making (managerial accounting) than it has done in the past. When the operation of enterprises was in no way disturbed by outside market forces, the main functions of accounting were to keep records of the financial conditions and to exercise control over the economic activities. There was little room for accounting to act as a decision-making instrument. In the future, however, the decision-making function of accounting presumably will assume much greater importance, with the ultimate aim of maximizing the potential productivity and efficiency of enterprises, both public and private, in the respective republics.

New Types of Financial Transactions

As economic structure reform progresses, it will bring numerous economic events and financial transactions that were unknown to accountants in the past and that demand proper accounting treatment. As an experiment in such reform, many enterprises will be permitted to issue stock and sell bonds to meet their financial requirements. Capital market institutions are to open in Moscow and St. Petersburg. Accounting for stocks and bonds therefore must be added to the list of new problems emerging from economic structure reform. This process started in 1990 with Minfin's Regulations 98 and 99.

Another example of a new economic event is the reform of the pricing system. Instead of all prices being set centrally, state enterprises now are authorized to sell the portion of their output that exceeds the production quota at a price they have determined. Further liberalization of prices is expected soon. Thus, a market for the producers' goods, in which prices are regulated in accordance with the law of supply and demand, will be established. The scope of state-controlled prices will be reduced gradually, and floating prices will exert greater influence on the economy. In this situation, market prices, floating prices, and state-controlled prices will function simultaneously, and all will contribute to the growth of the CIS economy.

Sometimes the differences among these three kinds of prices can be very significant. As a result, an intractable problem that Soviet accountants face in their practice is determining on what basis they should value the inventory and fixed assets, also taking into account price level changes. Inflation is an example. Currently, inflation in Russia and the other republics is expected to be in excess of 100% for 1992. Inflation accounting soon may become an important topic because inflation factors will remain very significant for at least the next few years.

With the coexistence of several prices for a given article instead of a single controlled price, the valuation problem in accounting is complicated beyond that of inventory and fixed assets. It is apparent that the pricing system affects the identification of product cost and determination of income as well as the assessment of economic sector performance. In short, the overall impact of accounting measurement (classification and valuation) must be taken into account.

In addition, the current reform has produced considerable horizontal contact among enterprises. This contact calls for special treatment in the accounts because a number of intangible items, such as specific technologies, patents, trademarks, and the right to use production sites, are involved. In this context, transfer pricing policy of an interorganizational and intracompany nature will have to be assessed—a matter of particular importance to joint venture operations and international transactions. Consequently, theoretical and practical solutions to these problems must be found. Besides intangibles, problems such as what kind of financial reports are to be prepared and whether consolidated financial statements similar to those used in Western countries are needed also challenge enterprises associated with other enterprises located in different areas and under different jurisdictions.

Although most of these problems have been identified, they have no ready solutions yet. It is evident that both academics and practitioners in accounting and auditing in the Soviet Union need to forge new theories, concepts, and methods, taking into account characteristics of the Soviet Union. They need to meet the requirements of economic structure reform, to review existing accounting principles, standards, and regulations, and to discard those that prove inconsistent with the spirit of reform. They must modify and improve the existing uniform accounting system. Furthermore, international accounting norms are to be appraised and reflected in practice. Specific important issues, such as accounting for price changes, foreign currency translation methods, transfer pricing methodology, consolidation accounting, segmental reporting, and foreign exchange risk management, should be addressed. One can be sure that the years to come will see much effort to overcome differences in accounting principles between Western countries and former Soviet states. The traditional Soviet accounting system did not take economic risk into account, but with the transition to a market-oriented economy, this element will become important. Funds and reserves may not increase in Soviet enterprises, but valuation of fixed assets and inventories may affect such funds and reserves.

General Trend of Development

Over many years, a number of accounting methods and approaches aimed at improving management and enhancing overall economic effectiveness have been used in the Soviet Union. Soviet accounting is classified principally according to industrial sectors. Although this kind of classification is easily understood and convenient for teaching accounting, it inevitably has led to much duplication in accounting textbooks and to a waste of time in training, education, and accounting development. To eliminate these shortcomings, it might be desirable to reclassify enterprise accounting into several branches—financial accounting, management accounting, and auditing. Enterprises should gradually implement the two accounting systems, one for management accounting and one for financial accounting, side by side. At the same time, the systems should be incorporated into the educational curriculum reforms.

Auditing, although closely linked with financial and managerial accounting, well may constitute a separate system. We have excluded here "governmental accounting" and "national accounting." The former especially also has a financial and managerial component.

As for future changes, the aspect of post-Soviet accounting most likely to change first will be dogmatism and the rigidity of the accounting structure and rules that have been inherited from the Stalinist era. Fruitless accounting methodological disputes pertaining to "the object and scope of accounting" or "accounting classification" and so on already have stopped, and practical steps are being taken instead to eliminate artificial barriers in sectoral accounting (that is, accounting by sectors of the economy such as retail trade, metal industry, agriculture, capital construction). The Western notion of three branches or systems of accounting—financial, managerial, and auditing—is now more widely accepted. Such an integral approach to accounting is especially important when multisectoral private enterprises are being established. Other Western accounting practices that are being introduced gradually include LIFO and FIFO valuation methods, consolidation principles, and inflation accounting (the latter already had an interesting development in the 1920s in the USSR). The identification of and catering to the users of accounting information will have a large impact on future accounting development.

Cost and Management Accounting Development

In Soviet accounting, management accounting as known in the West is not considered a separate branch or system of accounting but is treated as an adjunct to financial accounting. The term and concept of "management accounting" did not even exist until recently. The centralized planned economy in the USSR called for a rigid administrative control over resource allocation and output distribution, with little initiative in enterprise management. Western management accounting was found inappropriate and not applicable to the requirements of running businesses.

Management accounting now will face the most dramatic evolutionary prospects. Three elements of traditional Soviet accounting taken together may be considered prototypes of management accounting: (1) operational accounting, (2) cost accounting and calculation, and (3) analysis of economic activities. These embryos now will have to develop and merge into one coherent framework to become management accounting as it is known in the West.

Cost traditionally has been based on the Marxian labor theory of value. The distinct development of a separate area of cost/management accounting would be desirable for purposes such as product/process costing, variable costing, pricing, responsibility center accounting, budgeting, performance evaluation, variance analysis, standard costing, and feasibility studies. The notion of different costs for different purposes also may have to gain acceptance. Considerable interest in cost and management accounting developments has emerged in the Soviet Union. Cost and management accounting are subject to considerable review and adaptation there, and efforts are being made to enhance management accounting systems, training, and education. In the past, management accounting essentially consisted of the accumulation of costs, and such a redirection toward planning and control, as well as toward forecasting methods, undoubtedly will cause strain on existing management and accountants. Budgeting, long-range financial planning, the discounted cash flow method and its projections, performance measurements, and responsibility center concepts of accounting are some of the areas that need particular attention.

In view of an orientation toward the marketplace and its pricing system, attention also should be directed toward profitability analysis. Costing and pricing may be linked more closely. The appraisal and preparation of feasibility studies and the measurement of external factors (involving indirect and secondary costs and benefits) involve extensive management accounting techniques, which also need to be enhanced.

Standard costing, which in the past was norm costing (the best previous average cost), is another area that should be upgraded. The reform of direct or contribution margin costing and the allocation of overhead by means of cost drivers by cost center and products are other areas that need considerable evaluation. Profitability measurements, as they exist in the West, and similar profitability concepts in budgeting have gained new attention, although these systems themselves are not profit oriented but essentially consider profit as a measure of efficiency, effectiveness, and economy within economic development management. Sound management accounting can serve internal and external needs effectively, and cost-benefit appraisals can serve both micro- and macroeconomic purposes. It is recommended that management accounting concepts and practices be stressed also for planning and control. A problem at this point appears to be how to apply management accounting theory, and experimental research in this regard is lacking.

The development of a distinct interest group, either as part of the Association of Accountants in Russia and other republics or as a separate body, needs to be encouraged to disseminate management accounting knowledge to interested parties. The Association of Accountants may develop distinct branches, for example, financial accounting, management (cost) accounting, auditing, accounting systems, and education and research branches. In our opinion, such a structure would be warranted to give due attention to the necessary areas to be rethought and developed.

The Management Committee of the International Federation of Accountants (IFAC) and national management accounting bodies or institutes such as the Institute of Management Accountants (IMA) could be basic sources, together with exchange of practitioners and academics. Such organizations presumably would be willing to offer advice and assistance regarding the existing body of knowledge developed internationally.

Russian translations of certain good cost/management accounting textbooks would be useful. The publications of the IMA could contribute toward exposing Soviet accountants to literature and research carried on in this area of accounting, on such topics as transfer pricing and direct costing. Various areas of advanced managerial accounting also merit attention, and the study of extensive cases in management planning and control systems would help Soviet cost accountants to gain practical exposure.

Enterprises in the republics now have more autonomy, and their executives and directors are empowered to make more decisions on important issues. This situation inevitably creates an urgent demand on accounting in response to the complexities of organizational structure, internal control systems, personnel management, and the like. The shift of emphasis from administrative accounting control to scientific management will lead Soviet accountants to make greater efforts to devise a Soviet version of management accounting. To elaborate, Soviet accounting academicians and practitioners will have to define and conceptualize elements embodied in management accounting in their own way and will have to explore adapting methods and techniques from the Western world to conditions existing in the former Soviet republics.

Business executives and accountants now are armed with ideas with which they previously were not very familiar, such as cash flow, time-value of money, cost-benefit analysis, efficiency consciousness, direct costing, and activity-based costing. They surely will focus their attention on operational problems such as effectiveness in investments, responsibility centers, short-term and long-term financing plans, cost control, pricing policy, sales forecasting, feasibility studies, and cost-benefit analysis.

Examples of other issues that they may need to focus on are:

- Long-term investment decisions and control of the scale of capital construction,
- Implementation of cost-benefit analysis,
- Macroeconomic control of funds provided through credit and the financing plan of state enterprises,
- Control of comparative product costs and target costs,
- Pricing decisions and sales forecasting, and
- Quality control and quality cost.

Financial Accounting Development

In the past 60 years, financial accounting essentially has served national planning and control purposes in the USSR. It has not been geared effectively toward proper "income determination" (as the term is understood internationally), nor has it served as an information measurement system for a variety of external and internal economic and financial purposes. Currently, extensive efforts are being aimed at making the financial statements more relevant (in conformity with international accounting standards). A task force of the former USSR Ministry of Finance has been working on this matter, as well as on the underlying standards. Although considerable attention has been focused on the balance sheet, a properly geared income statement and cash flow statement also should be integral parts of such a recasting. Furthermore, a value-added statement, which has been adopted in several countries, would reflect how an enterprise can contribute to its own effectiveness and would serve national purposes as well.

Financial accounting has been oriented toward fund management; however, fund management should not be confused with flow of funds or cash funds statement. The actual source and the application of funds are not reflected directly in the financial statements, and a readaptation to rectify that lack might well be useful. The growing need for outside sources of enterprise financing and the consequent need for management to focus on debt management also make such cash flow statements desirable.

Another distinct feature is that fixed assets and inventories are valued at historical cost, with no adaptation for price changes. Although concepts of "accounting for price changes" have been explored in Soviet accounting, none has been adopted. The inflation rate in past years has been relatively low, about 5% to 8%, but it increased rapidly in 1990 and 1991 to about 20% to 50%. It is expected to be 100% to 200% in 1992. Other factors that affect prices, such as technological change, also should be taken into account. Therefore, in the future, some further appraisal of accounting for price changes could be urgent, as has been the case in many other economies. Accounting for price changes is appropriate not only for financial statement measurement and reporting but also for the system of cost/management accounting and its linkage with the national (macro) accounts. In this regard, gradual adherence by the republics to the U.N. System of National Accounts (SNA) would be helpful.

Adherence to accepted international accounting standards also would be desirable, although such standards should be appraised carefully in light of the socioeconomic conditions and objectives of the Soviet republics. Development of a conceptual framework of accounting, with the inductive and deductive process as part of its theory and norms, therefore is recommended.

Computerization also will demand extensive systems development. It is an area that will be of great benefit to the Soviet economy in the years to come. This development will help both computer systems and general accounting systems because sound systems (and procedures) improve not only accounting reporting and control but also efficiency and effectiveness, performance measurement, auditing, and resource allocation.

The identification of financial accounting as a distinct branch of accounting appears justified. Managers of business enterprises will be delegated much broader authority under the economic structure reform. They will be held fully responsible for properties and resources entrusted to them for profitable operations. They must make a large number of financial decisions, which cannot be reached without reliable financial information.

The current economic structure reform has given rise to a number of new problems, many of which are related to financial accounting, as previously stated. As a result of economic reform and the independence of republics, the scope of mandatory planning will be narrowed and that of planning using economic instruments may be expanded, causing widespread use of macroeconomic control instruments such as taxation, credit and interest rates, banking systems, and pricing. All these factors will bring enterprises more in line with market forces and the law of value. How extensively these economic controls will be exercised centrally by the CIS still needs to be worked out. Both managers and accountants, however, certainly will concentrate more attention on financial and managerial accounting than ever before.

The purposes of implementing the policies of reform (e.g., *perestroika* and *glasnost*) are not only to restructure the former Soviet economic and financial accounting system and to provide foreign investors with opportunities in the CIS but also to promote in the West a better comprehension of Soviet practices. The republics are aware of the necessity of involving themselves in international economic affairs and of casting an attentive eye to the trend of world economic development. As a result, an urgent need exists to train competent specialists so they can learn both accounting in foreign countries and (comparative) international accounting. The evolution of accounting has proved that mutual comparison and exchange of ideas and experiences between countries will accelerate the development of accounting in individual countries. Thus, it is clear that the task of formulating a framework of accounting theory, concepts, and methods in the former Soviet region cannot be undertaken properly without an understanding of international accounting and an in-depth comparison of Soviet accounting with its counterparts in the West.

Auditing Development

The concept of auditing has had a different connotation in the USSR in the past. Auditing essentially has been the verification of certain targets and funds without detailed appraisal of performance. Auditing as Westerners know it is emerging rapidly now, although it still has a long way to go from both theoretical and applied points of view. Auditing methods are being improved continuously.

Auditing under the economic structure reform has become a necessity to ensure that the policies of *perestroika* and stimulation of the economy are carried out. It also is needed for joint venture operations. The modernization and economic reform drives, geared toward economic results (for efficiency, effectiveness, and economy), have given auditing great impetus. A large number of auditing firms are appearing, but their qualifications have not yet been sorted out, nor is extensive literature available to explain how to conduct thorough audits, like those understood internationally. Various texts are being translated, and courses specifically in Western auditing are being offered. Auditing requires a thorough grasp of accounting, however, and auditors should first of all be accountants.

In addition to thorough financial auditing techniques, the notion of managerial, performance, or operational auditing is rapidly gaining acceptance in the republics. This type of auditing of course demands an insight into managerial accounting norms.

Auditing techniques are still subject to considerable refinement and implementation. Some form of integrated or "comprehensive" auditing—also known as "value for money" auditing—might well be a goal for the future, although the distinct auditing objectives to be achieved in the USSR must be recognized. The installation of computer-oriented systems also requires expertise in computer auditing techniques, another area where further enhancement may be warranted. Internal auditing is at present the least unified area.

Uniform auditing standards have not yet been developed, and it is hoped that they will be linked with international standards (for example, with IFAC) as much as possible. Standards and formats of audit reports have not yet been unified. The development of such auditing standards, reporting requirements, and a code of ethics also constitutes an important task for the (Soviet) Association of Accountants. This association may gradually set certification requirements, such as examinations and codes of conduct, and create a separate auditing section. No special qualifications currently are required for auditors.

Governmental Accounting Development

Our study did not focus on the governmental accounting system, and, accordingly, extended treatment of the subject is not warranted here. Many government units operated inefficiently in the USSR, and elsewhere, so good cost-effectiveness studies may well be appropriate in the context of a planning, programming, and budgeting structure. Governmental operations tend to be sizable both at the central and at the republic level, and therefore a thorough appraisal of governmental accounting and budgeting, better known as governmental financial management, appears warranted. Such an appraisal might be the subject of a separate study.

Accounting Research Development

Another area that needs the attention of Soviet accounting researchers is accounting and auditing research methodology. Marxist philosophy and political economics were the ideological grounds for the social sciences in the USSR, and one of the important features of research was the congruence of its methodology with Marxist dialectical materialism. Soviet researchers in accounting have been relying on this basic epistemology and methodology to investigate, analyze, explore, and evaluate reality. Marxism-Leninism was, and for many still is, the theoretical basis for guiding research. This fact does not mean that Soviet researchers should ignore or overlook other methodologies, especially when they are aware that we now live in an integrated world with rapid innovation in science and technology, when swift and radical structure shifts in society can be expected.

Soviet accountants must recognize that diversification of research methods also will be helpful in promoting research in accounting and auditing and in formulating a framework of accounting theory and methods with specific Soviet/CIS characteristics. As a result, Soviet accountants should explore the possibility of applying other scientific methods, such as systems analysis, normative and positive approaches, the empirical method, and the behavioral approach, to their research (in theory they already do, but more practical applications are needed). By employing these methodologies, the accountants will explore new frontiers in the field of accounting and auditing as an information measurement system.

Realization of a comprehensive framework of accounting is still a long way off, and a number of obstacles will have to be overcome. Although many Soviet accountants and officials have recognized that formulating a framework of accounting and auditing theory and methods is very necessary, doing it is by no means easy. The formulation is not simply a summing up of theories and methods of various branches of accounting and auditing.

Other Accounting Issues and Developments

The Accounting Profession

A United Nations publication [UNCTC Advisory Studies No. 7, UN 1990] describes the current state of affairs of the accounting profession:

> It is important to recognize that the development of accounting in any country is impossible without developing an accounting profession. Whereas, in many Western market economies, the accounting profession developed out of the need for "independent" financial opinions, Soviet accountants remain an integral part of the system of enterprise management. Furthermore, the auditing role of accountants in the USSR is quite restricted; an auditor does not need to be a qualified accountant, and many of his or her duties are nonfinancial in nature. Traditionally, the full potential of accounting has not been appreciated in the USSR, and insufficient attention has been paid to accounting activities. The process of economic restructuring, creating a new accounting environment, has given rise to the need for a strong accounting profession in the USSR. In addition, over 2 million accountants, accounting technicians, and bookkeepers must be retrained in the new system.

Currently, the regulations for senior accountants, ratified by a resolution of the Council of Ministers of the USSR on January 24, 1980, govern the organization of the accounting profession. The State Committee on Labor and Social Questions of the USSR established the qualifications required for the accounting profession in 1986. Specifically, senior accountants must have completed university education in economics and must have worked in leadership positions in the financial and accounting field for no less than five years. There are three classes of accountants:

1. *Class 1* accountants must have completed a university education in economics and must have worked as Class 2 accountants for no less than three years;
2. *Class 2* accountants either must have completed university education in economics without fulfilling the work-experience requirement or must have

completed special secondary education and must have worked as accountants for no less than three years;

3. *Class 3* accountants either must have completed special secondary education without fulfilling the work-experience requirement or must have received special training through an established course and must have worked in accounting and financial control for no less than three years. There are also three classes of economists working in accounting and the analysis of economic activities.

Until recently, the Soviets did not have an accounting profession, as Westerners know the term. The Soviet republics have three million "accountants," accounting technicians, and bookkeepers, but the term "accountant" has a different connotation in the Soviet Union. Traditionally, the accounting profession was not very popular and was underpaid. Therefore, many women fulfilled accounting functions. However, as a consequence of the changing role of accounting and because it has greater significance and offers more rewards, more men now are attracted to the job.

The Association of Accountants was established in December 1989 as a semiprivate organization. (The president is Professor A.D. Sheremet, and the vice presidents are Professors J.V. Sokolov, V. Palij, and S. Stukov.) Its members are public auditors and other experts. They have studied the need for an accounting organization to establish educational requirements for members of the profession and to set professional standards. At the present time, the Association is trying to establish refresher courses, to advise members to develop ethical norms, and to gather information on how the profession has been established in other countries.

The Association's objectives encompass the following:

- To decide on the level of education required before a person is permitted to become a student of the profession;
- To decide on the nature of theoretical and practical training that should be undertaken in the apprenticeship period;
- To establish an examination or licensing process and to determine the level of competency required to become a member of the accounting profession;
- To determine the continuing educational requirements necessary for continued membership;
- To establish a code of conduct for its members;
- To take measures to ensure that the interests of the public are protected;
- To comment on matters of public interest from the standpoint of the accounting profession.

Professional accounting activities need to be strongly enhanced in the USSR, and recognition should be given to the different "bodies of knowledge" forming the accounting information system network. Figure 6-1 sets forth the overall

**Figure 6-1
THE OVERALL ACCOUNTING INFORMATION SYSTEM**

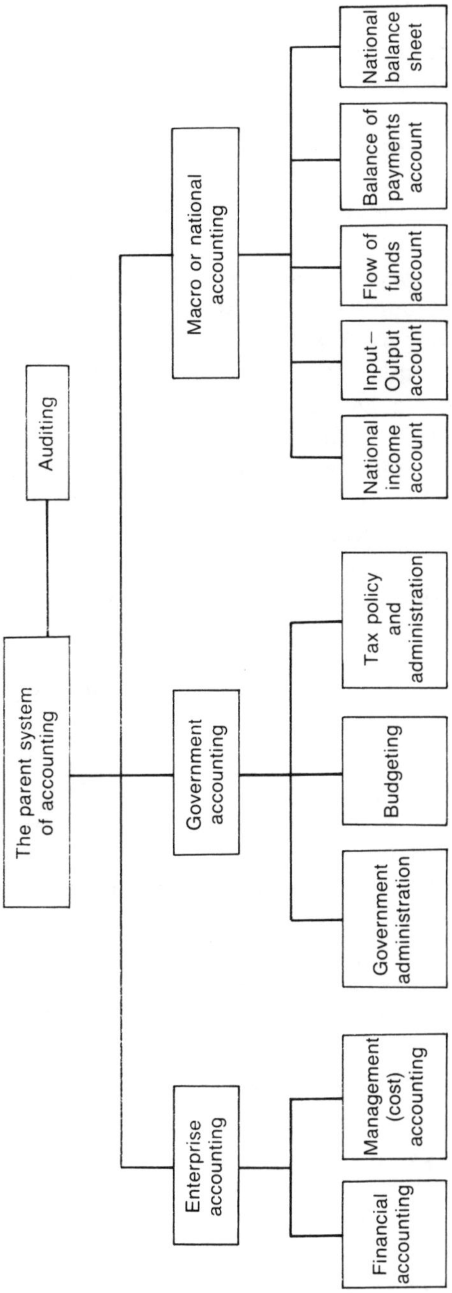

accounting information system, which should pay particular attention to the following areas of expertise and knowledge:

- Financial accounting,
- Management/cost accounting,
- Auditing,
- Accounting systems and procedures,
- Taxation,
- Governmental and not-for-profit accounting.

(Macro, or national, accounting is excluded because it falls somewhat outside the scope of regular accounting and is often the practice of economists and statisticians, although they work with the same data as enterprise accountants.)

From a professional development point of view, it would be desirable to set up separate interest or expert groups (subgroups of the profession) to concentrate on each area. Each group should develop its own field of required knowledge and should establish guidelines. Two separate tests of professional competence, one for middle-level and one for upper-level, might be developed gradually, along with a corresponding listing of middle- and upper-level skills and certifications or diplomas that could be acquired for each test.

The active development of Soviet accounting would require due attention to these distinct areas of accounting, the body of knowledge existing and required for each, and diploma/certification requirements to be established. Accounting has become too complex to recognize and develop just one type of accountant. Instead of developing accountants for different types of industries, as has been the case in the USSR (the course of accounting is divided into light industry, heavy industry, textile industry, trade accounting, and so forth), it might be advisable to outline the *basic* body of knowledge required in the various fields and then develop further specializations by area and/or specific industries. This development should be the subject of profound appraisals by professionals in the republics, and the profession should explore and set forth such appraisals in a detailed feasibility study. Furthermore, for each of those areas, they should prepare an outline of: (1) educational/training modules, (2) textbook development and adoption, and (3) research areas to be pursued.

The Crisis in the Accounting Profession

The accounting profession in the Soviet Union currently is experiencing a major crisis for the following reasons:

- Lack of a visible professional accounting organization;
- Abundance of vacant positions;
- Acute lack of qualified accountants capable of solving new methodological problems;

- The great number of controlling agencies that hamper the accounting profession's standing and effectiveness;
- Indifference of accountants to their discipline, its scientific element, its methodological principles, and its history;
- Lack of men in the accounting profession and low standing of the profession in the eyes of the public;
- Rapid increase in salaries of many accountants working for joint ventures and other enterprises, resulting in distortions in pay scales.

A principal condition that must be fulfilled before these problems can be solved is the transition toward a market economy (or social market economy), with corresponding changes in accounting education and the professionalization of accounting. Accounting, which is not a well recognized profession, should occupy a more important place within the field of economic sciences.

A market-oriented economy throughout the former Soviet Union inevitably will result in liquidation of unprofitable enterprises and reduction of jobs, including accounting staff. After the elimination of many marginal positions, the most qualified employees will fill vacant posts.

Needed Educational Changes

The institutions of higher learning and auditing organizations should be encouraged to offer courses in improving professional accounting skills. Such courses will demand radical changes in the system of higher education of accountants. These changes, in turn, may cause a considerable reduction in the number of accountants, for it may be difficult to find enough accountants who are qualified to teach up-to-date methodologies. Only some of the existing pool of teaching faculty are expected to be able to conduct accounting training at the higher theoretical and practical levels, and it will be necessary to limit the number of students in the accounting courses. Only those who are well qualified should be admitted. Accounting should be approached from the point of view of a single scientific discipline as an information measurement, analysis, and communication system. The new training methodology will require modern approaches involving experience at foreign universities, colleges, and business schools.

The accounting curricula need to be revised. For example, the teaching of economic sciences, including accounting, should be changed. Not less than 20% of the class hours for training accountants should be devoted to studying law (civil, business, labor, fiscal, and administrative). At institutions of learning, a historical perspective of accounting, stressing the development of ideas in accounting and economics, also should be taught.

The didactics of accounting education should be restructured. Currently, the instructors cover accounting first and only then do they teach analysis of business activities. This approach results in the isolation of accounting information in relation to analysis and financial management decision making. Under market economy conditions, it is necessary to combine form (accounting procedures) and content (analysis of business activities). These two areas should be brought together, and analysis should be integrated with the various aspects of accounting, such as financial, managerial, and auditing.

Modern accounting education seeks to make accountants computer literate. In addition, accounting faculties should expand and restructure the course of mathematics they offer. A course in advanced financial analysis and calculation must be included in the curriculum, because such knowledge will be essential in a market economy.

It will be desirable to provide internships in the Soviet Union and abroad for graduates of the institutes and to maintain close contact between institutions of learning and the business world.

Changes in the practice of publishing training manuals and textbooks also may be necessary. The institutes should be entitled to publish their own textbooks on accounting, on a commercial basis. The monopoly of publishing houses should be abolished to give the teaching staff as well as the students a free choice. Many textbooks with methodological and didactic contents, including questions, cases, and exercises, should be provided, and the use of overhead transparencies also could help students master the body of knowledge. (For details on accounting education, see Appendix C.)

Working Conditions for Accountants

In a market economy, the salary of the accountant should be set by contract with the employer. The chief accountant should have the right to hire the accounting staff, and these employees should report to the chief accountant, controller, or vice president for finance. With the improvement in professional skills and the growing use of computers, the number of accounting employees presumably could be reduced.

Financial agencies and independent auditing firms should maintain control, through audits, over the activities of organizations and accountants. It is worth noting that auditing in the republics is developing in the form of auditing firms, not as individual practitioners. To be an expert in auditing an accountant should have a college degree in accounting and no less than two years of work experience. Moreover, an applicant for an auditor's position should be able to enhance his or her professional auditing skills during a one-or two-year required work period because it is impossible to train an auditor who has no extensive business exposure.

Besides external auditing, effective *internal* auditing, that is, auditing within companies or departments, should be encouraged. The auditors carrying out this kind of control should be included on the staff of the controller or chief accountant.

Special attention should be paid to enhancing both the accounting profession and accounting as a scientific discipline. The accountant should not be regarded as a person bent on controlling and hampering operational activities but as one who assists management and others in carrying out progressive activities within the enterprise and who sets forth decision models for appraisals and actions.

In this regard it will be useful to differentiate accounting personnel by level of professional skills—for example, operator, bookkeeper, accountant, senior accountant, chief accountant, and auditor. Recognizing qualified experts will tend to stimulate the enhancement of professional skills. Written examinations should be used to help determine who can rise from one level of expertise to another. Financial organizations and accounting departments at learning institutions would offer such examinations once a year, and the Association of Accountants also might set uniform examinations. The applicants or their employers would pay for the examinations. Enterprises should recognize this approach in promoting accountants. Only after passing a qualifying examination should the accountant move to a higher position.

It appears necessary to restructure the activities of members of the Association of Accountants, including chief accountants and auditors. The organization should levy an entrance fee. It should promote the professional interests of its members, assisting in locating positions, settling labor conflicts, and developing the training of auditors, and should develop a code of professional ethics by which all members must abide. Its regional office should be entitled to expel violators from membership and deprive them of professional status.

International Accounting Organizations

In connection with professional development and the development of accounting and auditing standards (principles) or guidelines, close coordination with international accounting organizations would be desirable. Membership in the International Accounting Standards Committee (IASC), based in London, England, and the International Federation of Accountants (IFAC), based in New York, would be of considerable benefit to the republics, in our opinion, to develop sound standards, practices, and education and to advance in other accounting/auditing-oriented areas.

The Soviet profession also should develop closer ties not only with international accounting bodies but also with regional bodies such as the European Federation of Accountants (FEE), based in Brussels, Belgium, and the Confederation of Asian and Pacific Accountants (CAPA), based in Manila, Philippines. Furthermore, it is suggested that the distinct professional interest groups of the Soviet association should build close working relationships with Western professional accounting bodies.

As for technical assistance and funding requirements, membership in the International Monetary Fund (IMF), World Bank (IBRD), and European Bank for Reconstruction and Development (EBRD) certainly could spur development, for these organizations in the past have shown interest in enhancing private sector and public sector accounting and financial management for their member countries. Soviet membership in these agencies would make further assistance in the areas of accounting easier. One purpose of our study was to suggest areas where international cooperation could effect improvement. Although the former Soviet Union has, and wants to maintain, its own characteristics for accounting and auditing, extensive international cooperation would be warranted and welcomed. Such cooperation can be channeled through various sources, such as the World Bank, IMF, EBRD, United Nations, IFAC, bilateral national and professional bodies, regional institutions and agencies, professional firms, foreign academic institutions, and other groups. We expect that the various Western professional bodies in financial accounting, management accounting, internal auditing, and information systems would be very receptive to assisting Soviet colleagues with their needs and requests. It is anticipated and hoped that in due time the Soviet professions will become members of the International Accounting Standards Committee and the International Federation of Accountants, which would facilitate further international exchanges.

The areas where cooperative assistance appears particularly desirable are the following:

1. Education and training, including cooperation in supporting the updating of centers and text material, research funding, foreign scholarships, exchange of academicians, library enhancements, teaching aids (such as computers), and supply and exchange of study materials. Included should be extensive scholarships for potential accounting educators (Ph.D. students in particular) and grants for existing faculty for six to nine months of foreign study in specialized areas. Cooperation in course development and institutional aspects is another possibility. Foreign academic institutions, with the support of their respective governments, could adopt academic institutions in the Soviet Union, send them materials, and allow Soviet academics to visit their universities and colleges.

2. Active exchange of personnel and materials with foreign and international accounting organizations.

3. At the government level, visits to foreign governmental accounting agencies and active exchange of materials and information regarding comprehensive governmental audits, performance budgeting, and other related activities.

4. Extensive international exchange regarding accounting and auditing standards.

The Soviet Union already has made considerable strides under very difficult circumstances, and it is impressive to observe the commitment, dedication, and effort to enhance accounting, auditing, and related fields. However, considerable further advances are needed. Soviet accounting well may become a major force in accounting in the decades to come, but cooperation and assistance in a variety of fields are needed before the states can attain the goal of self-sustained accounting development and once again become valuable members of the international accounting community. It is hoped that this study may give an insight into the development and needs of accounting and auditing in the Soviet Union. It also is hoped that the Soviets will join hands with both the worldwide accounting profession and academic organizations and that such closer contacts will benefit both Soviet and international accounting.

Conclusion

As is pointed out in Appendix B on the history of accounting in Russia and the USSR, accounting developments in Russia before the 1917 revolution were in tune with those in Western Europe. After the revolution, accounting moved along different lines because of different socioeconomic objectives. Soviet accounting and auditing can be expected to be aligned again with international concepts and standards in the years to come, although retaining some distinctive characteristics.

Overcoming psychological barriers should be a major task of Soviet and Western accountants. Soviet accountants assume that Western accountants need their help in the Soviet region, but, underestimating the need to understand and work with international accounting principles in the new Soviet economic climate, they often believe they can work without the help of Western accountants.

Western accountants believe that Soviet accountants need their assistance in attracting investments and loans and in developing proper standards for student presentations and evaluations, but unfortunately Western accountants assume that their Soviet colleagues do not have the proper qualifications and professional knowledge to be updated rapidly. These misconceptions must be cleared up, and technical assistance in overcoming both the psychological and the technical professional barriers is an urgent necessity.

It is well recognized internationally that Soviet people are highly intelligent and well educated and have the basic abilities for rapid advancement. In our opinion, any reorientation and restructuring process in the accounting area could be achieved quickly. However, international technical cooperative assistance and materials undoubtedly will hasten and improve such an adaption process. As indicated above, not only are professional and international organizations expected to play a part, but academic institutions on a bilateral or multilateral basis could be vitally important. Exchange of students and faculty for specific programs would be one means. Another would be to supply supplemental texts and educational materials for such programs.

Such efforts, however, should be systematic and well organized, preferably spearheaded by international agencies in conjunction with Soviet officials and professional organizations and persons. It should be clear that the public sector will remain very large in the various republics of the CIS, and distinct socioeconomic conditions must be taken into account. The user orientation in the Soviet territories will continue to need strengthening in the foreseeable future.

Eventual growth of economic independence of the former Soviet republics now united in the Commonwealth of Independent States raises the issue of future uniformity and comparability of accounting, reporting, and auditing standards, and, even more, of tax regulations on the territory of the former Soviet Union. The rigidly centralized accounting organization, as well as the same historic accounting roots throughout the whole country and the similar educational background of all Soviet accountants, are the major factors ensuring a high degree of uniformity of accounting standards in all post-Soviet republics. However, as soon as market reforms in different republics accelerate at different speeds, some republics will face a more urgent need to adopt more radical steps in introducing international standards. The now-independent Baltic states are likely to be the first to take such steps and will tend to orient their accounting system toward German and European Community standards, although such standards will become more and more international, too.

The new emerging generation of Soviet entrepreneurs, managers, and accountants will have less of a burden of "centralized" accounting and will be more geared toward Western practices, though specific orientations (including American, German, French, and British) may vary. In these circumstances, efforts to spread international accounting knowledge may well serve the purpose of future harmonization of accounting standards in all republics. The Ministry or Ministries of Finance in the new Commonwealth are very likely to have a coordinating rather than a commanding role. The future CIS Minfin (if it exists) may become a good place to coordinate accounting harmonization efforts.

A great proliferation of accounting standards would be undesirable. We do not expect it to occur because the common economic ties among the republics will remain strong, and the whole internationalization of accounting also will have a positive influence on the uniformity of accounting systems. We therefore foresee that the splitup of the USSR will not seriously affect the trend toward westernization and internationalization of accounting and auditing in the Soviet region.

At the time we finished our study (early 1992), the future trends in economic centralization in the CIS were still unclear, and so were the accounting centralization efforts. However, we are confident that after initial confusion, common sense and wisdom will prevail, and the accounting developments to be carried out, as described in our study, will be pursued in a harmonized way in the CIS or whatever format (for example federation) may occur in the periods to come.

None of the desired changes may happen in the foreseeable future unless a new accounting profession is created, that is, training practicing accountants and forming a new generation of accountants. To reach this goal, the whole accounting education system in the ex-USSR needs to be restructured. Despite the fact that more than 100 universities and colleges train accountants, and numerous accounting short-term courses are offered, there is a shortage of qualified accountants. The program of accounting education launched by the

Centre for Transnational Corporations of the United Nations in Moscow, St. Petersburg, and Kiev has helped already to train the first groups of young accountants with new thinking, vision, and skills.

It is unreasonable to expect that, for example, Anglo-American accounting standards will be introduced into practice directly in the near future. Russia has its own accounting tradition, and it cannot be replaced overnight by new principles, even if they appear very attractive. However, the last years already have seen the amazing and dramatic process of bringing the centralized Soviet accounting closer to Western accounting principles. Like the transition to a market economy from the centrally planned economy, this process is irreversible.

Glossary and Bibliography

Glossary

Accounting Forms: Accounting procedures for recording data in formalized and standardized documents. Two main accounting forms are used by Soviet accountants: journal order and memorial order (see below).

Aggregated Cost: A method of cost accounting that provides calculation of cost for the whole output of a group of similar products.

"Activ": Russian equivalent of assets. By definition, the "activ" side of the balance sheet includes "means of economic activities, their allocation and utilization."

Amortization: Periodic allocations of the cost of fixed assets to finished products resulting in the depreciation of fixed assets and decrease in statutory fund.

Amortization Fund: Part of equity reserved to replenish fixed assets. It is mandatory for Soviet enterprises.

Analytic Accounts: See **Second-Level Accounts.**

Automated Control Systems (ACS): Computerized schemes for management of enterprises popular in the Soviet Union in the 1970s and '80s.

Auxiliary Production: Products other than basic (mainstream), accounted for separately by Soviet enterprises.

Bank Account: The principal bank account that every Soviet enterprise is required to have to make settlements with other entities. It is called the settlement account or current account.

Basic (Main) Production: Statutorily defined production of any enterprise (especially manufacturing). It is accounted for separately from auxiliary production.

Calculation of Cost: Key term in Soviet cost accounting that means determining the cost of finished products in monetary terms.

Chart of Accounts: Standardized, or national, chart of accounts effective for all Soviet enterprises nationwide. Accounting in different sectors of the Soviet economy uses specific subaccounts of the basic chart of accounts.

Chief Accountant: Controller of Soviet enterprise or organization. Functions of chief accountants are defined by the regulations of the Ministry of Finance and include subordination to the Ministry of Finance.

Circulated Assets: Close in meaning to "current assets" but with a different structure. According to traditional Soviet accounting concepts, all assets are divided into fixed, circulated, and "put-aside" assets.

Code: Account number attributed to each account in the national chart of accounts.

Depreciation: In Soviet methodology, the result of amortization allocations of the value of fixed assets. Accumulated depreciation decreases the statutory fund.

Documentation: Documentary evidence for every accounting entry. Documentation is considered one of the key elements of the accounting methodology.

Expenses in Future Periods: Those expenses included in costs within two accounting periods.

Economic Analysis (or analysis of economic operations): A separate part of Soviet accounting dealing with variances, forecasts, and ratios.

Feasibility Studies: Not mandatory but usually required by the Ministry of Finance when joint ventures are registered. The goal of feasibility studies is to show profitability, self-support in foreign currencies, and effects the joint venture would have on the Soviet economy. Requirements for feasibility studies vary, but usually such studies follow a preset standard.

Financial Investments: Item that appeared in Soviet balance sheets in 1990. It indicates both short-term (portfolio) and long-term (participation) investments.

First-Level Accounts (summary accounts): The principal accounts in the national chart of accounts (more than 70 in number) defining all main items in the balance sheet. First-level accounts are specified and adjusted in second-level accounts.

Fixed Assets (long-term assets): In Soviet methodology, long-lived items (usually of more than one year and beyond a determined value in rubles). Fixed assets are replenished from the amortization fund and from profit.

Foreign Currency Amount: An item introduced into the chart of accounts and balance sheet format so Soviet enterprises could account separately for foreign currencies, because of nonconvertibility of the ruble. It is recorded at the official exchange rate in rubles (total amount) and in specific currencies in analytic accounts.

Founding Documents (of a joint venture): Agreement between partners and statute (charter). Minfin requires other papers (application, permission, bank statement, notice from trade registers). Feasibility studies may be required.

Goods Delivered, Services Rendered: Sales of products at cost after dispatch until receipt of cash. This item is a result of the cash basis of accounting.

Inaudit: A joint stock company (controlled by Minfin) established in 1987 to perform audits for joint ventures. Until 1990 Inaudit was the first and only auditing organization in the USSR.

Inventorization (taking inventory): A key accounting method in Soviet methodology. Inventories usually are taken once a year.

Journal Order: The most commonly used standardized format for recording data in credits of different accounts (horizontally) while debits of related accounts are placed vertically. The total of credit entries during the month is computed in journal form for specific accounts.

Leased Assets: Property and equipment controlled by an enterprise under long-term lease agreement. Before the introduction of the category in 1991, such assets were accounted for as off-balance sheet items.

Long-Term Assets: See **Fixed Assets**.

Low-Value and Short-Life Items: Items that last less than one year or cost less than a specific number of rubles (e.g., R100). They are classified as assets and usually are depreciated within two years.

Main Production: See **Basic Production**.

Material Responsibility: An important element of Soviet accounting organization whereby employees (determined by the general manager of an enterprise) are personally liable for a specific amount of the value of items for which they are responsible. If an item is stolen or damaged the person in charge pays for the loss if he or she is unable to prove innocence.

Memorial Order: A standardized accounting form commonly used by small-scale Soviet enterprises to record similar transactions. Entries are posted from memorial orders to the general ledger.

Method of Accounting: Such elements as documentation, inventory taking, accounts, double entry system, calculation, valuation, balance sheet, and reporting.

Minfin: Russian abbreviation for Ministry of Finance, the principal Soviet accounting and reporting standard-setting body.

Norm Accounting: Soviet equivalent of a standard cost system. Norms are standards of cost that are set according to best previous average costs. Deviations of actual costs from norm costs are analyzed.

Off-Balance Sheet Accounts: Method used to account for items that do not belong on the balance sheet but that are used by an enterprise. It also is used for items (blanks of documents, guarantees, doubtful debts written off, and so on) that have no actual cost but that need to be recorded for purposes of control.

Operational Accounting: Accounting that provides managerial information other than financial information. Operational accounting is characterized by rapid data provision, approximations, use of ratios, informality (no strict documentation), and selectiveness.

"Passiv": In Soviet accounting, the offsetting part of the balance sheet to the assets. It is equivalent to liabilities and equity in Western balance sheets.

Profit Utilization: An item in the fixed assets section of the Soviet balance sheet. It is a purely imaginary item, however, with no real value but with controlling functions over allocations of the enterprise's profits.

Put-Aside Assets (sometimes called noncirculated asssets): An artificial category of traditional Soviet accounting which denotes use of profits for such purposes as tax payments or building up an enterprise's funds for economic and social development. It adds no real value to the assets.

Reporting: The system of providing indicators to reflect activities of enterprises or organizations during a definite period. Its purpose is to provide economic information to planning and controlling bodies.

Reserve Fund: An allocation of joint venture profits that is mandatory until it reaches 25% of the statutory (charter) fund. It is tax exempt.

Revision: Soviet version of auditing, performed by governmental agencies (Minfin, branch ministries, Gosbank).

Sales Tax: 5% tax on sales of many manufactured goods.

SCS: State Committee for Statistics.

Settlements: Key item in the national chart of accounts. Settlements stand for accounts receivable and payable, payments of taxes, payroll accounts, and so forth. The principal bank account of any Soviet enterprise is called the settlements account.

Second-Level (Analytic) Accounts: In the national and branch charts of accounts, accounts that support the first-level or summary accounts.

Special Crediting Accounts: Automatic credits provided by banks to enterprises under special agreements for some transactions (such as exports).

Special-Purpose Funds: A term that includes a number of funds (allocations of profit). Production development funds of joint ventures are not subject to taxes. Social welfare, economic stimulation, and other funds are not mandatory but typical of many Soviet enterprises.

Statutory (Charter) Fund: Initial equity of any Soviet enterprise, considered an offsetting item to fixed assets. In Soviet methodology, increase in fixed assets is followed by an increase in the statutory fund. Depreciation of fixed assets decreases the statutory fund.

Summary Accounts: See **First-Level Accounts**.

Synthetic Accounts: See **First-Level Accounts.**

Turnover Tax: Tax imposed on some categories of Soviet enterprises such as merchandising and on joint ventures. Turnover tax on joint ventures ranges from 15% to 90% of total sales.

Bibliography

Books and Monographs

Ash, Ehiel, and Robert Strittmatter. *Accounting in the Soviet Union*. Praeger Publishers, Westport, CT, 1991.

Coopers & Lybrand. *Joint Ventures in the USSR*. Coopers & Lybrand, London, 1989.

Erasmus University. *Joint Ventures in the Soviet Union: Accounting and Control Problems*. Erasmus University, Rotterdam, 1991.

International Monetary Fund, World Bank, OECD. *The Economy of the USSR*, Volumes I-III. OECD, Paris, 1991.

KPMG International. *Joint Venture Operations in the USSR*. KPMG International, Amsterdam, 1989.

KPMG International. *Joint Venture Accounting and Taxation in the USSR*. KPMG International, Helsinki, 1990.

Organization for Economic Cooperation and Development. *Accounting Reform in Central and Eastern Europe*. OECD, Paris, 1992.

Tverdohlebov, Stanislav, and Thomas P. Mullen. *Russia and Its Mysterious Market: Getting Started and Doing Business in the New Russian Marketplace*. Tradewinds Press, Closter, NJ, 1992.

United Nations. *Curricula for Accounting Education for East-West Joint Ventures in Centrally Planned Economies*. UNCTC No. 6. United Nations, New York, 1990.

United Nations. *Joint Venture Accounting in the USSR*. UNCTC No. 7. United Nations, New York, 1990.

United Nations Centre for Transnational Corporations. *Accounting for East-West Joint Ventures*. United Nations ST./CTC/122, New York, 1992.

Articles

Aurichio, Kenneth. "Western Accounting Principles Head East." *Management Accounting*, August 1991, pp. 54-56.

Bailey, Derek. "Accounting in the Shadow of Stalinism." *Accounting, Organization and Society* (London), Vol. 15N6, 1990, pp. 513-525.

Enthoven, Adolf J.H. "Accounting Developments in and for the Soviet Union." *De Accountant*. Netherlands Institute of Registered Accountants (NIVRA), Amsterdam, December 1990, pp. 210-214.

Lebow, M. and R. Tondkar. "Accounting in the Soviet Union." *The International Journal of Accounting*, Vol. 22, No. 1, 1986, pp. 61-79.

Sauvant, Karl. "Accountancy Development in the USSR." *The CTC Reporter*, No. 30, Autumn 1990, pp. 50-53.

Newsletter

Interflo: A Soviet Trade News Monitor. P.O. Box 42, Maplewood, NJ. Published monthly.

Appendices

Appendix A

Political and Socioeconomic Aspects of Change in the Soviet Union

This appendix covers the political and socioeconomic aspects of the former Soviet Union (USSR) and briefly touches on the structure of the new Commonwealth of Independent States (CIS) as of January 1992. In our opinion it is necessary to be familiar with the various eco-political developments that occurred in the Soviet Union to understand the present situation and regulations.

Basic Facts About the Soviet Union

The Union of Soviet Socialist Republics (USSR), as it was known, was the largest country in the world, with a territory of 22,402 square kilometers, crossing 11 time zones. The area has common borders with 12 nations and is washed by two oceans and 12 seas; 75% of the territory lies in Asia and 25% in Europe. The population is more than 290 million people, of whom slightly less than 50% are Russians.

Multinationality

One of the most striking peculiarities of the former Soviet Union is its multitude of nationalities—its population consists of about 150 ethnic groups. The 25 largest nationalities are listed in Table A-1. Any comparisons with such federal states as the United States may be very misleading for several reasons. Most large (and small) ethnic groups are concentrated in specific areas, and most of them preserve their national cultural and linguistic identity. Social, economic, religious, and cultural differentiation is very strong even among regions that share a certain Russian or Soviet heritage. This heritage has not been sufficient to homogenize the country.

The diversity of nationalities in the Soviet federation is reflected in the country's complex administrative and territorial structure (Table A-2). Multinational republics, especially Russia but also Georgia, Azerbaijan, and Uzbekistan, are further divided into autonomous republics, autonomous regions (*oblast*), and autonomous districts (*okrug*). Parallel to this, ethnically more homogeneous parts of the country are divided into administrative regions (*oblast*) or larger regions (*krai*). Cities may be subordinate to the republic, as is the case with Kiev and Sebastopol in Ukraine, or they may be subordinate to the district. Both regions and large cities are divided into districts (*raion*). Finally, towns and villages have their local administrations (soviets), which are the basic units of the administrative system in the rural areas.

Table A-1
25 LARGEST NATIONALITIES IN THE USSR

Nationality	Millions	% Speaking Primarily Their Native Language	Status
Russians	145.2	99.8	SR
Ukrainians	44.2	81.1	SR
Uzbeks	16.7	98.3	SR
Byelorussians	10.0	70.9	SR
Kazakhs	8.2	97.0	SR
Azerbaijans	6.8	97.7	SR
Tatars	6.7	83.2	AR
Armenians	4.6	91.7	SR
Tadjiks	4.2	97.7	SR
Georgians	4.0	98.2	SR
Moldavians	3.4	91.6	SR
Lithuanians	3.1	97.7	SR
Turkmens	2.7	98.5	SR
Kirghizians	2.5	97.8	SR
Germans	2.0	48.7	--
Chuvashians	1.8	76.4	AR
Latvians	1.5	94.8	SR
Bashkirs	1.4	72.3	AR
Jews	1.3	11.1	--
Mordovs	1.2	67.1	AR
Poles	1.1	30.5	--
Estonians	1.0	95.5	SR
Chechenians	1.0	98.1	AR
Mariis	0.7	80.8	AR
Avars	0.6	97.2	--

SR - Soviet republic
AR - autonomous republic within Russia

Table A-2
SOVIET ADMINISTRATIVE/TERRITORIAL SYSTEM
(01/01/1990)

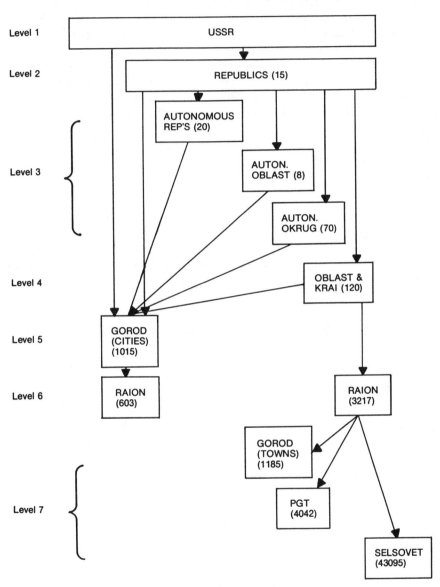

SOURCE: GOSKOMSTAT, USSR in FIGURES, 1989, 1990 pocket edition

Regulations that require registration with administrative agencies and/or approval for doing business from them apply to joint ventures as well as other enterprises. Foreign business people who engage in direct transactions with Soviet enterprises rather than transacting business in the usual place, Moscow, should be aware of the complexities of the former Soviet—now separate republics —administrative and territorial structure.

The explanation lies in the decision-making process in the Soviet Union as it concerns business authorization and registration. For example, before registration, joint ventures normally must obtain permission at the *oblat* or city level of administration. Partnerships or so-called "small-scale enterprises" are registered at the *raion* level.

Economic Performance

Although the estimated Soviet gross national product (GNP) is about 35% of the U.S. GNP, the USSR has accumulated tremendous economic wealth. Table A-3 shows how significant the Soviet output of certain products is. For several decades, production grew at the rate of 7% to 10% annually. The slowdown began only in the '70s (Table A-4) because of the country's inability to adapt to technological progress and to make a breakthrough into the postindustrial era. Other major problems of the centralized economy are mismanagement and the

Table A-3
SOVIET OUTPUT OF CERTAIN PRODUCTS
(USA = 100)

	1989	1980
Electric energy	58	53
Oil	158	142
Steel	169	142
Fertilizers	137	110
Synthetic fabric	38	30
Woolen fabric	424	525
Plastics	16	17
Paper	18	18
Tractors	580	256
Grain	74	70
Potatoes	432	486
Meat	68	56
Milk	164	156
Butter	335	267
Sugar	141	136

Source: USSR Statistical Abstract, 1990.

Table A-4
SOVIET GNP GROWTH
(Per annum %)

1976-1980	4.8
1981-1985	3.7
1986-1989	3.7
1990 (est)	(2.0)
1991 (projections)	(6.0-8.0)

poor infrastructure, which lead to enormous waste of the goods produced. For example, one-third to one-half of all vegetables produced in the state or collective farm sector are lost before reaching market because of transportation and storage problems, poor technology, and mismanagement. Lack of motivation on the part of suppliers remains the principal reason for such waste in a country that has experienced shortages in nearly every product from steel and oil to sugar and butter.

Soviet GNP structure (Table A-5) largely reflects the history of Soviet industrialization between 1930 and the 1960s, when emphasis was placed on heavy industry while new products, services, and consumer goods production remained largely underdeveloped. With energy, raw materials, and semifinished goods accounting for more than 90% of its exports, the Soviet Union must import a huge variety of products, from machinery to food.

Foreign Trade

The difficulty that the former centralized economy had in innovating and competing is reflected in the structure of Soviet foreign trade with the developed market economies (Tables A-6 and A-7). Agriculture constitutes a significant share of the GNP and yet there are substantial food shortages, a situation that indicates both waste and low productivity. Contrary to widespread belief, relevant raw materials are not always available in the USSR, and many Soviet manufacturers who use Western technologies have to purchase products of a certain quality and standard in international markets because of lack of

Table A-5
1989 SOVIET GNP STRUCTURE (%)

Mining and manufacturing	34
Agriculture	18
Construction	10
Services	36

Table A-6
BREAKDOWN OF SOVIET EXPORTS TO OECD
(Total = 100)

	1989	1980
Machinery and equipment	3.2	1.9
Energy	55.1	72.1
Raw materials and semifinished products	36.9	21.6
Food and consumer goods	4.8	4.4

Source: Soviet Statistical Abstract, 1990

Table A-7
BREAKDOWN OF SOVIET IMPORTS FROM OECD
(Total = 100)

	1989	1980
Machinery and equipment	34.3	29.6
Energy	0.9	1.1
Raw materials and semifinished products	38.5	40.3
Food and consumer goods	26.3	29.0

Source: Soviet Statistical Abstract, 1990

processing capacity at home. While the share of the country's exports attributable to commodities and semifinished goods has increased, the share attributable to energy has decreased, not only because of the fall of oil prices in the second half of the '80s but also because of the appearance of new commodities in Soviet foreign trade that helped to diversify Soviet exports.

Education

The educational system has five main stages:

1. Secondary school: from ages six to 17;

2. Vocational training: from ages 15 to 18, or 17 to 19;

3. Higher education: four or five years (daytime, part-time, by correspondence);

4. Postgraduate education: usually three years full-time or four years part-time; and

5. Training of specialists: variable, depending on the sector of the economy.

The first four stages are supervised by the State Committee on Education. Branch ministries usually organize training of specialists. There were several attempts to reform the educational system in the '80s. The key point of these reforms was to give the schools more autonomy. Schools and universities now have more independence from the State Committee on Education in designing their curricula, but they still must contend with the problem of very poor facilities because of shortages of state funding. Only schools directly supervised by "rich" ministries (such as Civil Aviation) can afford better material support and equipment.

Foreigners often are surprised by the high educational level of Soviet men and women they happen to meet. The knowledge of English and other foreign languages in a country that had been almost closed to the outer world for many decades is unprecedented. With 23 million university graduates and almost 39 million extended (two to three years) vocational training graduates in 1989, the Soviet Union has an impressive intellectual potential.

The centralized economy failed to avail itself properly of this tremendous brain resource, however. More than 10% of all university graduates remain officially unemployed, and many more do jobs for which they are overqualified. Before *perestroika*, lack of motivation and poor salaries pushed many young university graduates to accept less prestigious but better paid jobs, such as driving cabs or cutting meat (although due to meat shortages, the latter job is, in a way, prestigious). Now, for hundreds of thousands, there are cooperatives and individual business ventures.

Because the Soviet economy and management always have been production and technology oriented, many Soviet university graduates are manufacturing and construction engineers (one-third of all graduates in 1989), who dominate the Soviet class of industrial managers. The different educational background of Soviet and Western managers is an important factor that must be kept in mind in the processes of negotiation and cooperation. In contrast to the United States, graduates in economics and law combined were less than 8.5% of all university graduates in 1989. Moreover, even those specialists were not taught such subjects as marketing or financial management and accounting. It is only the advent of economic reforms that has created a huge wave of interest in these subjects, as well as in Western-style management. More and more private and quasi-private schools are being created, most of them concentrating on teaching Soviet managers how to do business in a market economy and how to engage in international transactions.

The Mechanism of the Centralized Economy

In 1990 the Soviet economy entered into a painful transition process. In order to understand how a superpower with a tremendous output of many basic products can encounter enormous economic disproportions, one must take a closer look at the centralized economic mechanism that prevailed in that country for almost 60 years—from the early 1930s to the late 1980s.

Because the Soviet economy is in the process of transition, it still retains basic features of the centralized, or command, mechanism at the republic level. Joint ventures, like other profit-oriented businesses, must operate in a highly controversial environment. Becoming acquainted with this environment requires considerable effort from international managers, who also must understand both historical roots and future trends.

The Soviet version of a centralized socialist economy was born as a result of the October Revolution in Russia in 1917. This major event, which reshaped not only the history of Russia but the history of the world in the 20th century, was a combination of numerous factors that probably made further developments inevitable. Thus, the centralized economy cannot be regarded as merely an idealistic experiment or even as the result of the evil will of a few individuals to use it as a platform for political dictatorship.

Also, some country had to try that experiment, and if it had not happened in Russia, it would have happened somewhere else. But again, in a different historical and cultural context, the socialist idea in managing the economy would have emerged in a different shape.

The Soviet economic system has three origins: (1) Marxist theories, (2) the global context, and (3) the Russian heritage.

Marxist Theories

The influence of the economic views of Karl Marx on Soviet economic policies resulted in the attempt to abandon the very idea of the market as the central element of the economic mechanism. Marx began his economic analysis of capitalism with the "values" of goods, which are determined in the process of production, and not prices, which are determined in the markets. Every specific value is determined by an average total amount of the time of labor input. The pricing system is based on the Marxian view of expenses incurred plus a percentage of overhead.

Because an enterprise could establish higher prices by including higher expenses plus an overhead margin, the decisive element of the economy is production, not the market. The equilibrium price, which is the market price, is not considered the best price. It is in the process of production of goods that surplus value, or profit, is created, and not in the process of circulation (selling and buying) of goods.

Marx concluded that profit earned by individuals must be made available to the whole society, a concept that requires public control over the means of production. Public ownership and control over production leave no room for competition, which must be replaced by planning. Market competition and profit earning by capitalists make economic growth disproportionate and lead to economic, social, and political crises. Public control and ownership of all wealth produced in a country where the economy is planned and proportionate—and where there is no basis for social (class) conflicts—was the ideal envisioned by Marx, which some society had to strive to attain.

The Global Context

The October Revolution of 1917 and the attempt to implement Marxist theories could hardly have been possible in any other global context than that of the years immediately after 1910. During World War I, in 1915 and 1916, the leader of the Russian left-wing socialists, Vladimir Lenin, analyzed two global economic megatrends. This analysis led him to a definite idea of the form a socialist or nonmarket economy should take.

The first trend began in the 1870s with the creation of the cartels in Germany, trusts in the United States, and syndicates in France. Though the names were different, the idea was the same. In most developed nations, the biggest manufacturers preferred to unite rather than compete and to form monopolies over the production of specific products that were extended to whole sectors of the economy. The trend toward monopolization in the world economy emerged in the 1870s and culminated in the 1930s, often called the "golden age" of cartels. One of Lenin's conclusions was that free competition is increasingly replaced by monopolistic control over the economy.

World War I gave birth to the second global trend—the "statization" of the economy by the growing interference of governments in economic life in the form of regulations, budgetary policies, and nationalization. Since the 1930s, and especially after the Great Depression, all the major economies of the world experienced growing regulation by the state. The Great Depression marked an end to the old "wild or laissez-faire capitalism" pattern of development. Social and economic policies of governments were the only way to preserve the stability of society.

In the 1930s the United States on the one hand, and Germany and Italy on the other, conducted similar policies in different ways. "Statization" continued even more dramatically after World War II. It was only in the late '70s that the Keynesian way of regulating the economy was reconsidered.

Because Lenin was far-sighted enough to see the birth of this trend, he formulated his idea of a socialist economy as a "state-monopolistic capitalism" where private ownership is replaced by public ownership and control over production. The fact that the Soviet economy was run as a state monopoly places this huge experiment still within, though at the extreme of, the global economic trends of the 20th century.

The Russian Heritage

Such a radical revolution as the Bolshevik revolution never would have occurred except in a country in the middle of economic, social, political, and moral crises, as was Russia during World War I. Sixty thousand Bolsheviks took and held power in a country of 170 million people because they were able to offer clear ideas and objectives—such as "peace to peoples," "land to peasants," and "factories to workers"—to a country falling into an abyss. But it took about 15 years of daring economic experiments to establish the centralized economy. Before that, Soviet economic development passed through two distinct phases.

From 1918 to 1920 the so-called "war communism" was introduced by force with the purpose of ultimate concentration of all available resources in the extreme situation of the civil war. At that time money, prices, and salaries did not exist. Products were distributed directly by the state.

In 1921, when the country was in ruins and at an economic impasse, Lenin introduced the NEP (new economic policy), which restored market instruments, created a mixed economy, and established a convertible ruble. The economy boomed for several consecutive years, but at the end of the 1920s the structural crisis deepened and prices were rising. The new Soviet leadership, headed by Stalin, started a new political and economic system, which by and large existed until the end of the 1980s. One should bear in mind that the economic mechanism described here is not only the result of "communist experiments." It also has deep roots in Russian history and in the fact that the state and its bureaucracy always have had significant control over the economy.

The large-scale economic debate that preceded the adoption of the first five-year plan in 1928 centered around the vital issue of finding ways and means of industrializing the country. One approach suggested slower rates of growth and a combination of centrally planned and market instruments. The other defended the idea of a "forced" industrialization on the basis of "state-monopolistic" socialism. However, both parties agreed the money for industrialization was to be taken from the agricultural production of the peasantry.

The major features of the Soviet centrally planned economy were designed in the early 1930s and were based on a dogmatic interpretation of Marxian socialist theory. The main principles include the following:

- The state owns and controls most of the nation's property.
- The plan is the main element of the economic mechanism; the plan is law.
- Plans are worked out within central economic agencies and are vertically imposed and controlled.
- Procurement and distribution of products are centrally planned and organized.
- Practically all prices are fixed centrally, and basically, so are wages.
- Accounting, reporting, auditing, and statistics are plan-oriented.
- The bank (actually, one) is a controlling rather than a credit institution.

- All foreign transactions are monopolized by the state through a few institutions.
- The whole economy is based on obedient execution of orders coming out of "the center," which "always knows best."

More or less productive in the period of emergency (massive industrialization, war economy, and reconstruction), the centrally planned system was losing impetus beginning in the late 1960s and ending in stagnation and impasse in the 1980s. The peculiarity of the centralized economic mechanism is that specific governmental agencies are responsible for the control over each particular element (see Table A-8).

Table A-8
GOVERNMENTAL AGENCIES RESPONSIBLE FOR CONTROL

PLAN	State Committee on Planning*	(Gosplan)
BUDGET	Ministry of Finance	(Minfin)
SUPPLIES	State Committee on Material Supplies	(Gossnab)
PRODUCTION	Sectoral ministries	
DISTRIBUTION	State Committee on Material Supplies	(Gossnab)
REPORTING	Ministry of Finance	(Minfin)
	State Committee on Statistics	(Goskomstat)
MEASUREMENT (money and prices)	State Bank	(Gosbank)
	State Committee on Prices	(Goskomtsen)
CONTROL	Ministry of Finance	(Minfin)
	State Bank	(Gosbank)

* Note: Most of these agencies changed their names in 1991; for example, Gosplan became Ministry of Economy and Forecasting and Gossnab became Ministry of Procurement. Changes in functions are still to follow.

As a substitute for profit making, group and individual motivation to support the system was secured largely by promoting faith (after several years of effort comes well-being) and fear (with *gulag* being the most important "ministry" in terms of production output).

As will be discussed below, most of the elements of the traditional centralized mechanism have largely been destroyed since the advent of *perestroika*, with the exceptions of Minfin and Gosbank. They have preserved most of their functions and to some extent are still standing in the way of the market economy. The new Soviet enterprise law rejects the traditional centralized economic mechanism, which actually no longer operates although the agencies still exist. However, market instruments are only now being introduced and largely contribute to the controversy and uncertainty of the current business environment. Between the changes that have already occurred and the transitions (attitudes, adaptation, and policies) that are on course lies a "neutral zone" characterized by political and economic turmoil.

The focus and the most striking evidence of the current economic crisis in the Soviet Union was the budgetary crisis. Table A-9 shows a dramatic increase in the budget deficit financed by Gosbank loans, which has led to the increase in state debt and to the printing of new money. The heaviest burden on the federal budget is caused by subsidizing money-losing enterprises and basic consumer

Table A-9
USSR FEDERAL BUDGET
(in billions of rubles)

	1989	1987	1985
Revenues			
Sales tax	111	94	98
State enterprise tax	115	127	120
Foreign trade	66	69	71
Other	64	53	51
Total from enterprises	356	343	340
Individual income taxes	45	35	32
Total revenues	401	378	372
Expenditures	493	435	390
Deficit financing - Gosbank loans	(92)	(57)	(18)

Source: USSR Statistical Abstract, 1990

products and services. Food subsidies alone exceed 15% of overall budgetary expenditures.

While expenditures and the deficit are growing, the principal source of government revenues—the state enterprise tax—is stagnating and even decreasing because of the gradual easing of former governmental fiscal policies under which the most profitable enterprises were practically deprived of their profits. The reforms of 1987, which aimed at increasing enterprise motivation, introduced more equality and greater order in the fiscal treatment of different Soviet enterprises. Now, most profitable enterprises pay less to the state than before 1987. Especially since April 1991 many more factories lose money and therefore pay no taxes.

Table A-10
MAJOR INFLATION FACTORS IN THE USSR

- Pricing gradually liberalized.
- Restrictions on individual earnings partially lifted.
- Party's command over the economy diminished.
- New money printed to cover the budget deficit.
- Confidence of citizens in government lost.

The budgetary deficit was one of the factors in the growing inflation in the Soviet economy brought to life by the process of reform. Those factors are listed in Table A-10. The introduction of free entrepreneurship in the old-style command economy has contributed a great deal to inflation, as the government gradually has been losing control over prices and individual incomes. The liberalization, which began in 1987, was not followed by consistent monetary policies. It was only in the fall and winter of 1990-91 that the government tried to regulate the money supply and cash in circulation. The most dramatic and desperate of these measures was the cancellation of the 50 ruble and 100 ruble bills in January 1991. But these restrictive measures came too late and were carried out in the old totalitarian style (a very similar kind of savings confiscation had been ordered by Stalin in 1947). This action was a chief cause of a further dramatic decrease in popularity of the Soviet governmental policies. In the summer of 1991 the government started printing new bills at high speed without withdrawing old ones (1961 series), thus boosting inflation.

The scale of inflation, in its peculiar form of shortages and black market price increases, is illustrated in Table A-11. While the state subsidized many commodities and controls basic prices in the state-owned sector, most of the goods and services are sold on free market terms. The profit usually goes to the people directly or indirectly engaged in the retail trade. Dramatic price increases (one and one-half to four times) for most products and services commanded by Prime Minister Pavlov as of April 2, 1991, did not fill shelves in stores but multiplied black market prices.

The Logic of Perestroika

The brief period since *perestroika* ("restructuring") was initiated has been characterized by the most rapid and significant changes in Russian history since the October Revolution. International managers who are seriously considering investing in the republics should not be misled by short-term political developments that could prevent them from seeing long-term trends. A rational and weighted approach to the dramatic political and economic changes could save

Table A-11
AVERAGE MARKET PRICES OF CERTAIN PRODUCTS IN RUSSIA
SEPTEMBER 1990
(R per kilo, unit, etc.)

Product	Official price	Number of times higher than official price
Meat	9	4.0
Sausage	19	3.0
Coffee	15	2.5
Vodka	24	2.4
Lady's winter coat	1,236	2.4
Man's winter footwear	293	4.0
Lady's winter boots	470	3.7
Soviet cigarettes	5	8.0
Gold chain	651	2.0
Refrigerator	1,138	2.4
VCR	6,148	2.8
Color TV	2,021	2.4
Lada car	32,900	3.6

Source: <u>Argumenti i facti</u>, October 1990.

potential investors from the extremes of both euphoria and skepticism. While it was unreasonable to expect that the exciting acceleration of economic reforms in the summer of 1990 could shorten the painful transition to a market economy after 60 years of unprecedented centralization, it also was short-sighted to consider that the events of early 1991 were an end to reform and heralded a revival of the cold war.

The meaning of *perestroika* in 1991 was very different from what it was in 1989, and even more so, in 1986. *Perestroika* has its own logic—the logic of a very difficult transition. Unpredictability is the uncomfortable reality in such circumstances. Actually, market-oriented programs adopted by Soviet parliaments (both federal and republican) in 1990 can hardly be called "restructuring" programs as they are programs of radical change in Soviet economic life. The principal logic of *perestroika* was: more change and transition. The events of the summer of 1991 indicated a forthcoming acceleration of economic reform in a certain degree of coordination with Western powers (for instance, Gorbachev's invitation to the "Big Seven" summit in London). However, the failed August 1991 coup in Moscow marked an end to the *perestroika* period and opened a new stage of reforms in what used to be the USSR.

The evolution of *perestroika* can be traced through a number of periods, beginning in 1985.

The "Acceleration Period" (March 1985 to September 1986)

Soon after Gorbachev came to power in March 1985, people realized that the country had a leader very different from previous ones. Actually, the expectation of change, or rather the belief in the necessity for change, was growing in the early 1980s. The advent of a younger leader was not unexpected. Gorbachev gained popularity quickly enough by appearing from time to time in the streets of Soviet cities, by making some changes in Politburo membership (Edward Shevardnadze's nomination to the Ministry of Foreign Affairs looked very exotic at that time), and by adopting a new tone in foreign policy. Gorbachev's main point in economic policy became the notion of "acceleration" as a natural response to the slowdown and stagnation of the early 1980s. The original idea was that with the restructuring of investment policies, promotion of scientific and technological progress, and increase in incentives for innovation, the economy would regain the high growth rates of past decades.

It was only at the party's congress in February 1986 that the notion of "restructuring" officially appeared. It was far from a "policy of *perestroika*" but was a recognition of the necessity to redirect the economic mechanism primarily toward innovation and profitability. New ideas were able to raise somewhat prudent enthusiasm, but there was little real change in the Soviet economic and political landscape. The party, according to its new program, was still "building communism," with Gorbachev fiercely defending the "socialist values" and "socialist choice."

Economists as TV Stars (Fall 1986 to Fall 1987)

It was only a year and a half after Gorbachev launched the idea of "acceleration" that serious discussions began about whether the existing economic
mechanism could assure an increase in economic growth, innovation, and a
better quality of life. The nation, which previously knew only one "economist,"
the Communist Party, suddenly discovered individuals who were able to provide
a very different analysis of the economic situation in the country. Professors
Leonid Abalkin, Abel Aganbegyan, Stanislav Shatalin, and Pavel Bunich appeared, in turn, during prime time on Soviet television. For several months those
shows, which were becoming more and more critical of the centralized economy,
gathered audiences of tens of millions of people.

Other economists, such as Nikolai Shmelev and Gennady Lisichkin, built
their popularity exclusively by articles demolishing Stalinist economic ideology.
Gavriil Popov became nationally famous several weeks after his article, "The
Administrative System," was published in February 1987. Most of these people
later became influential politicians (Abalkin became deputy prime minister;
Shatalin, the president's advisor; Popov, mayor of Moscow).

The first rumors about a conservative threat to the reforms started circulating
in January 1987 before an important session of the Communist Party Central
Committee, at which Gorbachev for the first time strongly condemned Stalin and
Stalinism. This condemnation seemed to ease the tension, and the entire spring
and summer of 1987 were characterized by the adoption of the first significant
package of economic reform-oriented measures. The most important was the
first law approving state enterprises, which introduced such ideas as profit-
making, antimonopolism, a contract system instead of central plans, wholesale
trade instead of centralized supplies, and taxes instead of withdrawal of
enterprise profits by the government. July 1987 marked the culmination of the
departure from the Stalinist economic system—new laws were passed, prices
and wages were partially decontrolled, and more new faces appeared in the
Soviet leadership.

The Controversial Winter of 1987-1988

While the economic situation was becoming more critical, reformers increasingly were insisting that economic changes could not be continued without the
democratization of the society. Conservatives became more aware of the threats
to their political and social position. For several months in the fall of 1987
literally nothing important happened to the country's policies. While Gorbachev
was working on his opus on "*Perestroika* and New Thinking," tensions were
growing. The climax came in October during a party plenum, when Boris Yeltsin
openly accused some Politburo members, namely Yegor Ligachev, of sabotaging
perestroika and Gorbachev of failure to act.

At that time, Yeltsin, as Moscow party boss, was already in serious conflict
with the almighty Moscow party *nomenklatura* (the bureaucratic elite of Soviet

society). Very soon he was ousted from both the Politburo and the Moscow party secretaryship in an atmosphere reminiscent of the 1930s. One major difference was that Yeltsin was not "annihilated politically" but demoted to a ministerial post.

The triumphant right-wingers continued their roll over *perestroika* until March 1988, when a previously unknown teacher from Leningrad, Nina Andreeva, published an article that made her famous: "I Cannot Denounce My Principles." It was the first published anti-*perestroika* manifesto, which many local party committees photocopied as required reading for rank-and-file party members.

The rescue of *perestroika* came in April from the main party paper, *Pravda*, which criticized Andreeva's manifesto and proclaimed the necessity for political reform. While the *nomenklatura* managed to block further economic reform and freeze the domestic political climate, the media were becoming bolder after having obtained Gorbachev's blessing to condemn the Stalinist past. At that time, most Soviets learned more about their not so distant past than they had known through all of their previous life. Disgust with Stalinism and Brezhnevism was growing, and criticism of Soviet history came very close to Lenin at one end and Gorbachev at the other. All the rest of the Soviet heritage, as Gorbachev bitterly recognized later, was "mixed with mud" by journals and magazines.

The Advent of Pluralism (May to November 1988)

The critical rethinking of history led to where it should lead, that is, criticism of today's policies. A Communist Party conference held in July 1988 adopted a number of important resolutions. Among them, political pluralism was legalized in the form of free discussions in society and in the party (no other party was yet permitted). Second, it was decided to reorganize and diminish the party apparatus and abolish its sectoral economic departments. This decision had the most important effects on the life of the country since the party's direct command over the economy ended in the fall of 1988. Meanwhile, some important laws and regulations in the economic sphere were passed at that time, including the law of cooperatives and gradual liberalization of foreign trade.

Preelection Tensions (December 1988 to March 1989)

The winter of 1988/1989 was marked by growing tensions in Soviet political life after a new law of elections was passed by the Soviet parliament in December 1988. For the first time in Soviet history, the parliament was to be elected from competing candidates, including those not nominated by the party leadership. As the registration campaign continued, more and more independent candidates were running for seats in the Soviet parliament. The law made public campaigning possible, so many public anti-party meetings took place in major Soviet cities in February and March for the first time in more than 60 years. The *nomenklatura* tried all possible means to prevent democratic candidates from running for parliament. In many cities, it succeeded in keeping the party nominees as the only candidates. Media controlled by the party used calumnies and hidden threats against alternative candidacies. Political opposition to the existing regime began crystallizing, and it was fiercely attacked by the authorities.

Preelection tensions were increased by the first serious political crisis in the Baltic republics, when Gorbachev strongly opposed and condemned an Estonian law requiring the approval of Soviet laws by the Estonian parliament before they could be enforced in the territory of the republic. Estonia was forced to retract the decision. In the economic arena, this period was marked by dramatic restrictions on foreign trade and operations of cooperatives.

The First Congress of People's Deputies and Its Impact (May 1989 to November 1989)

March 25, 1989, is a day that many Soviets probably will never forget. Large majorities voted for independent candidates and for reforms, especially in urban and industrial areas. In Moscow, Boris Yeltsin obtained more than 90% of the vote. In Kiev, Leningrad, and some other major cities the party nominees for parliament had no competitors but were unable to get a majority of the vote. It was probably the first time since the October Revolution that people felt that together they could influence the political future and impose their will. Mass rallies, which started during the election campaign, have become a permanent reality of Soviet political life.

The congress started its work in May. Its proceedings were broadcast live on television for several months and greatly surpassed all other television shows in popularity. Soon, the opposition to the Communist party leadership was organized in the parliament in the form of the so-called "interregional group of deputies," with Boris Yeltsin and Andrei Sakharov among its leaders. During that period there was much more criticism of the government without any practical steps being taken toward reform, but the political climate became radical enough to prepare for future breakthroughs.

More Headaches for the Kremlin (December 1989 to April 1990)

With the economic situation deteriorating, inflation growing, lines getting longer, the government engaging in fights with the opposition in parliament, and a political bribery scandal electrifying the country, ethnic problems became the hottest spot on the Soviet domestic policy scene. After a year of talks about economic autonomy within the Soviet Union, the Baltic republics took more practical steps toward political independence. As nationalist movements and feelings were growing, Gorbachev rushed to Lithuania to try to cool down the emotions, but it was already too late. The first free elections to republican parliaments brought nationalist movements to power. Immediately, the Lithuanian parliament issued a declaration of independence.

This action was the first serious political crisis of the Soviet federation. At first Gorbachev tried to solve it in the traditional manner by forcing the Lithuanians to back down. The USSR split into those who supported the action taken by the Lithuanians and those who condemned the way it was done, but almost everyone agreed that no one could deny the right of any republic to decide its own future. What seemed unthinkable before—the splitting up of the Soviet Union—since that early spring has become the dominant feature of Soviet domestic politics.

In the meantime, facing the growing inability of a government in constant fights with the parliament to rule the country effectively and to deal precisely with the independence crises, Gorbachev gave himself additional powers by creating the post of president of the USSR.

Breakthroughs Toward the Market (May 1990 to October 1990)

The beginning of this period of the most far-reaching economic and political changes, unprecedented in Soviet history since the 1920s, was marked by two dramatic events. First, new, more radical parliaments were elected in a number of republics, including Russia, where Boris Yeltsin was elected president of the Supreme Soviet. The Russian parliament soon passed its own declaration of sovereignty, accepted quietly this time by Gorbachev. Other republics did not wait long to follow. An unprecedented situation emerged: Republican parliaments began adopting independence-minded laws usually more radical than the federal laws. The country was plunged into a real legal crisis with conflicting federal and republican laws.

Second, the Soviet parliament turned down the governmental plan for price increases in June 1990. This event significantly radicalized Soviet economic policies. Also, after 1987, a major package of regulations was adopted including taxation and enterprise laws, corporation and partnership acts, and stocks and bonds regulations. This step marked a clear departure from the centralized economic mechanism toward the market economy.

The process culminated in September and October when the Russian parliament adopted the "500-day plan," until that time the most comprehensive and radical program of transition to a market economy. Later, on October 19, 1990, the Soviet parliament passed a resolution with a somewhat vaguer plan but a very clear statement: There is no alternative to the transition to the market.

The Major Challenge to *Perestroika* (November 1990 to March 1991)

The two big gaps in Soviet domestic policy resulted in profound crisis by the end of 1990. The first gap was the quasi-vacuum between the reforms of 1987 and 1990 (the latter still not radical enough) and the inconsistent governmental policies, which disrupted the established economic links, ruined the consumer market, and destabilized the ruble, as well as the federal budget. The second was Gorbachev's inability to find a timely and innovative solution to ethnic conflicts that had been growing since 1987. These conflicts led to the crisis of the Soviet federation, which started falling apart much faster than anyone expected.

One can hardly imagine a less propitious environment for the hardline policies that Gorbachev actually adopted. Moreover, after several years of defeats and retreats, the old *nomenklatura* and its supporters finally organized themselves into a "conservative opposition" to reform, in such entities as the newly born Communist Party of Russia and the hardline faction in the federal parliament, the *soyuz.*

Criticism of *perestroika* in general had flourished in hard-line papers. Crackdowns on republics proclaiming independence (Lithuania), on media (liberal television journalists), and on private business (confiscation of high denomination bills and assaults on cooperatives) were desperate attempts by the government to bring the country to order by traditional means.

The conservative counterattack on liberal reforms culminated in March 1991 with two events: (1) a referendum vote on the future of the USSR boycotted by six republics, in which no party could claim victory; and (2) a failed attempt by Russian hardliners to make Yeltsin resign from his post as chairman of the Russian parliament. April's Allied victory in Desert Storm and Gorbachev's defeat of challenging conservatives at the party plenum marked an end to this first period of real threats to reforms.

Toward a New Union (April 1991 to December 1991)

The period of Soviet policies up to December 1991 clearly was dominated by the key problem of the future of the Soviet federation. The sensational "9+1" agreement between leaders of nine republics and Gorbachev brought hopes for a peaceful solution to interethnic conflicts and wars between union republics and "the center." The text of the new union treaty was finalized in July and opened for official signing beginning August 20. Domestic policies also were marked by Yeltsin's triumphant popular election as Russia's first ever president, democratic elections of mayors of Moscow and Leningrad (St. Petersburg), turmoil inside Russia's Communist Party, and the evident impotence of both federal and Russian parliaments. The culmination of foreign policy came in July, with Gorbachev's invitation to the "Big Seven" summit in London and the Soviet-American summit in Moscow. Economic developments, unlike those in previous periods, were not characterized by adoption of dramatic new laws or regulations. Lawmaking obviously became almost useless during this period.

A number of events marked further considerable moves toward a new business environment in the Soviet republics. Republics continued to gain more and more important economic powers from "the center." Economic decision making, with the exception of monetary areas, shifted de facto to the governments of the republics. New market structures boomed. Embryos of commodity and stock exchanges became the watchword of Soviet business in the summer of 1991. Privatization accelerated and "Soviet millionaires" were born daily. Signs of economic liberalization appeared (such as the abolition of Pavlov's draconian customs duties) as republics acquired more regulatory powers.

In December 1991 the Commonwealth of Independent States (CIS) was established in Minsk. The CIS at present comprises 11 of the 12 remaining states (excluding Georgia). The actual economic, political, and military structure of the CIS still needs to be fully worked out. Foreign investors will not have to negotiate directly with the respective republics instead of first with the central government. The economic integration between the republics is subject to specific evaluations at this time.

The End of *Perestroika*

Already, in early 1991, many spoke of the death of *perestroika*. Actually, as a "restructuring" policy, it had died a long time before. The "command" economy presumably cannot be restored, so political struggles in 1991 mainly revolved around two issues: what the future of the union would be and who would have the political power in the new economic system.

Since August 1991, *perestroika* is officially dead, and its creator has resigned. However, it only means the beginning of a new era of reforms that will continue for years. No change ever occurred rapidly in Russia.

Strangely enough, for the last five years the ups and downs of *perestroika* had a clearly seasonal character. What is even more amazing is that even in the "post Soviet" and "post *perestroika*" period the seasonal character of political developments continues. This is probably related to the tensions that the always-feared Russian winter creates. In the CIS winter of 1991-1992, the following factors reactivated new conservative attacks on reforms:

- Crop failures raised the specter of famine.
- It was feared that continued disruption of established interrepublic economic links would cause production to fall.
- Hardliners rallied, calling for "strong power" and "social guarantees."
- Russian chauvinist feelings were being heated up by conservative nationalists against "traitor" Ukrainians and others (disputes over Crimea and the Black Sea fleet). Calls for restructuring of "great Russia" were heard.
- The most important factor—dramatic price increases—created unprecedented tensions in the population.

The Political and Social System in Transition

The most dramatic occurrence from 1988 through 1990 was the radical reshaping of Soviet society. The changes that took place within this short period will continue to have a long-range effect on political and economic developments in this part of the world and beyond well after the year 2000.

Those three years were practically lost for economic reform, and the result was the disastrous state of the Soviet consumer market by the fall of 1990. But any movement toward a market economy never would have been possible without the democratic breakthrough of those years. Because of these changes, Russia and the other republics will never be the same, and periods of reactionary policies may slow down but never stop further reform.

Electoral System

A constitutional law passed in December 1988 changed the electoral system profoundly from the former single-slate, formalized, and useless procedure. Every five years all citizens age 18 and over (with the exception of certain categories, such as criminals) elect the deputies of the congress. Also, the supreme soviets of different republics are elected every five years. In many republics, uncontested elections are prohibited. The number of candidates is unrestricted, and registration requirements have been simplified. Under the law of 1988 a number of deputies were elected not by the people but by so-called "public organizations," such as the Communist Party, trade unions, Komsomol, Academy of Sciences, and so on. This regulation, which made the first elected congress of deputies more conservative, was criticized bitterly by the media, lawyers, and deputies. As a result, many republics adopted their own laws, which prohibit elections by public organizations.

There was considerable progress in the conduct of elections to republican parliaments in 1990 as compared with elections to the Soviet parliament in the spring of 1989. One of the results was much more radical and reform-minded republican parliaments.

Structure of Traditional Soviet Political Power

After the political reorganization of Soviet society in 1988, 1989, and 1990, and before the republics became independent in 1991, the political structure had the following characteristics:

The Congress of Peoples' Deputies had the ultimate power in the country. It consisted of 2,500 members, elected on both territorial and national principles, and elected the president and the Supreme Soviet. The first session was held in May 1989.

The first president was elected in March 1990. The president has the ultimate power between the sessions of the Congress, which has the power to impeach him. The Presidential Council existed between March and December 1990. It was replaced by the Security Council, with members nominated by the president. The Security Council lasted until August 1991.

The Supreme Soviet (parliament) is the permanent body of the Congress. It consists of 500 deputies, equally divided between the Soviet of the Union and the Soviet of Nationalities.

The Communist Party and the New Parties

The Communist Party, which since 1918 had been the only political party in the country, has been undergoing profound changes in recent years. This process was launched in June 1988 at the 19th Party Conference. Party apparatus was simplified and reorganized. Elections of party officials became more democratic.

In February 1990, the Communist Party officials recognized the right of other parties to be formed but insisted on maintaining control of Soviet political life. The democratic wing of the party rejected this idea as undemocratic, and finally its leaders left the Communist Party at its 28th Congress.

The process of creation of new parties began in 1988. National fronts created in most of the republics gradually were transformed into political parties (actually, they became a coalition of different opposition parties). Political pluralism was institutionalized in March 1990 when the Congress of People's Deputies abolished Article 6 of the Soviet constitution, which proclaimed the Communist Party as the "leading force" in Soviet society and the "core" of the Soviet political system. Since August 1991 all party committees (organizational structures) in Russia are prohibited by Yeltsin's decree. Communist Party structures are allowed only at the territorial level. New parties, including those of the extreme left and right wings, became more important (an extremist candidate to the Russian presidency, Mr. Zhirinovsky, obtained about 8% of the votes in June 1991).

Major New Laws and Regulations

Since the first session of the new Soviet parliament in May 1990, some major laws have been adopted that have transformed significantly the Soviet political and economic system. Although beset by controversy, they have succeeded in laying the foundation for future reforms. Among the most significant laws are the following:

- The law of property,
- The law related to land,
- The laws of individual taxation,
- The law governing relations between the Soviet Union and its republics,
- The law related to the presidency (as an amendment to the constitution),
- The law on enterprises,
- The law on taxation of enterprises,
- The law on mass media,
- The law on political parties,
- The law on emigration and immigration; and
- The law on foreign investments.

The enterprise law passed in June 1990 by the Supreme Soviet replaces the very first *"perestroika* law" on state enterprises passed in June 1987. The latter was very much criticized later and never fully implemented because of bureaucratic opposition but still remained an important landmark in the transformation of Soviet economic philosophy. Enforcement of the new law most probably will encounter enormous difficulties, primarily because of the continuing disintegration of the former Soviet Union. Its major importance, however, is that it has legalized the departure from the centralized economic mechanism, as described above, in such crucial areas as the following:

- Profit making: It now is considered the primary goal of any enterprise.
- Ownership: Different forms of ownership are permitted, including joint-stock companies, partnerships, and quasi-private ownership.
- Property rights: Neither the state nor any person has any claim to the enterprise's property, other than by investment or loan.
- Management: The owners of the enterprise design and control its management, and the employees may have an influential role.
- Planning: Central planning is no longer mandatory; planning is left entirely up to the discretion of enterprises.
- Contracts: Contracts no longer are imposed on enterprises, which are now free to find partners and negotiate deals.
- Supplies: The centralized system of material supplies is no longer part of the economic mechanism and must be replaced by wholesale and retail trade companies and agreements.
- Pricing: Enterprises are free to sell their products at negotiated (contractual) prices except when direct governmental regulations are in effect; such regulations are supposed to decrease in scope.
- Foreign economic activities: Any enterprise has an undeniable right to engage directly in international business so long as it abides by applicable regulations.

Although proclaiming a very different philosophy from the previous central planning system, this law actually can be enforced only if it is followed by other regulations and laws introducing market instruments. Gorbachev's *ukases* (decrees) of the fall of 1990, with the exception of two decrees of October 26, were far from bringing the country closer to the market and even further from stabilizing the economy. One can hardly define the logic of these decrees as other than chaotic in the attempt to face the numerous and growing problems in the Soviet Union.

Social Structure and Trade Unions

The social structure of Soviet society is undergoing changes similar to those in many industrialized nations. The traditional ideological scheme—working class, laboring peasantry, people's intelligentsia—is disintegrating.

The number of people engaged in agriculture is decreasing constantly although it still remains high, about 25%. Even so, it is not high enough for self-sufficiency in food production.

The so-called intelligentsia includes mostly state employees—18 million people are engaged directly in the party/state apparatus. For many years a distinct line was drawn between the bureaucratic elite (the *nomenklatura*) and the rest of the population. Nowadays the privileges of the *nomenklatura* in procurement and services are shrinking but are still far from disappearing, especially in decision making and use of state-owned assets.

Workers are becoming increasingly politicized and engage in the creation of independent trade unions that are replacing the official trade unions. The latter long ago merged with the state bureaucracy. The process of creating new independent trade unions started in the summer of 1989 when the first major coal miners' strikes took place in the country. The "strike committees" (*stachkom*) in some places replaced local authorities because they had popular backing and later developed into independent unions.

Today, the intelligentsia and mining and manufacturing workers are the most politically active strata of Soviet society. The peasantry, as elections show, still remains a more conservative and less dynamic, but very influential, class.

Soviet Republics: National Problems

The 15 former Soviet republics include the three Slavic republics (Russia, Ukraine, and Byelorussia), Moldavia, the three Baltic republics (Latvia, Lithuania, and Estonia), the three trans-Caucasian republics (Armenia, Azerbaijan, and Georgia) and five Asian republics (Kazakhstan, Uzbekistan, Kirgizia, Turkmenia, and Tajikistan). The rigid centralization of the Soviet federation left little room for the republics' independence.

The trend toward independence of different republics started in 1988, when national fronts were created in the Baltic republics. The movement toward economic and political sovereignty accelerated enormously in 1990, when most of the republics, including Russia, passed legislation according to which republican laws take precedence over Soviet laws. Combined with increasing economic decentralization in the USSR, these developments are creating a new business environment, in which management of cultural/regional differences is becoming more important.

The national problems that emerged in 1987 with the Nagorny Karabakh conflict, followed by others, have their roots in the deep economic crises of the Soviet Union and have led to the transformation of the USSR into a loose federation, in the form of the CIS.

Gorbachev for the last several years had been trying to use U.S. federal models for the future Soviet Union. As soon as the failure of such policies became obvious, he made several apparently desperate attempts to use the iron fist. The "pro-Union" referendum campaign before March 1991 did not bring comfortable popular support for his idea of "a strong center and strong republics." The idea of a possible union in which republics voluntarily decide to grant certain powers to the federal agencies finds much stronger support.

In the meantime the economic and legal disintegration of the USSR continued. The republics preferred to negotiate directly without the Kremlin's participation. For example, in June 1991, heads of foreign economic agencies of all 15 republics gathered to reject new federal customs regulations and to work out coordinated foreign economic policies.

The economic environment of Soviet republics differs. Lithuania and Estonia introduced free market prices on staples. Both republics tried to introduce international accounting standards, an effort that was not entirely successful because for the last three centuries, including the period of independence of 1918-1940, Baltic accountants adhered to Russo-German accounting standards.

Latvia is trying to secure transition to a market economy with price stability by using ration coupons.

In 1991, Ukraine instituted its independent economic policies. It increasingly has separated its industrial and foreign economic policies from federal policies and also has liberalized fiscal policies. (Medical instruments, baby food, and other products were tax exempt, and for a number of other consumer-oriented industries, income taxes were reduced by 15%.) State-fixed purchasing prices for wheat and other cereals also were increased significantly. However, managers of numerous kolkhozes (collective farms) and sovkhozes (state-owned farms) preferred to sell agricultural products to buyers from other republics at high market prices. The Ukrainian government tried to stem the crisis by imposing restrictions on the export of most agricultural products and by increasing incentives for farmers to sell their products to the Ukrainian government.

The Byelorussian government, like Kazakhstan and some other republics, invited an American economist (Scott Norwood) to serve as economic advisor. It adopted measures to stimulate agricultural production, and, to prevent manufactured products from being exported from the republic, it imposed a 120% surcharge on exported items, compared to domestic prices for similar products.

Moldavia's leadership is firm in its independent policy and its refusal to sign the Union treaty. It has established close links with ethnically close Romania. One-third of its population (which represents half of the industrial output) does not wish to remain within an independent Moldavian state but wants to join Romania.

Armenia has finished the privatization of land and introduced other independence-minded reforms. However, the Armenian government has on numerous occasions shown its desire to maintain stable relations with the other republics of the former Soviet Union and probably will sign the Union treaty. Armenian policies are very much determined by its bellicose relations with Azerbaijan.

Georgia faces a complex economic and political situation while output decreases and shortages and budget deficits grow.

Azerbaijan is engaged in trying to stimulate American investments in the oil and gas industry.

Kazakhstan was more radical than any of the "nine" republics in taking control over former federal property in its territory. Its President Nazarbayev shows significant independence in foreign economic policies, especially those oriented toward Turkey, Israel, Saudi Arabia, and the Pacific nations.

Uzbekistan, unlike many other republics, does not prevent its commodities from being exported but levies customs duties.

Turkmenistan, Kirgizia, and Tajikistan still depend very much on economic aid from the federal government and richer republics, which shape their current policies toward the new union.

Many observers agree that further splitting of the republics' economies may be unavoidable. However, many important factors will hold the Soviet republics' economies together and provide a basis for coordination. Accounting principles are likely to be among the most synchronized aspects of economic policies of the different republics under the federal Minfin's guidance.

The New Business Environment in the Soviet Union

The socioeconomic and political developments in the Soviet Union show that reform is a long-term cyclical process. It is a process that has brought radical changes to the Soviet political system. The "traditional" Soviet Union has been disintegrating, and the centralized economic mechanism is being destroyed as the privatization of the economy continues. As a result, the enormous economic potential of the Soviet Union has been abused as the country has entered a most painful period of transition.

The developments described above are creating a new business environment. Understanding them is the key to success in doing business in the Soviet Union today, even with the present political and legal uncertainty.

Adopting long-range strategies always has been recommended to potential business partners in the USSR. This long-term view remains the dominant feature of most business and investment strategies there, but the reasons have changed. Under the central economy dominated by the Communist Party, one of the main reasons for adopting long-range strategies was the unnerving length of negotiations. Building a long-term relationship and securing a long-term market usually required an enormous amount of patience. Developing special relationships with Soviet foreign trade officers of the Ministry of Foreign Trade was crucial.

Now, the country is changing and the whole of foreign business organization is being reshaped. The main reason for encouraging long-range strategies is the true opening of markets in the Soviet republics, with the introduction of market tools and convertibility of the ruble.

Another important long-term consideration is the development of trust between Soviet and foreign partners. Soviet negotiators would not appreciate a *veni, vidi, vici* approach from the foreign partner.

New Business Realities

Foreign companies will find that new business partners in great variety are available today in the Soviet area, the result of reforms in foreign business organization. The V/Os, described more fully in Chapter 5, are foreign trade organizations directly supervised by the Ministry of Foreign Trade. V/Os no longer monopolize foreign trade but instead act as trade agents. Soviet state enterprises or companies may use their services as middlemen, but more often the enterprises deal directly with their foreign partners. The nonstate sector (private and quasi-private business entities, including cooperatives, business associations, and joint ventures) is becoming more and more active in international business, as the advent of new business partners encourages entrepreneurial spirit and diversity.

Cultural variety is another business reality that international managers need to comprehend. Soviet business culture and negotiating style have been dominated by Moscow, but increasingly the unique historical and cultural traditions, work ethic, and peculiar legal and administrative environments of different parts of the Soviet Union are influencing business style.

A third aspect is that the negotiation-authorization relationship is changing. The endless negotiations typical of past contracts occurred because decision making and approval were usually parallel step-by-step processes. Negotiations with new Soviet partners may be much faster, more informal, and more successful, but allowance must be made for the red tape involved in obtaining authorization from regulatory agencies. Western negotiators who understand the situation will apply themselves to learning their new partners' capabilities and the relevant Soviet procedures. Doing so will give them a realistic view of the whole process of making a deal in the republics. Some tips for negotiating and doing business in the changing Soviet Union are listed in Table A-12.

Table A-12
SOME TIPS FOR DOING BUSINESS IN THE CHANGING USSR

- Learn the new environment.
- Know your partner's capabilities.
- Identify decision makers and evaluate power distances.
- Create confidence.
- Respect Soviet standards for documents.
- Be known.

The taxation climate may appear horrendous at first glance, but two things must be kept in mind. Draconian governmental fiscal policies are largely explained by the budget deficit. The Ministry of Finance is still guided by the old command-style philosophy, which denies the very idea of laissez-faire. However, the financial robbery of profit-making enterprises, dominant prior to 1987, no longer exists. The current taxation climate cannot be regarded as other than temporary as the transition to a market economy continues, especially when it is probable that the various republics of the USSR will be adopting more liberal tax policies.

Secondly, the practical absence of competition permits joint ventures and many other profit-oriented businesses to realize profit margins enormous by Western standards. After-tax profits in the Soviet Union today are much higher than in most competitive environments—it is almost impossible to find a company with foreign participation already in business in the Soviet Union that would like to withdraw.

The whole currency situation in the Soviet Union today is quite a mess. As of August 1991, three of the exchange rates were the "touristic" exchange rate, at $1 = R33; the market exchange rate, at $1 = R30-35; and the auction rate, at $1 = R35-50. As of December 31, 1991, these rates were $1 = R100-110. Two trends characterize the growing monetary crisis in the Soviet Union and clearly indicate that confidence in the ruble will not be restored until the government undertakes measures to reshape the banking and pricing systems and introduces a realistic official exchange rate. First, more and more domestic transactions, between both companies and individuals, are carried out in dollars. Second, various republics (such as Ukraine since November 1990) will take steps to protect their domestic market by adopting their own currencies.

For the ruble, 1992 may be a critical year. Unless the ruble is stabilized by the federal government, it faces a mortal threat. Its precarious situation means that the long debated issue of convertibility of the Soviet currency will have to be resolved much sooner than the government had expected.

Appendix B

The Historical Development of Accounting and Auditing in the Soviet Union

The impetus for the development of accounting in Russia was the emergence of an enormous state in Eastern Europe. During the more than 11 centuries that have elapsed since the inception of this state in A.D. 862, the evolution of its accounting system has reflected the many changes in its administrative and economic functions. Based on three historic turning points, the development of accounting in Russia can be divided into three periods: (1) 862-1700, development of a simple Russian accounting system; (2) 1700-1917, introduction and development of the European double entry accounting system; and (3) 1917-present, adaptation of the established European double entry accounting system to the requirements of a new socioeconomic order.

The First Period

The first period (862-1700) is closely related to the development of writing, the adoption of Christianity (988), the promulgation of the first code of laws, "Russkaya Pravada" (1016), and the influence of monastery accounting, which originated in the Eastern Roman Empire. This accounting system reached its peak in the 17th century. Three of its specific features are connected with socioeconomic aspects of the nation's development—the serf system, prevention of theft, and the combination of economy with unlimited waste.

The pervasiveness of the serf system led to serfs' being treated as units of accounting. An accounting instruction of the 18th century ordered, "In January take a census of all serfs of both sexes, male and female, with their belongings, noting the craft of each one, how many sowed this year for himself and for you (the landowner), taxes paid, gain or loss of persons in comparison with the previous census, the monthly allowance for each servant, what each is doing..." It is noteworthy that cattle, arable land plowed, and agricultural implements were counted against the number of serfs. Serfs were considered as persons financially responsible for the property entrusted to them by their landlords, and what a serf sowed for himself was only "allowable" to him from the landowner's income.

Accounting for material values had only one object: prevention of property theft. As in most Western European countries, accounting for income was separated from accounting for expenditures because this method provided more reliable control over the safety of property. The persons financially responsible for the property did not know the remaining balances. First, physical inventory was taken; then the accounting balances were determined.

The principal contradiction confronting the accounting of that period was the combination of economy, even miserliness, in details, with unlimited waste and embezzlement. More than half of the tax payments made by peasants did not reach the treasury but stayed in the pockets of the officials.

Major Obstacles to Accounting Development

During this period there were four major obstacles to successful development of accounting. One was dogmatism in thinking. An accounting bureaucrat year after year mindlessly copied the practices of his predecessors, following the rule: Don't do anything without an order.

A second obstacle was undeveloped legal consciousness. Gennady, the Archbishop of Novgorod, in 1647 wrote, "Our people are very simple-minded and cannot speak according to the books," with the result that in a court "there is no need for speeches." The purposes of courts were "only to execute, burn, and hang." Gennady could not understand that there was no need for a court to execute, burn, and hang. Another obstacle was the low level of literacy. "...Such is our country, we couldn't find anybody who is well educated," wrote the same Archbishop Gennady.

The fourth obstacle was the low level of mathematics. For example, letters stood for numerals adopted from the Eastern Roman Empire. Use of the "devil's" Arabic numerals was forbidden in order "not to lose Orthodoxy." The first book published with Arabic numerals in Moscow was confiscated because the unfamiliar numerals were considered to be "the devil's and against God's law." These factors greatly restricted the possibility of efficient bookkeeping.

The Second Period

The second period (1700-1917) was shaped by the reforms of Czar Peter I, aimed at making Russia more European. Market relations were established, followed by the abolition of serfdom in 1861, after which all aspects of the national economy were reformed.

Feverish work on the translation and publication of instructions adopted from the practice of Western European countries had already begun in the time of Peter I. This work on the economic development of the country intensified under Peter's successors. Highlights of the period were adoption of merchants' regulations (1727), establishment of the first bank in the country (1733), establishment of the first joint stock company (1757), and first translation from English to Russian of a book on the double entry accounting system, *The Key to Commerce*.

At the beginning of the 19th century, Russia's own accounting system came into being. It was based on the principles of double entry accounting, called the Italian system, but it included many original ideas. The most prominent representatives of this school were I.F. Valitsky and F.V. Ezersky.

Valitsky introduced two essential ideas. He divided a firm's balance sheet into two—the balance of principal activities and the balance of investments. This idea was adopted by the Soviet government. He also established an accounting system for the entire national economy, an idea partially used in the balance of the national economy of the Soviet Union.

Ezersky called his system "Russian" or "triple-form" bookkeeping because it consisted of three main aspects, each of which was subdivided into three parts. Transactions were recorded in three groups—sales, expenditures, and others—which he called "three step-up boxes." Three books were used as registers—the journal, the general ledger, and a report book used instead of the balance sheet. He compared these three books to a three-story building.

Ezersky's system used only three accounts—cash, assets, and capital—"three windows," as he called them. The ideas on which Ezersky based the "Russian form of bookkeeping" were ahead of their time and carried forward many new objectives that could not be met by old, traditional accounting methods.

The most important of Ezersky's ideas were:

- The possibility of computing the results of economic activities from the books at any time,
- Use of purchase price only for cost,
- Organic relationship of "analytic" and "synthetic" accounting,
- "Automatic" internal control by use of presupposed equality of control sums,
- Use of the "retail trade markup" (sales commission) account; Ezersky introduced in Russia methods of calculation of retail trade markups through average interest rates,
- Use of the perpetual system rather than the periodic system to track inventory,
- Determination of the "dead point."

The first Russian professional accounting journal appeared in 1888. During the period from 1783 to 1917, 1,356 books on accounting were published. The monetary reform of 1897 was a powerful new impulse to the economic development of the country. This reform introduced the gold ruble, which became convertible. Adoption of a tax on profits (the industrial tax) in 1898 and the requirements that balance sheets of joint stock companies be published resulted in many new tasks for accountants. As a whole these objectives were met successfully.

The Third Period

The third period (since 1917) has been characterized by radical social and economic changes. For the purposes of accounting history, this period began on July 27, 1918, when the Soviet of People's Commissars of Russia adopted and Lenin signed the decree on commercial books. But this document was only partially related to accounting. Radical changes in the organization of accounting began to take place in the fall of 1918.

The ideas of cost accounting and profit were rejected. "Extraordinary accounting" replaced commercial accounting. Its basic ideas were adopted officially in the *Basic Regulations on State Bookkeeping and Reporting* (1920). These regulations were consistent with ideas proclaimed by party and state leaders. The contents of the regulations may be summarized as follows:

- A natural gauge was used instead of a monetary one.
- The accounting process was organized not by factories (firms) but by local executive committees of people's deputies, which became the control offices of accounting.
- Material values were the only objects of accounting; all others were excluded.
- The use of registers was the only method of accounting permitted—the method was "set in stone."
- Cards were the only kind of register adopted; all other registers were declared to be "bourgeois prejudice."

Lenin stated four requirements for socialist accounting:

1. *Openness.* There is no place for commercial secrets; all registers must be accessible to everyone. Without this requirement a serious struggle against shortcomings and violations of law is impossible.
2. *Mass character.* All the adult population of the country must participate in the process of accounting.
3. *Responsibility.* Not only values and the process of their creation and circulation must be under control but also the activities of executives responsible for them.
4. *Simplicity.* Accounting must be clear to every literate man.

Of these four requirements, only the third survived. "Extraordinary accounting" was abolished in 1921. After the New Economic Policy (NEP) was initiated in the same year, the traditional accounting methods, practice, and principles gradually were reintroduced. While the NEP was in effect, joint stock companies and joint ventures with foreign firms were established, and foreigners were given the right to take concessions in Soviet territory. The use of commercial credit and notes became widespread.

In addition, the sphere of interest of accountants included three other areas during the first stage of the NEP.

1. *Organization of inflation accounting.* Two basic approaches were revaluation of items according to the price index and constant price accounting. In the latter approach, inflation was recorded in the Sales account. The purchase cost of goods was debited to this account, and the selling price of realized value was credited to the same account.

2. *Development of principles of balance construction and rules of balance interpretation* (financial analysis). The work of I. F. Scher, T. Gerstner, and A. Kalmas was influential in this area, amd the work of A.T. Rudanovsky and W.A. Blatov was distinguished among other original work. These authors created a special branch of accounting—"setting up balances"—which in turn became transformed into financial analysis.

3. *Accounting not in books but on cards.* This practice was a legacy of "extraordinary accounting" and was reinforced by the close economic relations with Germany then prevailing. The "card copying system" of bookkeeping became widespread.

Development After 1930

The NEP had begun to be eliminated by 1930, a process that had a serious negative effect on further development of accounting in the Soviet Union. First, almost all accountants were labeled as "bourgeois," and those who were accused of bringing harm to the national economy were physically eliminated. Second, the economic life of the country was simplified radically. Joint ventures and joint stock companies were stigmatized, as was commercial credit. Trusts were forced out, and management of factories passed to the commissariats (ministries). Factories remained formally responsible for their own accounting, with more and more official propaganda being devoted to the subject, but in reality, the more this self-accounting was advertised, the less it was implemented in practice.

Under the new conditions, the so-called "self-accounted factory" could not become bankrupt. Both profitability and nonprofitability were of symbolic character, and the main criterion for every factory became the plan. When a factory fulfilled its plan, losses were not taken into account, but if the plan was not fulfilled, even giant profits could not help the management escape punishment (including capital punishment).

Thus, fulfillment of plans became the most important objective of accounting. This approach fully corresponded to the principles of the "administrative command system" and led to the unique concept of socialist accounting, which retained the basic principles of the double entry system but introduced many original features.

For one thing, every aspect of accounting was proclaimed an integral part of national economic accounting. This national economic accounting itself comprised three kinds of accounting—bookkeeping, statistical accounting, and operational accounting—but their unity was mostly for show. Accounting was carried out in factories, and the information was taken from the system of accounts. Financial statements of factories were summarized first by central branch administrative boards and then by ministries. Thus, all the information required to be reported to the upper levels of the hierarchy was provided by accounting, which summarized but did not consolidate balance sheets. Statistical accounting included all forms required by the state offices of statistics. Operational accounting, which provided financial statistics on operations, was carried out by the factory for its own rather than external use. The peculiarity of the administrative command system was and is that all the subordinates always must present any information required, so, in practice, operational accounting was carried on by accountants who drew up different reports required by numerous higher administrators.

Centralized management of accounting had as its goal the unification of every sphere of accounting activity. Until recent times, the objective was complete uniformity, even as to the forms of all the documents. Special albums of forms were issued, and these forms were the only ones authorized for use anywhere in the country.

The chart of accounts was unified first of all through the branches of the national economy and in the last 30 years has been unified for most of these branches. This fact has been of major importance for the organization of all the economic information in the country and has implications for the way Soviet accountants think.

Accounting procedures were in the sphere of interest of the top level of the administrative hierarchy. Until 1949 the obligatory basic procedure for most factories was the "memorial order" form. It required that each document be accompanied by "order entries," which then were summarized in cross-section journals and, finally, in financial statements. In 1949, the "journal order" form of accounting, in which all credit entries in each account were recorded in separate journals along with debits of the accounts, began to be widely used. The results of the journals were collected monthly in the ledger. This procedure is still in use.

Centralization and decentralization are contrary poles of the organization of accounting. When accounting is centralized, all the accountants are in one place, and the whole process is carried on by enterprises (legal persons). When it is decentralized, affiliated branches of the central accounting office are organized in all structural subdivisions. Every affiliated branch of the central accounting office performs the complete accounting cycle and summarizes separate balance sheets. Central accounting offices then consolidate these separate balance sheets. The whole history of Soviet accounting during the last 50 years can be viewed as a process of jumping from one organizational form of accounting to the other.

"Norm" cost accounting and prime cost calculation are integral parts of industrial accounting. In theory they are close to standard cost accounting in Western economies, but their practical usage is limited by the instability of economic processes. As a result, more deviations than stable standard costs are computed beforehand. Revelations of such deviations only serve to make managers at different levels nervous.

Mechanization and automation began to become widespread in the 1930s, but the principal shortcoming of these processes was that they were instigated by people from the administrative command system, not by accountants. Only two objectives became universally and justly acknowledged: (1) recording of material values and (2) calculation of payroll (calculated in accordance with fulfilled order, not by time sheets).

The financial analysis that replaced "setting up balances" resulted in a situation in which principles of examination of the financial position of a factory lost their importance. They mostly were replaced by pure statistical exercises aimed at abstract and retrospective conclusions.

Modeling as a methodological approach emerged in the 1970s. Its objective was to replace the pure branch-oriented approach to accounting, still used today, with a technological and structural one, but the efforts in this direction were mainly theoretical.

In 1985, it became clear that the national economy was in deep depression and that the established accounting system was inadequate for actual economic processes and sometimes even distorted the real picture. As a result, the question of restructuring the national economy arose, as did the probably even more complicated objective of reorganization of the accounting system. It became apparent that, to further this objective, all the better practices accumulated by accountants of the past would have to be revived.

Peculiarities of Management Accounting Development

Even the term "management accounting" is foreign to the Russian accounting tradition, evoking absolutely inadequate associations in the minds of Soviet administrators and accountants. Management accounting often is considered to be cost accounting and prime-cost calculation of produced goods. In the Soviet Union cost accounting and prime-cost calculation never have been treated as an independent branch of accounting but only as an integral part of the whole accounting system. In fact, only financial accounting has existed in the Soviet Union. Cost accounting is nothing more than an analytical expansion of the Main Production account. The idea of two parallel accounting branches—financial and management—seems extravagant.

At the same time, cost accounting in the Soviet Union has a long history. It came into being in the Middle Ages in monasteries that used it to calculate the results of their economic activities.

The Early Days

In the 18th century, when Czar Peter I first began Russian industrialization, serious efforts were made to organize accounting for the production process. Accounting regulations adopted in the West were translated and published. The most important of these was *Regulations of Admiralty and Shipyard Management,* which appeared in 1772. Foreign accountants were brought to Russia. For example, the Dutchman V. L. Genhin organized excellent accounting for metallurgical factories in 1735.

Both state-owned and private industry were under strong government control. The government tried to force the management of both state-owned and private factories to make reports of prime-cost calculation of produced goods. The managers ignored this requirement, however, and accounting was limited to the recording of expenditures. Before adoption of the double entry system, the ideas of natural accounting procedures dominated industrial bookkeeping. Expenditures were registered as they were made. For example, if logs were purchased for 20 rubles, logs were entered on the books only as logs, without monetary value, and 20 rubles were deducted from cash.

At the same time, the registration of expenditures had the following characteristics: (1) complete registration in written form of all the facts of economic activity, (2) regular inventory taking and reporting, and (3) analytic nature of accounting data, providing in many cases the possibility of developing decisions.

Not until the second half of the 19th century was the double entry system adopted in practice in industrial enterprises. Its evolution passed through three stages:

1. The scheme of commercial bookkeeping was fully accepted. Such accounts as Production and Finished Goods did not appear in the chart of accounts. Finished goods were shown in the same account as materials, and information from the ledger could not answer the questions: What is the stock of materials? and What is the cost of manufactured goods?

2. Introduction of the Finished Goods account helped to solve these problems, but production costs remained outside of accounting procedure. Production costs were accounted for as cash deductions.

3. Introduction of the Production account made it possible to concentrate the accounting for all production costs and provided conditions for the prime-cost calculations. At the same time the problem of work-in-process valuation arose because the sum of actual expenditures depends on this valuation.

Russian accounting passed through these three stages during the second half of the 19th century. They also reflected the stages of the second Russian industrialization. Close economic ties to Germany strongly influenced the development of the ideas of cost accounting and prime-cost calculation. Simultaneously, proliferation of knowledge, establishment of the first Russian accounting magazine, *Scheto-Vodstvo* (Bookkeeping), in 1885, and the formation of societies promoting accounting led to the appearance of many original ideas in the sphere of cost accounting. For example, in 1872 S. F. Ivanov argued in favor of the Production account and showed the possibility of recording only direct costs in this account. He suggested placing all general (indirect) costs in a special account without correspondence and distribution among produced goods.

In 1888 E. E. Feldhausen regarded accounting as a method of management of industrial enterprises. This same system worked out in practice was called norm accounting. The gist of this system was that all the expenses were estimated by a commission of experts once every 10 years, and on the basis of this estimate, the commission fixed norm rates. Accounting offices registered only deviations from these rates and showed them on the Gains and Losses account.

The cost structure according to norm accounting was as follows: materials + fuel + salaries - cost of byproducts + defects and spoilage = factory cost + percentage of direct expenses distributed in proportion to technical costs = commercial price.

Another new idea, the original calculation method, was devised by L.I. Gomberg in 1895. The cost of the remainder of production (waste) and sum of gross profits were deducted from sales to estimate the total expenses of production of the principal products. Then the sum of expenses was deducted from sales to estimate the net profit realized from the principal products. This sum was divided by the quantity of calculated units to compute the profit per unit. Profit was deducted from the cost of goods of each type in calculation (selling price x quantity of goods sold) to calculate the cost per unit of each type. These operations can be expressed with the formula shown in Table B-1.

Approaches adopted from Germany were dominant in this period before the revolution because they were promoted by R.Y. Weitzman. Accounting for expenses was concentrated in the Main Production account. Product or order was assumed as a calculated unit. Indirect expenses were distributed in proportion to direct labor included in the expenses incurred in producing each individual finished product or order. It was assumed that value was created by labor, so indirect expenses had to be covered in proportion to the labor involved, and the total expenses had to be divided by the number of calculated units of this product. This approach has been in use since before the revolution up to the present.

After the Revolution

Revolution and civil war caused gigantic losses in the national economy, which could not but be reflected in the country's accounting. On July 27, 1918, the Soviet of People's Commissars of Russia adopted a decree on commercial books, which as a whole assumed a traditional scheme of accounting. As the process of nationalization of factories and socialization of the economy progressed, however, directive bodies rejected the monetary unit as a unit of measurement and prime-cost calculation.

The New Economic Policy (NEP) restored traditional accounting principles. On August 12, 1921, the Council on Economy and Defense issued the Decree on Basic Measures to Reconstruct Large-Scale Industry and Develop Production, which restored accounting on the basis of inventory sheets, valuation of inventory assets in gold rubles (based on the year 1914), and valuation of materials on the basis of London market prices. The practice of centralizing accounting at the regional level began to shift to decentralization.

In 1923 the party leadership began to stress the necessity of calculation. In that year organized systematic prime-cost calculation was introduced by the Order of the All-Union Council on National Economy No. 406. From that

Table B-1
GOMBERG'S FORMULA

$$A - W - B = C \tag{1}$$
$$A - C = P \tag{2}$$

$$\frac{P}{\Sigma q} = a \tag{3}$$

$$\left. \begin{array}{l} (pq)_1 = (aq)_1 = B_1 \\ (pq)_N = (aq)_n = B_N \end{array} \right\} \tag{4}$$

and besides $\displaystyle\sum_{i=1}^{N} B_1 = C \quad \sum_{i=1}^{N} a_i = p$

and always $p < B$

A = total sales revenue from selling main finished products
W = wastes during production process

B = gross profit
C = cost of main finished products
P = gross profit from sales of main finished products
q = calculated units

$\displaystyle\sum_{c-1}^{N} q_1$ = sum of calculated units

a = profit per calculated unit
n = number of types of calculated units/types of finished
        products
p = selling price
b = cost of unit of realized product

moment, calculation assumed top priority as an accounting objective. The tendency toward greater complexity and expansion of prime-cost calculation developed as complicated systems were elaborated.

The Order of the All-Union Council on National Economy issued on October 1, 1929, introduced obligatory monthly calculation for products manufactured by factories. Reports on the calculations had to be presented not later than the 15th to 20th day of the month following the current period, while annual and seasonal reports were due within a month after the current month. Monthly reports on factory and commercial (factory prime cost plus expenses on realization) prime costs also were required.

Such close attention from the party and state was not surprising. An economic coup took place, the NEP was canceled, and the country returned to the principles of military communism, but the leadership did not like to recognize that fact and tried to cover up its actions by complicating and muddling the accounting system.

In 1931 I.V. Stalin issued an order "to increase the rate of industrial accumulation of capital." Decreasing prime costs was considered most seriously as a source of industrial accumulation. This decrease was stimulated by all the methods available—replacing raw materials then in use with cheaper ones, decreasing depreciation allowances, decreasing wage rates, and so forth. Apparent decreases in costs were realized by debiting some expenses to Gains and Losses instead of costs.

The economic role of prime-cost calculation also was apparent in the substantial decrease in prices. Stalin thought that prices must be determined by costs, that is, materialized socially necessary labor. Price as monetary expression of cost was treated as inversely proportional to labor efficiency—the higher the labor efficiency the lower the costs, making it possible for government to decrease prices. It was not by chance that from 1932 forward enterprises were required by plan to decrease costs.

The early 1930s also were marked by a very important event—the introduction of norm accounting, which came from three sources:

1. The experience of E.E. Feldhausen with norm reporting mentioned above;
2. The suggestion of A.P. Rudanovsky that two costs be calculated—one based on actual expenses, the other the norm cost—with their difference determining the commercial policy of the factory; and
3. The acquaintance of Soviet accountants with the standard cost system, which had become familiar to them through the works of Charles Harrison, translated into Russian. Norm accounting was put into practice for the first time in 1930 at the Hammer and Sickle factory in Kharkov.

Two contradictory tendencies characterized the postwar period: (1) the requirement for absolute precision in the calculation of costs and (2) the tendency to simplify accounting. The former was registered in the *Basic Regulations on*

Planning, Accounting, and Cost Calculation of Industrial Products issued in 1955 by the Ministry of Finance of the Soviet Union and the Central Statistics Committee. The latter tendency was apparent in the widespread usage of the "pool" method.

Organizing the Soviets (councils) of People's Enterprises (1957-1965) was an effort to decentralize accounting methodology and encourage local initiative. At that time the organization of accounting was differentiated between geographical areas (regions) rather than branches of industry. Each region had its own Soviet of People's Enterprises with its own accounting departments that determined accounting procedures.

With the economic reform of 1965, enterprises acquired some additional rights. Norm accounting was strengthened, but despite forced popularization, this method did not become dominant in Soviet industry. By the end of the 1960s, however, many factories used some elements of it. Since then, no other radical changes in the theory and practice of cost accounting and cost calculation have occurred.

Viewing the events associated with the formation of the principles of cost accounting and cost calculation in the Soviet Union, we can formulate those principles as follows:

- Highly centralized control of methodology,
- Increasing uniformity in methods of calculation and presentation of information on cost calculation,
- Treatment of cost accounting as an integral part of financial accounting,
- Integration of cost accounting with cost calculation (cost calculation as a necessary consequence of cost accounting), and
- Precision of calculated results as the ideal.

Today cost accounting and cost calculation are in crisis, as existing methods do not adequately reflect the various kinds of ownership that are appearing in the course of economic reform. Changes must take place to meet the needs of the numerous joint ventures and joint stock companies that are being established in the Soviet Union.

The Development and Status of Auditing

Auditing, as the term is understood in the West, has never existed in Russia or the USSR. Throughout the history of Russia, the pervasive power of the state and the absence of private ownership (or the very strict limits on it) have made the emergence of an auditing profession impossible. The notion of an independent controller is absolutely alien to the consciousness of people living in the eastern European plains and northern Asia. They do understand that their performance must be monitored, but they believe that the evaluator should report what he is told, rather than what he thinks or has discovered about an organization's activities.

Nor do government officials have any use for independent auditors. They regard all subordinate enterprises as being under their full control and would not want an outsider to investigate their operations. The independent auditor is a stranger who meddles in other people's affairs. Because Russia is a country of administrative rather than civil law, where vertical ties have always dominated over horizontal ones, the concepts of "control" and "controller" are used instead of "audit" and "auditor." Also the term "revision" (inspection) is widely used. Inspection usually is understood as documentary verification, and an inspector (revisor) is an accountant who performs the inspection. Inspection is a part of control, and an inspector is a kind of controller. All kinds of control and inspection always have been governmental functions in this country.

The Background

Organization of systematic control was accomplished in the 17th century when Prikaz (Ministry of Calculation Affairs) was formed under Czar Alexei Mikailovich. Prikaz employees exercised control over calculation (accounting) ledgers of different organizations, state investments in the custody of officials, and withdrawals of unused assets in the state budget. For an inspection by Prikaz, officials from the province with all their ledgers and documentary evidence were called to Moscow.

It is worth mentioning that while officials of the Ministry of Calculation Affairs were checking ledgers and other documents in Moscow, other officials might at the same time be taking inventory in the province. This second inspection (inventory) was regarded as more important than the first (documentary inspection).

The system of state control was very ineffectual, however. Historians contend that more than half of the peasants' payments due under the state budget went into the pockets of officials. Reforms of Peter I (the Great) and his followers resulted in adaptation of the state control function to a new pseudo-European system.

A new phase began in 1811 when the principal agency of state accounts inspection was organized under the influence of the great reformer, Speransky. Later this office was renamed the Ministry of State Control. The activities of V. A. Tatarinov in the 1860s promoted adoption of the best examples of Western European practice and led to formation of the main principles of control, which to a certain extent exist today.

Control over some institutions was forbidden, thereby putting limits on the system of state control. For example, the very liberal law of 1892 stipulated that certain organizations were exempt from state inspection:

- Ministry of Court,

- Personal Office (Chancellory) of His Imperial Majesty,
- Personal Office (Chancellory) of His Imperial Majesty for Tsarina Maria's Institutions,
- State Credit Agencies and the Credit Office,
- Holy Synod for Special Funds allocated in the budget for ecclesiastical educational institutions,
- All ministries concerning appropriations to programs known to His Imperial Majesty,
- To some extent, other offices.

At the very end of the 19th century, some prominent Russian statesmen tried to create the Institution of Barrister Accountants and developed all the necessary statutory documents, but their initiative found support neither in the government nor from the public nor among professionals. The government was afraid of competition from independent professional groups of accountants and inspectors. The public was afraid of additional expense because as one accountant put it, "We have no money for real needs but only for disgraceful things." Professional groups skeptical that the emergence of an accountancy elite could improve the overall social and material position of accountants believed that an "accounting aristocracy" would appear deeply alien to the ideas and tastes of the Russian people. The revolution had some influence on the fate of control in Russia, but most of the changes were of a structural character.

On January 18, 1918, Lenin signed the Decree of People's Commissars' Council "on creation of a central control board and local commissions," and on May 9, 1918, the People's Commissariat (Board) of State Control was created. The functions of the board were to provide for the security of cash and other assets. On that date (May 9, 1918) began the history of the institutions that control the economic activities of all Soviet enterprises.

Lenin wrote: "The goals of control are twofold: the simple inspection of inventories, stocks, and products; and the most complex, control of correctness of work . . . control of the work organization system: guarantee of the highest efficiency, and so forth." (V. I. Lenin, *Collected Works*, V. 37, p. 339.)

All the practical work fell in line with this directive. First of all, assets (inventory) were inspected to assure safekeeping. Second, activities were analyzed to determine their economic effectiveness. In spite of the theories of economists, the effectiveness of work was measured by the fulfillment of the state plan. The more the state plan was exceeded, the better the performance, but if performance fell short of the plan, it was regarded as a state crime. From the 1930s to the 1980s, in many cases the data on fulfillment of plans were distorted. The attention of inspectors was directed chiefly to this phenomenon.

In the USSR, a complex and multistructural system of control institutions existed and often competed with and hindered each other. The Committee of People's Control of the USSR, which performs the functions of the Ministry of State Control, exercised intersectoral state control. Its structure is very broad, and its sphere of influence encompasses diverse activities, from the economic activity of enterprises to the analysis of quorums at the meetings of advisory boards. However, in 1990 some republics, including Russia and Ukraine, terminated the activities of the Committee of People's Control and dismissed its bodies.

The branches of the Ministry of Finance of the USSR, as well as the ministries of finance of the individual republics, pursue fiscal purposes related to taxation. These ministries also define the methodology of accounting, which determines the financial results (gains and losses). The regulations of the republican and federal ministries are contradictory. Republican bodies refer to the sovereignty declared by their supreme soviets and therefore affirm the primacy of republican laws over those of the USSR, but the Ministry of Finance of the USSR proceeds from the assumption that the federal government has priority in questions of foreign policy, defense, and finance. Where finance is concerned, the boundary between federal and republican jurisdiction remains unclear and intricate. Sometimes local authorities refer to the normative documents that are more beneficial for taxpayers and wage earners at the moment. As a punishment, financial branches use the compulsory confiscation of the assets of enterprises.

State and commercial banks exercise control only if they are creditors of the enterprise, but sometimes this control may take an extraordinary form. For example, a bank inspector may arrive at a trade company and begin to check its inventory, visit stocks, and try to find out whether the management of the company is hiding the goods that are in short supply. Nowadays banks can use as sanctions measures that were not available to them before: they can impose fines, raise the interest rate, and close credit lines.

At both the federal and republican levels are branches of a state committee on quality control and standards, although there are some contradictions among them. They may take low-quality or irregularly produced goods out of circulation. The persons found guilty usually are fined.

Governmental agencies for automobile inspection, sanitary inspection, and fire inspection also exercise control, and a very tight control over the security of property is maintained by the militia bodies of the Ministry of the Interior. A department devoted to the struggle against theft of socialist property investigates cases of theft, embezzlement, and misuse of state property.

Departmental (sectoral) control is exercised on both the interdepartmental and intercompany levels. The first gives special control-inspection authority to industrial ministries, state committees, state industrial consolidations, and sectoral consolidations. The second provides for the formation of special control-inspection groups at the levels of the enterprises, consolidations, associations, or concerns. Throughout the history of the USSR, the intercompany levels were subordinate to the chief accountant or to the director of the enterprise. In the first case, the chief accountant is regarded as the principal controller. In the second case, the director of the company officially bears the responsibility for all control work although the chief accountant is still responsible for financial discipline and for security of assets and cash. In practice, control and inspection services remain subordinate to the chief accountant. The usual punishments resulting from interdepartmental and intercompany inspections are administrative measures such as fees, warnings, or dismissal.

Public control takes the form of "workers' control" by trade unions and control groups formed by municipal bodies for special inspections. For example, these groups may check stores for unauthorized price increases or hidden goods that the administrators of the shops do not sell for some reason. Punishment in this case may be of an administrative or even criminal type. Employees of the enterprise are permitted to exercise control, and according to Soviet law on "working collectives," they can request a report from the administration on its activities. Councils of working collectives can issue orders to the administration resulting from inspections.

The role of trade unions must be especially stressed. Trade unions control the use of human resources, workplace discipline, work security, and improvement of working conditions. Representatives of trade unions are required to participate in production-related meetings.

Finally, organizations of court-accounting experts must be mentioned, such as the Bureau of Court-Accounting Expertise. Expert witnesses could be called to testify by investigative bodies or by a court. Before the revolution, expert witnesses were authorized for both the prosecution and the defense, creating difficulties for the work of the court. In the Soviet judicial system, experts are enlisted by courts to aid in impartial fact-finding rather than by attorneys representing one side in an adversarial proceeding. As a rule, attorneys cannot reject the conclusions of experts. Accounting experts must pass tests of their knowledge once every five years to be certified as expert witnesses.

In addition to the numerous state control institutions, collectives form control bodies, a situation that causes instability in the functioning of enterprises. Because there is no coordination of the activities of all these bodies, any enterprise can be in a state of constant inspection, and some inspectors could approve its activities while others disapprove.

The many centuries of experience in control and inspection in this country have led to the following conclusions:

1. The objects of control are not organizations but people—first of all administrators and then people responsible for assets. If these people are good from the point of view of control bodies or bodies authorized to exercise control, the results of inspection will be favorable. Otherwise, inspectors face the very difficult task of finding in normative documents specific rules that have been violated, and then punishing the offenders according to law. The remaining conclusions follow logically from this one.

2. Inspectors analyze the substance of a violation, not its form. The inspector must not only understand the situation at the enterprise but determine who was in control and what the purpose of the inspection is. The objective is not to state

that laws have or have not been violated but to help the administrator correct the error or to dismiss him. If company management enjoys the confidence of officials, it need not fear inspection; the moral intent is more important than the result of the infraction.

3. As the object of control is a person, his or her personal attitudes observed by the inspector, such as style of dress, personal property, what cigarettes he or she smokes, his or her use of alcoholic beverages, and so forth, are more significant than documents.

4. State assets are in the custody of persons, and therefore inventory taking is more important than documentary inspection.

5. Respectability of control envisages its definition as a science. A special theory of financial and economic control was created in Russia and the Soviet Union, based on an old idea of the Italian accountant, Fabio Sesta (1845-1923), about the division of control into preliminary, operating, and subsequent aspects. This idea colors almost all discourses on accounting and control.

6. Confidentiality is combined with openness. Deep distrust of managers is the basis of inspection. It is widely believed that administrators do not do the work with which they are charged, that in the best case they neglect their duties and in the worst case they abuse the state's property. Only by confronting an administrator unaware can one see his or her true face. Hence, the element of surprise is highly valued.

7. The complex nature of control envisages inspection of all sides of the economic activity of the enterprise. This rule usually does not work in real life and causes the dispersion of inspection forces.

8. Lenin predicted the mass character of control. He thought that under socialism the entire adult population of the country would be engaged in control. Until recently, two aphorisms were widely heard: "Socialism is control" (Lenin) and "Communism is control squared" (folk saying). The mass character of control is achieved when the inspector finds additional sources of information about possible bad attitudes or acts of persons under inspection. To accomplish this objective, all employees of the enterprise are informed about the inspection beforehand, with the inspectors' telephone numbers publicized and special inspectors' mailboxes installed. Any employee can provide inspectors with revelations about any other employee at the enterprise.

With the advent of *perestroika*, the methods of control and inspection are becoming more democratic. First, auditing companies were launched. The Soviet firm Inaudit was created for control of joint ventures, and such international accounting firms as Arthur Andersen, Coopers & Lybrand, Deloitte & Touche, Ernst & Young, KPMG Peat Marwick, and Price Waterhouse have moved into the Soviet republics. But auditing as an independent control institution is still absent. Foreign companies as a rule provide consulting services, training, and internal inspection.

Accounting Education and Research in the Soviet Union

This appendix describes both the prevailing accounting educational structure in the former Soviet Union and the ways in which accounting education, training, and research need to be changed—and adapted—to serve the new socio-economic requirements of the republics.

Current System of Training and Research

Accounting education and training in the Soviet Union currently are subject to considerable evaluation and restructuring. We have described the current system first, to give an idea of what is involved in the educational process for training accountants. Accounting education in the republics is conducted at universities, colleges, and vocational schools, in specialized courses, and directly at the workplace.

Comprehensive Studies

The most comprehensive studies take place at universities and other institutions of higher education. In the Soviet Union 150 such schools have accounting faculties; anyone with 10 years of secondary education can enroll after passing entrance exams. No tuition is charged for the five-year degree program. In fact, most students are paid allowances by the state and are housed in dormitories for nominal fees. No more than 6% of students leave the universities before graduating.

The prestige of accounting has been extremely low in the USSR. In the past, secondary school graduates rated it 91st of 92 professions. Therefore, university graduates receive degrees with their specialty shown as "economist"; only a special code in the degree—06.08.04.08—indicates that the graduate's field is accounting.

During their five years (10 semesters) of study, students must pass examinations in the following courses:

Courses	Classwork Hours
1. Twentieth-Century Political History	250
2. Political Economy	482

41.	Accounting in Automated Managerial Systems	76
42.	Secretarial Administration and Business Correspondence	80
43.	Foreign Economic Operations	78

The following courses also are available:

1.	Foreign Language(s)	124
2.	History and Theory of World Cultures	36
3.	Modern Forms of Cooperation	88
4.	Psychology and Professional Ethics	36
5.	Scientific Atheism	26
6.	Physical Training (required for all students who are not certified as having health problems; strangely enough, future accountants spend more time on this than on accounting itself)	604

At the end of the five-year program, each student has to prepare a graduate (diploma) study in the field of accounting. University studies can be pursued on a full-time basis in daytime courses or part-time through evening classes and by correspondence (the latter making it possible to combine work and study). The best universities offer courses of continuing education for practitioners who already have their university degrees.

Basic Required Knowledge

Accountants with higher education are required at a minimum to know:

1. Theory and methods of research to solve various accounting, controlling, planning, and financing problems;
2. Methodology for planning and forecasting major indicators of an enterprise's performance, accounting techniques, and preparation of reports;
3. Economic and technological processes and the organizational structure of enterprises in different branches of the economy, as well as mathematical models and their applications;
4. Modern means of data processing, including electronic data processing;
5. The basics of law and of labor and environmental protection.

The accountant with a higher education should be able to:

1. Organize the accounting process and financial control of enterprises based on different types of property;
2. Use and increase modern accounting knowledge;
3. Ensure that cash and materials are used legitimately;

4. Prepare timely reports and controlling documents;

5. Set up instructions and rules to improve the organization of accounting within an enterprise;

6. Control the organization and the techniques of accounting within an enterprise;

7. Provide expertise related to settlement of commercial disputes;

8. Introduce electronic data processing systems;

9. Make independent decisions on all issues of accounting and control;

10. Organize continuing education of subordinate employees;

11. Conduct research and present analytical papers.

Higher education provides not only professional skills but also career opportunities. A university graduate can be appointed chief accountant or deputy to the chief accountant, accounting analyst, revisor (auditor), expert in law-enforcing agencies, or professor of accounting at vocational training schools or courses. Those gifted in research can continue with postgraduate studies and later work in universities or research institutes.

Specialized Accounting Courses

The State Committee on Statistics supervises a broad network of specialized accounting courses. Attending such courses enhances skills and provides job opportunities. In recent years, the growing prestige and the increasing importance of the accounting profession have led to a revival of private accounting courses, which were widespread before the 1917 revolution. These courses are being organized by cooperative and other private or semiprivate firms and provide, for a fee, the accounting knowledge necessary under market conditions.

Vocational Training Schools

After eight or 10 years of secondary school, a young person may decide to enter one of the 750 vocational training schools in the Soviet Union. Training will last either two or three years.

Earning a vocational training school diploma also brings significant job opportunities, ranging from inventory accountant to inspector for an accounting group to task supervisor. Graduation with honors from such a school provides immediate opportunity to enter a university for daytime courses. With an ordinary vocational training school diploma, a person can attend evening courses or take correspondence courses from a university.

Education in the Workplace

Anyone with basic accounting education who is willing to learn accountancy can start working in an accounting department as a trainee. Such work provides some basic empirical knowledge. This education can be supplemented later by more in-depth studies in one of the forms described above.

Research Work

The training of accounting specialists often is combined with research concentrated in universities and institutes. The Ministry of Finance of the USSR also supervised a specialized research center. Any Soviet accounting professor could conduct research in a specific field. Research topics are divided into those funded by the state budget and those funded by interested enterprises. The former topics are approved by the relevant ministries and universities, and the research constitutes a part of the faculty member's regular job. The latter are conducted with special task groups for extra pay from funds obtained from customers.

The results of accounting research are implemented in the form of regulations and instructions, and the most important results are published in monographs, textbooks, *Accounting* (a journal with nationwide circulation), and other publications.

Reforms in Accounting Education

The republics have clearly recognized the importance of sound accounting education, an area that had been much neglected.

The following organizational structure is envisioned for the training of accountants:

- Practical training and study of accounting techniques (under experienced supervision at a firm) for young employees;
- A network of courses (studies held both at employer organizations and in class sessions);
- Technical school training (professional schools can provide a sizable number of accountants);
- Academic institutes with strict admission requirements both for entry and during the process of study.

One way to enhance accounting education efficiently might be to prepare an *accounting manpower inventory* and *accounting development plan* that would set forth the future needs of the various areas of accounting and auditing. Because of the great shortage of educators and trainers, the development of accounting training centers and the types of updating to be undertaken could be based on the manpower needs of various sectors of the economy. In this regard, too, the areas requiring greater concentration and more text materials may have to be spelled out. For example, considerably more training might be needed in electronic data processing (EDP) systems and procedures, management accounting, computer auditing, and related areas. The teaching of accounting at institutes and universities could benefit by the case method approach, and closer contacts with enterprises and governmental departments also could give students some sound practical exposure. Good interaction between the educational institutions and the Association of Accountants would be beneficial, and international accounting firms might be helpful in conducting certain courses and supplying course materials. Specialties to be covered in accounting also might be appraised and set forth. Methods to be used for continuing accounting education also need to be addressed specifically.

As part of the accounting planning framework, the deficiencies in accounting and auditing education and research should be described in detail. International and regional development agencies (such as the UN, the World Bank, IMF, and the European Bank for Reconstruction and Development) might review these areas in regard to technical and financial assistance. In essence, such an accounting planning framework may constitute the basis for educational feasibility studies to be submitted to international and regional development agencies and for bilateral support and cooperative requirements.

Internally, a manpower inventory could serve as a framework for resource programming and capital investment and help shape educational directions. Such a comprehensive accounting development program should fit existing and projected needs in: (1) manpower development, including foreign scholarships; (2) expatriate manpower needs; (3) teaching aids and materials; (4) building requirements; (5) short-course programs, for instance, travel cost; (6) research and translation funding; and (7) miscellaneous elements.

The contemplated redirection of accounting and auditing clearly will pose a considerable strain on the educational and training process and institutions. As accounting has not in the past been adequately recognized as a desirable field of learning and practice because of its dogmatic methods and statistical orientation, a new emphasis may have to be put on educational aspects of accounting. The existing training institutes may have to be reoriented, and new directions for education and training, including teacher training, may have to be offered. A number of institutes, for example, Institute of Commerce and Economics (LESTI) in St. Petersburg (Leningrad), already have taken a new approach. This whole reorientation process needs careful appraisal in the context of Soviet socioeconomic objectives, taking into account such factors as:

- The existing setup and teaching materials,
- The desired direction of various fields of accounting,
- Text materials to be translated and developed,
- Updating and reorienting existing and new faculty,
- Funding needs to execute the new direction,
- Desired foreign technical assistance,
- Physical requirements, including teaching aids.

Under the auspices of the United Nations Centre for Transnational Corporations (UNCTC) and with the direct involvement of the Center for International Accounting Development of The University of Texas at Dallas (UTD), various training programs have been developed (training students, practitioners, and above all, accounting faculty) and are being executed. However, more profound and continuing programs need to be in place to update and reorient the existing and new accounting faculty. Funding from various foundations is being sought to carry out a coherent long-term accounting development program. In our opinion, this program should have high priority. A set of course programs and modules geared toward specific examinations to identify qualified candidates for certificates or diplomas needs to be developed for training accountants at various levels. As discussed above, specialization qualifications also need to be developed, and specific examinations should be offered with special designations. Also, continuing education materials and requirements may have to be generated. As for some specific educational/training activities to be pursued, the following are suggested:

1. Elaborate new conceptual frameworks and basic curricula for new guidelines in accounting education need to be implemented, because former narrow specialization for training accountants by sectors of economy is losing its importance.

2. The conceptual framework for the new curricula should include training in distinct areas such as financial accounting, managerial accounting, and auditing (as opposed to existing accounting specialization by accounting branches of the economy).

3. The role and scope of training of accountants in legal issues and mechanisms of the market economy should be increased dramatically, and accountants should acquire a deeper understanding of international economic activities and their accounting implications.

4. Accounting training/education needs to be enhanced for three main categories: students, practitioners, and teachers. Further differentiation is needed in training accountants and bookkeepers for specific functions and levels of responsibility.

5. Case studies, a powerful educational tool, should be used and applied in teaching.

6. Leading Western and international accounting texts and cases should be translated from English, French, German, and other Western languages for Soviet educational and practice purposes. Domestic authors should be stimulated as well to prepare textbooks.

Research and Development

The further development of accounting education and training in the various areas should go hand in hand with research covering the areas and topics of accounting to be developed. Faculty at the various institutions should be able to carry out such research and should write scholarly and applied materials, textbooks, and the like. This process may require a complete educational reorientation.

The amount of research in accounting and auditing has been relatively limited (except for the work of certain scholars), partially because of the lack of funding but also because accounting has not been considered a discipline of high standing. Undoubtedly this attitude is and will be changing, and accounting research, both applied and theoretical, will be brought up-to-date. Applied research deals, for example, with the development of accounting and auditing standards, a conceptual accounting framework, transfer pricing, and accounting for price changes, whereas the more theoretical, basic accounting research should delve into the normative and conceptual, as well as historical, aspects of accounting.

The organizational framework for accounting in the Soviet Union also needs to be researched. The objective would be to study current problems and promote the development of accounting and auditing, integrating theory and practice. In the past, methodology was based on both dialectical and historical materialism. A fundamental task now is to establish a framework of accounting and auditing theory and methodology adapted to the new economic order and circumstances.

Presumably, the Association of Accountants could play a vital role in the development and distribution of research materials and bulletins devised for this purpose. The focus of such research materials should be well thought through, and their relevance should be outlined in a funding request. Updated materials also should be developed for accountants who may need reorientation and may well be required to pass new qualifying examinations.

Research methodology of both an inductive and a deductive nature, and its linkage with other disciplines (such as behavioral science, quantitative methods, and information systems), might need to be stimulated further, preferably also with extensive outside aid. The current research may well be more prescriptive, involving profound research methodologies. The research also should be linked to the developmental aspects of accounting and auditing because the results are to be disseminated for educational and training purposes.

Among the tasks of the Soviet associations would be motivating research, summarizing past experiences to serve the economy, investigating new requirements and problems, carrying out international exchanges, and fostering friendly relations with foreign organizations. A nationwide survey—an inventory—also could be useful to set forth the need for, and ranking of, accounting information for enterprise management; to explore the needs of managers, and to combine micro- and macroeconomic requirements effectively.

Many accounting issues still must be resolved, and the training and education of Soviet accountants and auditors demand extensive appraisal and foreign technical assistance, especially initially. We have offered some suggestions for expediting the transformation process for Soviet accounting. Because accounting traditionally was not recognized as a separate discipline in the Soviet Union but was taught in conjunction with economics and finance, the development of a specific accounting concentration with distinct areas of knowledge may be necessary. Furthermore, the trend toward a market economy requires a distinct reorientation, including accounting for capital market institutions (stock exchange), costing for pricing, performance measurement, and so forth. Such an orientation also will be needed for effectively appraising the financial activities of prevailing state enterprises and outlining better courses of action to follow (in the form of cost-benefit/effectiveness appraisals).

Western Curricula for Training Soviet Students and Academics

An important underlying element in improving accounting in the USSR is the development of curricula for educating/training students, practitioners, and academics in Western accounting. Several training programs were developed jointly by Soviet academics, practitioners, the United Nations Centre for Transnational Corporations, and Western academics, especially at the Center for International Accounting of The University of Texas at Dallas.

The training programs cover a mixture of international and Soviet accounting, so that the focus will be on *comparative* aspects. A series of eight modules within those programs cover such specifics as: comparative evaluation of the historical development of accounting in centrally planned and Western economies; legal and accounting aspects of joint ventures; financial accounting, disclosure, and reporting; management/cost accounting; corporate finance; financial and operational auditing; taxation; accounting information systems; and critical issues in international accounting and auditing.

Three types of training programs were developed.

1. An academic program for students in their last year of studies at institutions of higher learning, covering approximately 60 hours of class work spread over the semester or in the form of an intensive two- to three-week concentrated seminar. International accounting instructors teach two-thirds of the class. They are highly qualified certified public or chartered accountants from major internationally recognized accounting firms familiar with educational aspects of the subject. The other one-third is taught by national accounting instructors/professors. At the end of the course, to be offered twice by foreign accounting firms, the Soviet instructors will be teaching this program on their own. Approximately two-thirds of the sessions center on international accounting and one-third on accounting elements of centrally planned economies, on a comparative basis. In essence, therefore, the sessions are of a comparative nature with a focus on aspects of joint ventures. As part of the program, textbooks are being translated into Russian, and other study materials are being developed.

To date, the following institutions in the USSR have participated: Moscow Plekhanov Institute of National Economy; Moscow Finance Institute; Moscow

State University; Kiev State University; Leningrad Institute of Soviet Trade; and Moscow State Institute for International Relations. The following international accounting firms have provided pro bono instructors: Arthur Andersen, Coopers & Lybrand, Deloitte & Touche, Ernst & Young, KPMG Peat Marwick, and Price Waterhouse. Approximately 30 students at each institution participated in the first program, offered at different times at each institution.

2. Short-term intensive programs for practitioners, in the form of workshops, covering two weeks with six class hours per day. The workshops essentially conform to the same pattern as the university program above, except for the following:

- More attention will be given to practical versus conceptual aspects and issues;
- Somewhat less study material will be covered, so that topics will have to be selected more carefully. This program will be offered at two or three locations in the USSR. The purpose of the workshops is to update and retrain practitioners in state enterprises, the administration, and government in the requirements of accounting and auditing for joint venture operations.

3. Program of "training the teachers," a full-time program for professors and educators spread over an entire semester (18 weeks). This program is meant to update accounting-oriented faculty at academic institutions in concepts, standards, procedures, and practices of international accounting. It is intended for instructors in accounting, auditing, and related areas. The program is structured along lines similar to the outlined curriculum for the university course. The contents of the modules will, however, be much more elaborate.

The program for "training the teachers" would have the following specific features and requirements:

- Approximately 120 accounting instructors will be selected to participate in the program, with extensive course materials, textbooks, and guidelines for study (in English) made available to each participant. Those materials are to be selected, and produced, by UNCTC/UTD.
- The instructors selected are expected to spend an entire academic semester (12-18 weeks) on the course materials and to complete the course requirements in a satisfactory way. At the end of the semester, a comprehensive two-day examination will ascertain the instructors' level of knowledge in the module areas. After the completion of the program, 20 to 40 participants will be selected to go to Western Europe, the United States, or Canada for an eight- to nine-week period or possibly an entire semester (three or four months) for additional studies to acquire specific insight and knowledge in particular aspects and elements of international accounting.

This latter program, "training the teachers," is expected to start during the fall of 1992 in the USSR. Furthermore, it is anticipated that a number of selected Soviet academics could spend three or four months in Western European countries or North America to become familiar with Western accounting and auditing norms and practices. They will undergo a combination of training and updating in practice, at accounting firms or industry, and at academic institutions.

Prospects in Education and Training

Progress in Auditing Education and Training

Facing the task of auditing several hundred thousand business enterprises (which annually use and generate enormous amounts of wealth) and numerous widely scattered nonprofit entities, the Soviet Union needs a great many competent external and internal auditors. In addition, a large number of professional certified public accountants, certified management accountants, chartered accountants, and other such persons are needed to answer the increasing demand for professional accounting services. In this regard, management services, including the building of better accounting systems and procedures, will be an urgent need.

It is imperative to accelerate the development of accounting and auditing education and training to a degree never seen before. The following trends can be noted:

1. Establishment of more accounting and auditing training centers and schools, and auditing concentrations in related departments, institutes, and universities.

2. Increase in the number of accounting and auditing educators, including teachers, lecturers, and professors, to meet the requirements of schools of different levels. The rate at which accounting education (including managerial, financial, auditing, and systems accounting) can develop depends largely on the competence of educators. To ensure the availability of an adequate number of competent accounting educators, special training centers may have to be set up. Also, outstanding educators and teachers may have to serve as visiting scholars abroad, and foreign scholars should be invited to the CIS to introduce new ideas, developments, and experiences.

3. Compilation of complete sets of accounting and auditing textbooks to meet various training needs. The lack of a sufficient variety of appropriate textbooks is a serious impediment to the progress of accounting education. It is hoped that textbooks dealing with different topics and addressing students at various levels will appear. Achieving this goal will require efforts of both older and younger educators.

4. Development of an accounting education network offering junior, senior,

and advanced programs. Students at the junior level will be taught elementary accounting techniques. The senior level mainly comprises undergraduate students in institutes, academies, and universities. Candidates for the master's and doctoral degrees form the advanced level.

Various refresher courses for off-the-job training of personnel from different organizations will supplement the network. Refresher courses are necessary because during the process of revival and expansion of accounting organizations, many persons with little or no accounting/auditing experience and training are being transferred from other lines of work to strengthen the teams temporarily. In view of the rapid development of accounting/auditing and its branches as a discipline, even those who have had accounting education or experience should undergo a short period of condensed training every few years, to update their knowledge.

Ongoing Reform in Accounting Education in the CIS

The realization of *perestroika* and its economic reforms demands a great number of competent accountants with comprehensive professional knowledge and practical skill. They should be versed not only in accounting and auditing but also in law, management, economics, mathematics, computer science, and similar subjects. Graduates of institutes should have had adequate training in basic techniques and theory of accounting and auditing and also should have had some primary practical experience to enable them to get acquainted quickly and easily with accounting and auditing work.

Accounting education reform has a long way to go. In the future, such reform might cover several aspects. For example, teaching methods would be reformed. More emphasis would be placed on class discussion about case studies than on lectures and more on encouraging students' enthusiasm than on passive acquisition of information. Educators also would put greater emphasis on developing the ability to analyze and solve practical and theoretical problems and cases independently.

Advanced programs of accounting education for postgraduates would be perfected. Both quantity and quality of the program would be stressed to meet the urgent requirement for high-level accounting specialists.

A new set of textbooks would be developed and published according to the needs of the new accounting education program. Educational reform in accounting has far-reaching effects not only on education but on research and practice as well. Ongoing educational reform is expected to extend to professional schools and other training programs in the coming years. The influence of educational reform on accounting education cannot be ignored. The republics of the former Soviet Union currently are reappraising their educational structure, and due attention needs to be given to educating and training a large number of various types and levels of accountants and auditors. The current big demand for accountants is reflected in the sizable salaries accountants are able to command today.

In our opinion, the CIS and its republics need to carry out a well-thought-through and systematic approach to stimulate accounting and auditing education, training, and research and development. To this end, we recommend first a feasibility study comprising a comprehensive inventory and planning framework for accounting practices and education, as referred to earlier. We hope that our study has contributed to paving the way for such an accounting structural reform as a vital element in enhancing economic growth and development in the USSR and to integrating its economy fully with that of the outside world.